YOUR 15-MONTH
COMPLETE AND INDIVI

SCORPIO
October 23 - November 22

1988
SUPER HOROSCOPE

ARROW BOOKS LIMITED
62-65 Chandos Place
London WC2N 4NW

CONTENTS

THE PUBLISHERS REGRET THAT THEY CANNOT ANSWER INDIVIDUAL LETTERS
REQUESTING PERSONAL HOROSCOPE INFORMATION.

FIRST PUBLISHED IN GREAT BRITAIN BY ARROW BOOKS 1987
© GROSSET & DUNLAP, INC., 1974, 1978, 1979, 1980, 1981, 1982
© CHARTER COMMUNICATIONS, INC., 1983, 1984, 1985
COPYRIGHT © 1986, 1987 THE BERKLEY PUBLISHING GROUP

PRINTED IN GREAT BRITAIN BY
GUERNSEY PRESS CO. LTD
GUERNSEY C.I.
ISBN 0 09 948860 4

NOTE TO THE CUSP-BORN

First find the year of your birth, and then find the sign under which you were born according to your day of birth. Thus, you can determine if you are a true Scorpio (or Libra or Sagittarius), according to the variations of the dates of the Zodiac. (See also page 7.)

Are you *really* a Scorpio? If your birthday falls during the third to fourth week of October, at the beginning of Scorpio, will you still retain the traits of Libra, the sign of the Zodiac before Scorpio? And what if you were born late in November—are you more Sagittarius than Scorpio? Many people born at the edge, or cusp, of a sign have difficulty determining exactly what sign they are. If you are one of these people, here's how you can figure it out, once and for all.

Consult the following table. It will tell you the precise days on which the Sun entered and left your sign for the year of your birth. If you were born at the beginning or end of Scorpio, yours is a lifetime reflecting a process of subtle transformation. Your life on Earth will symbolize a significant change in consciousness, for you are either about to enter a whole new way of living or are leaving one behind.

If you were born at the beginning of Scorpio, you may want to read the horoscope book for Libra as well as Scorpio, for Libra holds the keys to much of the complexity of your spirit and reflects many of your hidden weaknesses, secret sides and unspoken wishes.

You have a keen way of making someone feel needed and desired, whether you care deeply or not. Sex is a strong directive in your life and you could turn your talents toward superficiality in relationships, merely winning people over with your sexual magnetism and sheer magic.

You can love with an almost fatal obsession, a bigger-than-both-of-you type thing, where you will blind your eyes to facts to keep the peace in a relationship—then suddenly declare war.

No one in the whole Zodiac is as turned on to the passions of life as you. You can survive any crisis, for deep in your spirit lie the seeds of immortality and you know it. Above all you are the symbol that life goes on—the personification of awakening passion.

If you were born at the end of Scorpio, you may want to read the horoscope book for Sagittarius as well as Scorpio. You are the symbol of the human mind awakening to its higher capabilities. What you are leaving behind is greed, blind desire and shallow lust, as you awaken to your own ability to learn, create, understand. You *want* to travel, see new places, see how people live, figure yourself out, acquire knowledge—yet you are often not quite ready to take the plunge. When you shift your behavior patterns significantly and permanently, new worlds open up and you turn on to immortality and the infinite possibilities of your own mind.

DATES SUN ENTERS SCORPIO
(LEAVES LIBRA)

October 23 every year from 1900 to 2000, except for the following:

October 22:	October 24:			
1992	1902	1911	1923	1943
96	03	14	27	47
	06	15	31	51
	07	18	35	55
	10	19	39	59

DATES SUN LEAVES SCORPIO
(ENTERS SAGITTARIUS)

November 22 every year from 1900 to 2000, except for the following:

November 21:		November 23:		
1976	1992	1902	1915	1931
80	93	03	19	35
84	96	07	23	39
88		10	27	43
		11		

HISTORY AND USES
OF ASTROLOGY

Does astrology have a place in the fast-moving, ultra-scientific world we live in today? Can it be justified in a sophisticated society whose outriders are already preparing to step off the moon into the deep space of the planets themselves? Or is it just a hangover of ancient superstition, a psychological dummy for neurotics and dreamers of every historical age?

These are the kind of questions that any inquiring person can be expected to ask when they approach a subject like astrology which goes beyond, but never excludes, the materialistic side of life.

The simple, single answer is that astrology works. It works for tens of millions of people in the western world alone. In the United States there are 10 million followers and in Europe, an estimated 25 million. America has more than 4000 practicing astrologers, Europe nearly three times as many. Even down-under Australia has its hundreds of thousands of adherents. The importance of such vast numbers of people from diverse backgrounds and cultures is recognized by the world's biggest newspapers and magazines who probably devote more of their space to this subject in a year than to any other. In the eastern countries, astrology has enormous followings, again, because it has been proved to work. In countries like India, brides and grooms for centuries have been chosen on the basis of astrological compatibility. The low divorce rate there, despite today's heavy westernizing influence, is attributed largely to this practice.

In the western world, astrology today is more vital than ever before; more practicable because it needs a sophisticated society like ours to understand and develop its contribution to the full; more valid because science itself is confirming the precepts of astrological knowledge with every new exciting step. The ordinary person who daily applies astrology intelligently does not have to wonder whether it is true nor believe in it blindly. He can see it working for himself. And, if he can use it—and this book is designed to help the reader to do just that—he can make living a far richer experience, and become a more developed personality and a better person.

Astrology is the science of relationships. It is not just a study of planetary influences on man and his environment. It is the study of man himself.

We are at the center of our personal universe, of all our relationships. And our happiness or sadness depends on how we act, how we relate to the people and things that surround us. The emotions that we generate have a distinct affect—for better or worse—on the world around us. Our friends and our enemies will confirm this. Just look in the mirror the next time you are angry. In other words, each of us is a kind of sun or planet or star and our influence on our personal universe, whether loving, helpful or destructive, varies with our changing moods, expressed through our individual character.

And to an extent that includes the entire galaxy, this is true of the planetary bodies. Their radiations affect each other, including the earth and all the things on it. And in comparatively recent years, giant constellations called "quasars" have been discovered. These exist far beyond the night stars that we can observe, and science says these quasars are emitting radiating influences more powerful and different than ever recorded on earth. Their effect on man from an astrological point of view is under deep study. Compared with these inter-stellar forces, our personal "radiations" are negligible on the planetary scale. But ours are just as potent in the way they affect our moods, and our ability to control them. To this extent they determine much of the happiness and satisfaction in our lives. For instance, if we were bound and gagged and had to hold some strong emotion within us without being able to move, we would soon start to feel very uncomfortable. We are obviously pretty powerful radiators inside, in our own way. But usually, we are able to throw off our emotion in some sort of action—we have a good cry, walk it off, or tell someone our troubles—before it can build up too far and make us physically ill. Astrology helps us to understand the universal forces working on us, and through this understanding, we can become more properly adjusted to our surroundings and find ourselves coping where others may flounder.

Closely related to our emotions is the "other side" of our personal universe, our physical welfare. Our body, of course, is largely influenced by things around us over which we have very little control. The phone rings, we hear it. The train runs late. We snag our stocking or cut our face shaving. Our body is under a constant bombardment of events that influence our lives to varying degrees.

The question that arises from all this is, what makes each of us act so that we have to involve other people and keep the ball of activity and evolution rolling? This is the question that both science and astrology are involved with. The scientists have attacked it from different angles: anthropology, the study of human evolution as body, mind and response to environment; anatomy, the study of bodily structure; psychology, the science of the human mind; and so on. These studies have produced very impressive classifications and valuable information, but because the approach to the problem is fragmented, so is the result. They remain "branches" of science. Science generally studies effects. It keeps turning up wonderful answers but no lasting solutions. Astrology, on the other hand approaches the question from the broader viewpoint. Astrology began its inquiry with the totality of human experience and saw it as an effect. It then looked to find the cause, or at least the prime movers, and during thousands of years of observation of man and his *universal* environment, came up with the extraordinary principle of planetary influence—or astrology, which, from the Greek, means the science of the stars.

Modern science, as we shall see, has confirmed much of astrology's foundations—most of it unintentionally, some of it reluctantly, but still, indisputably.

It is not difficult to imagine that there must be a connection between outer space and the earth. Even today, scientists are not too sure how our earth was created, but it is generally agreed that it is only a tiny part of the universe. And as a part of the universe, people on earth see and feel the influence of heavenly bodies in almost every aspect of our existence. There is no doubt that the sun has the greatest influence on life on this planet. Without it there would be no life, for without it there would be no warmth, no division into day and night, no cycles of time or season at all. This is clear and easy to see. The influence of the moon, on the other hand, is more subtle, though no less definite.

There are many ways in which the influence of the moon manifests itself here on earth, both on human and animal life. It is a well-known fact, for instance, that the large movements of water on our planet—that is the ebb and flow of the tides—are caused by the moon's gravitational pull. Since this is so, it follows that these water movements do not occur only in the oceans, but that all bodies of water are affected, even down to the tiniest puddle.

The human body, too, which consists of about 70 percent water, falls within the scope of this lunar influence. For example the menstrual cycle of most women corresponds to the lunar month; the period of pregnancy in humans is 273 days, or equal to nine lunar months. Similarly, many illnesses reach a crisis at the change of the moon, and statistics in many countries have shown that the crime rate is highest at the time of the full moon. Even human sexual desire has been associated with the phases of the moon. But, it is in the movement of the tides that we get the clearest demonstration of planetary influence, and the irresistible correspondence between the so-called metaphysical and the physical.

Tide tables are prepared years in advance by calculating the future positions of the moon. Science has known for a long time that the moon is the main cause of tidal action. But only in the last few years has it begun to realize the possible extent of this influence on mankind. To begin with, the ocean tides do not rise and fall as we might imagine from our personal observations of them. The moon as it orbits around the earth, sets up a circular wave of attraction which pulls the oceans of the world after it, broadly in an east to west direction. This influence is like a phantom wave crest, a loop of power stretching from pole to pole which passes over and around the earth like an invisible shadow. It travels with equal effect across the land masses and, as scientists were recently amazed to observe, caused oysters placed in the dark in the middle of the United States where there is no sea, to open their shells to receive the non-existent tide. If the land-locked oysters react to this invisible signal, what effect does it have on us who not so long ago in evolutionary time, came out of the sea and still have its salt in our blood and sweat?

Less well known is the fact that the moon is also the primary force behind the circulation of blood in human beings and animals, and the movement of sap in trees and plants. Agriculturists have established that the moon has a distinct influence on crops, which explains why for centuries people have planted according to moon cycles. The habits of many animals, too, are directed by the movement of the moon. Migratory birds, for instance, depart only at or near the time of the full moon. Just as certain fish, eels in particular, move only in accordance with certain phases of the moon.

Know Thyself—Why?

In today's fast-changing world, everyone still longs to know what the future holds. It is the one thing that everyone has in common: rich and poor, famous and infamous, all are deeply concerned about tomorrow.

But the key to the future, as every historian knows, lies in the past. This is as true of individual people as it is of nations. You cannot understand your future without first understanding your past, which is simply another way of saying that you must first of all know yourself.

The motto "know thyself" seems obvious enough nowadays, but it was originally put forward as the foundation of wisdom by the ancient Greek philosophers. It was then adopted by the "mystery religions" of the ancient Middle East, Greece and Rome, and is still used in all genuine schools of mind training or mystical discipline, both in those of the East, based on yoga, and those of the West. So it is universally accepted now, and has been through the ages.

But how do you go about discovering what sort of person you are? The first step is usually classification into some sort of system of types. Astrology did this long before the birth of Christ. Psychology has also done it. So has modern medicine, in its way.

One system classifies men according to the source of the impulses they respond to most readily: the muscles, leading to direct bodily action; the digestive organs, resulting in emotion, or the brain and nerves. Another such system says that character is determined by the endocrine glands, and gives us labels like "pituitary," "thyroid" and "hyperthyroid" types. These different systems are neither contradictory nor mutually exclusive. In fact, they are very often different ways of saying the same thing.

Very popular and useful classifications were devised by Dr. C. G. Jung, the eminent disciple of Freud. Jung observed among the different faculties of the mind, four which have a predominant influence on character. These four faculties exist in all of us without exception, but not in perfect balance. So when we say, for instance, that a man is a "thinking type," it means that in any situation he tries to be rational. It follows that emotion, which some say is the opposite of thinking, will be his weakest function. This type can be sensible and reasonable, or calculating and unsympathetic. The emotional type, on the other hand, can often be recognized by exaggerated language—everything is either marvelous or terrible—and in extreme cases they even invent dramas and quarrels out of nothing just to make life more interesting.

The other two faculties are intuition and physical sensation. The sensation type does not only care for food and drink, nice clothes and furniture; he is also interested in all forms of physical experience. Many scientists are sensation types as are athletes and nature-lovers. Like sensation, intuition is a form of perception and we all possess it. But it works through that part of the mind which is not under conscious control—consequently it sees meanings and connections which are not obvious to thought or emotion. Inventors and original thinkers are always intuitive, but so, too, are superstitious people who see meanings where none exist.

Thus, sensation tells us what is going on in the world, feeling (that is, emotion) tells us how important it is to ourselves, thinking enables us to interpret it and work out what we should do about it, and intuition tells us what it means to ourselves and others. All four faculties are essential, and all are present in every one of us. But some people are guided chiefly by one, others by another.

Besides these four types, Jung observed a division into extrovert and introvert, which cuts across them. By and large, the introvert is one who finds truth inside himself rather than outside. He is not, therefore, ideally suited to a religion or a political party which tells him what to believe. Original thinkers are almost necessarily introverts. The extrovert, on the other hand, finds truth coming to him from outside. He believes in experts and authorities, and wants to think that nature and the laws of nature really exists, that they are what they appear to be and not just generalities made by men.

A disadvantage of all these systems of classification, is that one cannot tell very easily where to place oneself. Some people are reluctant to admit that they act to please their emotions. So they deceive themselves for years by trying to belong to whichever type they think is the "best." Of course, there is no best; each has its faults and each has its good points.

The advantage of the signs of the Zodiac is that they simplify classification. Not only that, but your date of birth is personal—it is unarguably yours. What better way to know yourself than by going back as far as possible to the very moment of your birth? And this is precisely what your horoscope is all about.

What Is a Horoscope?

If you had been able to take a picture of the heavens at the moment of your birth, that photograph would be your horoscope. Lacking such a snapshot, it is still possible to recreate the picture—and this is at the basis of the astrologer's art. In other words, your horoscope is a representation of the skies with the planets in the exact positions they occupied at the time you were born.

This information, of course, is not enough for the astrologer. He has to have a background of significance to put the photograph on. You will get the idea if you imagine two balls—one inside the other. The inner one is transparent. In the center of both is the astrologer, able to look up, down and around in all directions. The outer sphere is the Zodiac which is divided into twelve approximately equal segments, like the segments of an orange. The inner ball is our photograph. It is transparent except for the images of the planets. Looking out from the center, the astrologer sees the planets in various segments of the Zodiac. These twelve segments are known as the signs or houses.

The position of the planets when each of us is born is always different. So the photograph is always different. But the Zodiac and its signs are fixed.

Now, where in all this are you, the subject of the horoscope?

You, or your character, is largely determined by the sign the sun is in. So that is where the astrologer looks first in your horoscope.

There are twelve signs in the Zodiac and the sun spends approximately one month in each. As the sun's motion is almost perfectly regular, the astrologers have been able to fix the dates governing each sign. There are not many people who do not know which sign of the Zodiac they were born under or who have not been amazed at some time or other at the accuracy of the description of their own character. Here are the twelve signs, the ancient zodiacal symbol, and their dates for the year 1988.*

ARIES	Ram	March 20–April 19
TAURUS	Bull	April 19–May 20
GEMINI	Twins	May 20–June 20
CANCER	Crab	June 20–July 22
LEO	Lion	July 22–August 22
VIRGO	Virgin	August 22–September 22
LIBRA	Scales	September 22–October 23
SCORPIO	Scorpion	October 23–November 21
SAGITTARIUS	Archer	November 21–December 21
CAPRICORN	Sea-Goat	December 21–January 20
AQUARIUS	Water-Bearer	January 20–February 19
PISCES	Fish	February 19–March 20

The time of birth—apart from the date—is important in advanced astrology because the planets travel at such great speed that the patterns they form change from minute to minute. For this reason, each person's horoscope is his and his alone. Further on we will see that the practicing astrologer has ways of determining and reading these minute time changes which dictate the finger character differences in us all.

However, it is still possible to draw significant conclusions and make meaningful predictions based simply on the sign of the Zodiac a person is born under. In a horoscope, the signs do not necessarily correspond with the divisions of the houses. It could be that a house begins half way across a sign. It is the interpretation of such combinations of different influences that distinguishes the professional astrologer from the student and the follower.

However, to gain a workable understanding of astrology, it is not necessary to go into great detail. In fact, the beginner is likely to find himself confused if he attempts to absorb too much too quickly. It should be remembered that this is a science and to become proficient at it, and especially to grasp the tremendous scope of possibilities in man and his affairs and direct them into a worthwhile reading, takes a great deal of study and experience.

*These dates are fluid and change with the motion of the Earth from year to year.

If you do intend to pursue it seriously you will have to learn to figure the exact moment of birth against the degrees of longitude and latitude of the planets at that precise time. This involves adapting local time to Greenwich Mean Time (G.M.T.), reference to tables of houses to establish the Ascendant, as well as making calculations from Ephemeris—the tables of the planets' positions.

After reading this introduction, try drawing up a rough horoscope to get the "feel" of reading some elementary characteristics and natal influences.

Draw a circle with twelve equal segments. Write in counterclockwise the names of the signs—Aries, Taurus, Gemini etc.— one for each segment. Look up an ephemeris for the year of the person's birth and note down the sign each planet was in on the birthday. Do not worry about the number of degrees (although if a planet is on the edge of a sign its position obviously should be considered). Write the name of the planet in the segment/sign on your chart. Write the number 1 in the sign where the sun is. This is the first house. Number the rest of the houses, counterclockwise till you finish at 12. Now you can investigate the probable basic expectation of experience of the person concerned. This is done first of all by seeing what planet or planets is/are in what sign and house. (See also page 72.)

The 12 houses control these functions:

1st.	Individuality, body appearance, general outlook on life	(Personality house)
2nd.	Finance, business	(Money house)
3rd.	Relatives, education, correspondence	(Relatives house)
4th.	Family, neighbors	(Home house)
5th.	Pleasure, children, attempts, entertainment	(Pleasure house)
6th.	Health, employees	(Health house)
7th.	Marriage, partnerships	(Marriage house)
8th.	Death, secret deals, difficulties	(Death house)
9th.	Travel, intellectual affairs	(Travel house)
10th.	Ambition, social standing	(Business and Honor house)
11th.	Friendship, social life, luck	(Friends house)
12th.	Troubles, illness, loss	(Trouble house)

The characteristics of the planets modify the influence of the Sun according to their natures and strengths.

Sun: Source of life. Basic temperament according to sun sign. The will.
Moon: Superficial nature. Moods. Changeable. Adaptive. Mother.
Mercury: Communication. Intellect. Reasoning power. Curiosity. Short travels.
Venus: Love. Delight. Art. Beautiful possessions.
Mars: Energy. Initiative. War. Anger. Destruction. Impulse.
Jupiter: Good. Generous. Expansive. Opportunities. Protection.
Saturn: Jupiter's opposite. Contraction. Servant. Delay. Hardwork. Cold. Privation. Research. Lasting rewards after long struggle.
Uranus: Fashion. Electricity. Revolution. Sudden changes. Modern science.
Neptune: Sensationalism. Mass emotion. Devastation. Delusion.
Pluto: Creates and destroys. Lust for power. Strong obsessions.

Superimpose the characteristics of the planets on the functions of the house in which they appear. Express the result through the character of the birth (sun) sign, and you will get the basic idea of how astrology works.

Of course, many other considerations have been taken into account in producing the carefully worked out predictions in this book: The aspects of the planets to each other; their strength according to position and sign; whether they are in a house of exaltation or decline; whether they are natural enemies or not; whether a planet occupies his own sign; the position of a planet in relation to its own house or sign; whether the planet is male, female or neuter; whether the sign is a fire, earth, water or air sign. These are only a few of the colors on the astrologer's pallet which he must mix with the inspiration of the artist and the accuracy of the mathematician.

The Problem of Love

Love, of course, is never a problem. The problem lies in recognizing the difference between infatuation, emotion, sex and, sometimes, the downright deceit of the other person. Mankind, with its record of broken marriages, despair and disillusionment, is obviously not very good at making these distinctions.

Can astrology help?

Yes. In the same way that advance knowledge can usually help in any human situation. And there is probably no situation as human, as poignant, as pathetic and universal, as the failure of man's love.

Love, of course, is not just between man and woman. It involves love of children, parents, home and so on. But the big problems usually involve the choice of partner.

Astrology has established degrees of compatibility that exist between people born under the various signs of the Zodiac. Because people are individuals, there are numerous variations and modifications and the astrologer, when approached on mate and marriage matters makes allowances for them. But the fact remains that some groups of people are suited for each other and some are not and astrology has expressed this in terms of characteristics which all can study and use as a personal guide.

No matter how much enjoyment and pleasure we find in the different aspects of each other's character, if it is not an overall compatibility, the chances of our finding fulfillment or enduring happiness in each other are pretty hopeless. And astrology can help us to find someone compatible.

History of Astrology

The origins of astrology have been lost far back in history, but we do know that reference is made to it as far back as the first written records of the human race. It is not hard to see why. Even in primitive times, people must have looked for an explanation for the various happenings in their lives. They must have wanted to know why people were different from one to another. And in their search they turned to the regular movements of the sun, moon and stars to see if they could provide an answer.

It is interesting to note that as soon as man learned to use his tools in any type of design, or his mind in any kind of calculation, he turned his attention to the heavens. Ancient cave dwellings reveal dim crescents and circles representative of the sun and moon, rulers of day and night. Mesopotamia and the civilization of Chaldea, in itself the foundation of those of Babylonia and Assyria, show a complete picture of astronomical observation and well-developed astrological interpretation.

Humanity has a natural instinct for order. The study of anthropology reveals that primitive people—even as far back as prehistoric times—were striving to achieve a certain order in their lives. They tried to organize the apparent chaos of the universe. They had the desire to attach meaning to things. This demand for order has persisted throughout the history of man. So that observing the regularity of the heavenly bodies made it logical that primitive peoples should turn heavenwards in their search for an understanding of the world in which they found themselves so random and alone.

And they did find a significance in the movements of the stars. Shepherds tending their flocks, for instance, observed that when the cluster of stars now known as the constellation Aries was in sight, it was the time of fertility and they associated it with the Ram. And they noticed that the growth of plants and plant life corresponded with different phases of the moon, so that certain times were favorable for the planting of crops, and other times were not. In this way, there grew up a tradition of seasons and causes connected with the passage of the sun through the twelve signs of the Zodiac.

Astrology was valued so highly that the king was kept informed of the daily and monthly changes in the heavenly bodies, and the results of astrological studies regarding events of the future. Head astrologers were clearly men of great rank and position, and the office was said to be a hereditary one.

Omens were taken, not only from eclipses and conjunctions of the moon or sun with one of the planets, but also from storms and earthquakes. In the eastern civilizations, particularly, the reverence inspired by astrology appears to have remained unbroken since the very earliest days. In ancient China, astrology, astronomy and religion went hand in hand. The astrologer, who was also an astronomer, was part of the official government service and had his own corner in the Imperial Palace. The duties of the Imperial astrologer, whose office was one of the most important in the land, were clearly defined, as this extract from early records shows:

"This exalted gentleman must concern himself with the stars in the heavens, keeping a record of the changes and movements of the Planets, the Sun and the Moon, in order to examine the movements of the terrestial world with the object of prognosticating good and bad fortune. He divides the territories of the nine regions of the empire in accordance with their dependence on particular celestial bodies. All the fiefs and principalities are connected with the stars and from this their prosperity or misfortune should be ascertained. He makes prognostications according to the twelve years of the Jupiter cycle of good and evil of the terrestial world. From the colors of the five kinds of clouds, he determines the coming of floods or droughts, abundance or famine. From the twelve winds, he draws conclusions about the state of harmony of heaven and earth, and takes note of good and bad signs that result from their accord or disaccord. In general, he concerns himself with five kinds of phenomena so as to warn the Emperor to come to the aid of the government and to allow for variations in the ceremonies according to their circumstances."

The Chinese were also keen observers of the fixed stars, giving them such unusual names as Ghost Vehicle, Sun of Imperial Concubine, Imperial Prince, Pivot of Heaven, Twinkling Brilliance or Weaving Girl. But, great astrologers though they may have been, the Chinese lacked one aspect of mathematics that the Greeks applied to astrology—deductive geometry. Deductive geometry was the basis of much classical astrology in and after the time of the Greeks, and this explains the different methods of prognostication used in the East and West.

Down through the ages the astrologer's art has depended, not so much on the uncovering of new facts, though this is important, as on the interpretation of the facts already known. This is the essence of his skill. Obviously one cannot always tell how people will react (and this underlines the very important difference between astrology and predestination which will be discussed later on) but one can be prepared, be forewarned, to know what to expect.

But why should the signs of the zodiac have any effect at all on the formation of human character? It is easy to see why people thought they did, and even now we constantly use astrological expressions in our everyday speech. The thoughts of "lucky star," "ill-fated," "star-crossed," "mooning around," are interwoven into the very structure of our language.

In the same way that the earth has been created by influences from outside, there remains an indisputable togetherness in the working of the universe. The world, after all, is a coherent structure, for if it were not, it would be quite without order and we would never know what to expect. A dog could turn into an apple, or an elephant sprout wings and fly at any moment without so much as a by your leave. But nature, as we know, functions according to laws, not whims, and the laws of nature are certainly not subject to capricious exceptions.

This means that no part of the universe is ever arbitrarily cut off from any other part. Everything is therefore to some extent linked with everything else. The moon draws an imperceptible tide on every puddle; tiny and trivial events can be effected by outside forces (such as the fall of a feather by the faintest puff of wind). And so it is fair to think that the local events at any moment reflect to a very small extent the evolution of the world as a whole.

From this principle follows the possibility of divination, and also knowledge of events at a distance, provided one's mind were always as perfectly undisturbed, as ideally smooth, as a mirror or unruffled lake. Provided, in other words, that one did not confuse the picture with hopes, guesses, and expectations. When people try to foretell the future by cards or crystal ball gazing they find it much easier to confuse the picture with expectations than to reflect it clearly.

But the present does contain a good deal of the future to which it leads—not all, but a good deal. The diver halfway between bridge and water is going to make a splash; the train whizzing towards the station will pass through it unless interfered with; the burglar breaking a pane of glass has exposed himself to the possibility of a prison sentence. Yet this is not a doctrine of determinism, as was emphasized earlier. Clearly, there are forces already at work in the present, and any one of them could alter the situation in some way. Equally, a change of decision could alter the whole situation as well. So the future depends, not on an irresistible force, but on a small act of free will.

An individual's age, physique, and position on the earth's surface are remote consequences of his birth. Birth counts as the original cause for all that happens subsequently. The horoscope, in this case, means "this person represents the further evolution of the state of the universe pictured in this chart." Such a chart can apply equally to man or woman, dog, ship or even limited company.

If the evolution of an idea, or of a person, is to be understood as a totality, it must continue to evolve from its own beginnings, which is to say, in the terms in which it began. The brown-eyed person will be faithful to brown eyes all his life; the traitor is being faithful to some complex of ideas which has long been evolving in him; and the person born at sunset will always express, as he evolves, the psychological implications or analogies of the moment when the sun sinks out of sight.

This is the doctrine that an idea must continue to evolve in terms of its origin. It is a completely non-materialist doctrine, though it never fails to apply to material objects. And it implies, too, that the individual will continue to evolve in terms of his moment of origin, and therefore possibly of the sign of the Zodiac rising on the eastern horizon at his birth. It also implies that the signs of the Zodiac themselves will evolve in the collective mind of the human race in the same terms that they were first devised and not in the terms in which modern astrologers consciously think they ought to work.

For the human race, like every other kind of animal, has a collective mind, as Professor Jung discovered in his investigation of dreams. If no such collective mind existed, no infant could ever learn anything, for communication would be impossible. Furthermore, it is absurd to suggest that the conscious mind could be older than the "unconscious," for an infant's nervous system functions correctly before it has discovered the difference between "myself" and "something else" or discovered what eyes and hands are for. Indeed, the involuntary muscles function correctly even before birth, and will never be under conscious control. They are part of what we call the "unconscious" which is not really "unconscious" at all. To the contrary, it is totally aware of itself and everything else; it is merely that part of the mind that cannot be controlled by conscious effort.

And human experience, though it varies in detail with every individual, is basically the same for each one of us, consisting of sky and earth, day and night, waking and sleeping, man and woman, birth and death. So there is bound to be in the mind of the human race a very large number of inescapable ideas, which are called our natural archetypes.

There are also, however, artificial or cultural archetypes which are not universal or applicable to everyone, but are nevertheless inescapable within the limits of a given culture. Examples of these are the cross in Christianity, and the notion of "escape from the wheel of rebirth" in India. There was a time when these ideas did not exist. And there was a time, too, when the scheme of the Zodiac did not exist. One would not expect the Zodiac to have any influence on remote and primitive peoples, for example, who have never heard of it. If the Zodiac is only an archetype, their horoscopes probably would not work and it would not matter which sign they were born under.

But where the Zodiac is known, and the idea of it has become worked into the collective mind, then there it could well appear to have an influence, even if it has no physical existence. For ideas do not have a physical existence, anyway. No physical basis has yet been discovered for the telepathy that controls an anthill; young swallows migrate before, not after, their parents; and the weaverbird builds its intricate nest without being taught. Materialists suppose, but cannot prove, that "instinct" (as it is called, for no one knows how it works) is controlled by nucleic acid in the chromosomes. This is not a genuine explanation, though, for it only pushes the mystery one stage further back.

Does this mean, then, that the human race, in whose civilization the idea of the twelve signs of the Zodiac has long been embedded, is divided into only twelve types? Can we honestly believe that it is really as simple as that? If so, there must be pretty wide ranges of variation within each type. And if, to explain the variation, we call in heredity and environment, experiences in early childhood, the thyroid and other glands, and also the four functions of the mind mentioned at the beginning of this introduction, and extroversion and introversion, then one begins to wonder if the original classification was worth making at all. No sensible person believes that his favorite system explains everything. But even so, he will not find it much use at all if it does not even save him the trouble of bothering with the others.

Under the Jungian system, everyone has not only a dominant or principal function, but also a secondary or subsidiary one, so that the four can be arranged in order of potency. In the intuitive type, sensation is always the most inefficient function, but the second most inefficient function can be either thinking (which tends to make original thinkers such as Jung himself) or else feeling (which tends to make artistic people). Therefore, allowing for introversion and extroversion, there are at least four kinds of intuitive types, and sixteen types in all. Furthermore, one can see how the sixteen types merge into each other, so that there are no unrealistic or unconvincingly rigid divisions.

In the same way, if we were to put every person under only one sign of the Zodiac, the system becomes too rigid and unlike life. Besides, it was never intended to be used like that. It may be convenient to have only twelve types, but we know that in practice there is every possible gradation between aggressiveness and timidity, or between conscientiousness and laziness. How, then, do we account for this?

The Tyrant and the Saint

Just as the thinking type of man is also influenced to some extent by sensation and intuition, but not very much by emotion, so a person born under Leo can be influenced to some extent by one or two (but not more) of the other signs. For instance, famous persons born under the sign of Gemini include Henry VIII, whom nothing and no-one could have induced to abdicate, and Edward VIII, who did just that. Obviously, then, the sign Gemini does not fully explain the complete character of either of them.

Again, under the opposite sign, Sagittarius, were both Stalin, who was totally consumed with the notion of power, and Charles V, who freely gave up an empire because he preferred to go into a monastery. And we find under Scorpio, many uncompromising characters such as Luther, de Gaulle, Indira Gandhi and Montgomery, but also Petain, a successful commander whose name later became synonymous with collaboration.

A single sign is therefore obviously inadequate to explain the differences between people; it can only explain resemblances, such as the combativeness of the Scorpio group, or the far-reaching devotion of Charles V and Stalin to their respective ideals—the Christian heaven and the Communist utopia.

But very few people are born under one sign only. As well as the month of birth, as was mentioned earlier, the day matters, and, even more, the hour, which ought, if possible, to be noted to the nearest minute. Without this, it is impossible to have an actual horoscope, for the word horoscope means literally, "a consideration of the hour."

The month of birth tells you only which sign of the Zodiac was occupied by the sun. The day and hour tell you what sign was occupied by the moon. And the minute tells you which sign was rising on the eastern horizon. This is called the Ascendant, and it is supposed to be the most important thing in the whole horoscope.

If you were born at midnight, the sun is then in an important position, although invisible. But at one o'clock in the morning the sun is not important, so the moment of birth will not matter much. The important thing then will be the Ascendant, and possibly one or two of the planets. At a given day and hour, say, dawn on January 1st, or 9:00 p.m. on the longest day, the Ascendant will always be the same at any given place. But the moon and planets alter from day to day, at different speeds and have to be looked up in an astronomical table.

The sun is said to signify one's heart, that is to say, one's deepest desires and inmost nature. This is quite different from the moon, which, as we have seen, signifies one's superficial way of behaving. When the ancient Romans referred to the Emperor Augustus as a Capricornian, they meant that he had the moon in Capricorn; they did not pay much attention to the sun, although he was born at sunrise. Or, to take another example, a modern astrologer would call Disraeli a Scorpion because he had Scorpio rising, but most people would call him Sagittarian because he had the sun there. The Romans would have called him Leo because his moon was in Leo.

The sun, as has already been pointed out, is important if one is born near sunrise, sunset, noon or midnight, but is otherwise not reckoned as the principal influence. So if one does not seem to fit one's birth month, it is always worthwhile reading the other signs, for one may have been born at a time when any of them were rising or occupied by the moon. It also seems to be the case that the influence of the sun develops as life goes on, so that the month of birth is easier to guess in people over the age of forty. The young are supposed to be influenced mainly by their Ascendant which characterizes the body and physical personality as a whole.

It should be clearly understood that it is nonsense to assume that all people born at a certain time will exhibit the same characteristics, or that they will even behave in the same manner. It is quite obvious that, from the very moment of its birth, a child is subject to the effects of its environment, and that this in turn will influence its character and heritage to a decisive extent. Also to be taken into account are education and economic conditions, which play a very important part in the formation of one's character as well.

However, it is clearly established that people born under one sign of the Zodiac do have certain basic traits in their character which are different from those born under other signs. It is obvious to every thinking person that certain events produce different reactions in various people. For instance, if a man slips on a banana skin and falls heavily on the pavement, one passer-by may laugh and find this extremely amusing, while another may just walk on, thinking: "What a fool falling down like that. He should look where he is going." A third might also walk away saying to himself: "It's none of my business—I'm glad it wasn't me." A fourth might walk past and think: "I'm sorry for that man, but I haven't the time to be bothered with helping him." And a fifth might stop to help the fallen man to his feet, comfort him and take him home. Here is just one event which could produce entirely different reactions in different people. And, obviously, there are many more. One that comes to mind immediately is the violently opposed views to events such as wars, industrial strikes, and so on. The fact that people have different attitudes to the same event is simply another way of saying that they have different characters. And this is not something that can be put down to background, for people of the same race, religion, or class, very often express quite different reactions to happenings or events. Similarly, it is often the case that members of the same family, where there is clearly uniform background of economic and social standing, education, race and religion, often argue bitterly among themselves over political and social issues.

People have, in general, certain character traits and qualities which, according to their environment, develop in either a positive or a negative manner. Therefore, selfishness (inherent selfishness, that is) might emerge as unselfishness; kindness and consideration as cruelty and lack of consideration towards others. In the same way, a naturally constructive person, may, through frustration, become destructive, and so on. The latent characteristics with which people are born can, therefore, through environment and good or bad training, become something that would appear to be its opposite, and so give the lie to the astrologer's description of their character. But this is not the case. The true character is still there, but it is buried deep beneath these external superficialities.

Careful study of the character traits of different signs can be immeasurable help, and can render beneficial service to the intelligent person. Undoubtedly, the reader will already have discovered that, while he is able to get on very well with some people, he just "cannot stand" others. The causes sometimes seem inexplicable. At times there is intense dislike, at other times immediate sympathy. And there is, too, the phenomenon of love at first sight, which is also apparently inexplicable. People appear to be either sympathetic or unsympathetic towards each other for no apparent reason.

Now if we look at this in the light of the Zodiac, we find that people born under different signs are either compatible or incompatible with each other. In other words, there are good and bad interrelating factors among the various signs. This does not, of course, mean that humanity can be divided into groups of hostile camps. It would be quite wrong to be hostile or indifferent toward people who happen to be born under an incompatible sign. There is no reason why everybody should not, or cannot, learn to control and adjust their feelings and actions, especially after they are aware of the positive qualities of other people by studying their character analyses, among other things.

Every person born under a certain sign has both positive and negative qualities, which are developed more or less according to his free will. Nobody is entirely good or entirely bad, and it is up to each one of us to learn to control himself on the one hand, and at the same time to endeavor to learn about himself and others.

It cannot be repeated often enough that, though the intrinsic nature of man and his basic character traits are born in him, nevertheless it is his own free will that determines whether he will make really good use of his talents and abilities—whether, in other words, he will overcome his vices or allow them to rule him. Most of us are born with at least a streak of laziness, irritability, or some other fault in our nature, and it is up to each one of us to see that we exert sufficient willpower to control our failings so that they do not harm ourselves or others.

Astrology can reveal our inclinations and tendencies. Our weaknesses should not be viewed as shortcomings that are impossible to change. The horoscope of a man may show him to have criminal leanings, for instance, but this does not mean he will definitely become a criminal.

The ordinary man usually finds it difficult to know himself. He is often bewildered. Astrology can frequently tell him more about himself than the different schools of psychology are able to do. Knowing his failings and shortcomings, he will do his best to overcome them, and make himself a better and more useful member of society and a helpmate to his family and friends. It can also save him a great deal of unhappiness and remorse.

And yet it may seem absurd that an ancient philosophy, something that is known as a "pseudo-science," could be a prop to the men and women of the twentieth century. But below the materialistic surface of modern life, there are hidden streams of feeling and thought. Symbology is reappearing as a study worthy of the scholar; the psychosomatic factor in illness has passed from the writings of the crank to those of the specialist; spiritual healing in all its forms is no longer a pious hope but an accepted phenomenon. And it is into this context that we consider astrology, in the sense that it is an analysis of human types.

Astrology and medicine had a long journey together, and only parted company a couple of centuries ago. There still remain in medical language such astrological terms as "saturnine," "choleric," and "mercurial," used in the diagnosis of physical tendencies. The herbalist, for long the handyman of the medical profession, has been dominated by astrology since the days of the Greeks. Certain herbs traditionally respond to certain planetary influences, and diseases must therefore be treated to ensure harmony between the medicine and the disease.

No one expects the most eccentric of modern doctors to go back to the practices of his predecessors. We have come a long way since the time when phases of the moon were studied in illness. Those days were a medical nightmare, with epidemics that were beyond control, and an explanation of the Black Death sought in conjunction with the planets. Nowadays, astrological diagnosis of disease has literally no parallel in modern life. And yet, age-old symbols of types and of the vulnerability of, say, the Saturnian to chronic diseases or the choleric to apoplexy and blood pressure and so on, are still applicable.

But the stars are expected to foretell and not only to diagnose. The astrological forecaster has a counterpart on a highly conventional level in the shape of the weather prophet, racing tipster and stock market forecaster, to name just three examples. All in their own way are aiming at the same result. They attempt to look a little further into the pattern of life and also try to determine future patterns accurately.

Astrological forecasting has been remarkably accurate, but often it is wide of the mark. The brave man who cares to predict world events takes dangerous chances. Individual forecasting is less clear cut; it can be a help or a disillusionment. Then welcome to the nagging question: if it is possible to foreknow, is it right to foretell? A complex point of ethics on which it is hard to pronounce judgment. The doctor faces the same dilemma if he finds that symptoms of a mortal disease are present in his patient and that he can only prognosticate a steady decline. How much to tell an individual in a crisis is a problem that has perplexed many distinguished scholars. Honest and conscientious astrologers in this modern world, where so many people are seeking guidance, face the same problem.

The ancient cults, the symbols of old religions, are eclipsed for the moment. They may return with their old force within a decade or two. But at present the outlook is dark. Human beings badly need assurance, as they did in the past, that all is not chaos. Somewhere, somehow, there is a pattern that must be worked out. As to the why and wherefore, the astrologer is not expected to give judgment. He is just someone who, by dint of talent and training, can gaze into the future.

Five hundred years ago it was customary to call in a learned man who was an astrologer who was probably also a doctor and a philosopher. By his knowledge of astrology, his study of planetary influences, he felt himself qualified to guide those in distress. The world has moved forward at a fantastic rate since then, and in this twentieth century speed has been the keyword everywhere. Tensions have increased, the spur of ambition has been applied indiscriminately. People are uncertain of themselves. At first sight it seems fantastic in the light of modern thinking that they turn to the most ancient of all studies, and get someone to calculate a horoscope for them. But is it *really* so fantastic if you take a second look? For astrology is concerned with tomorrow, with survival. And in a world such as ours, those two things are the keywords of the time in which we live.

HOW TO USE
THESE PREDICTIONS

A person reading the predictions in this book should understand that they are produced from the daily position of the planets for a group of people and are not, of course, individually specialized. To get the full benefit of them he should relate the predictions to his own character and circumstances, co-ordinate them, and draw his own conclusions from them.

If he is a serious observer of his own life he should find a definite pattern emerge that will be a helpful and reliable guide.

The point is that we always retain our free will. The stars indicate certain directional tendencies but we are not compelled to follow. We can do or not do, and wisdom must make the choice.

We all have our good and bad days. Sometimes they extend into cycles of weeks. It is therefore advisable to study daily predictions in a span ranging from the day before to several days ahead; also to re-read the monthly predictions for similar cycles.

Daily predictions should be taken very generally. The word "difficult" does not necessarily indicate a whole day of obstruction or inconvenience. It is a warning to you to be cautious. Your caution will often see you around the difficulty before you are involved. This is the correct use of astrology.

In another section, detailed information is given about the influence of the moon as it passes through the various signs of the Zodiac. It includes instructions on how to use the Moon Tables. This information should be used in conjunction with the daily forecasts to give a fuller picture of the astrological trends.

THE MOON

Moon is the nearest planet to the earth. It exerts more observable influence on us from day to day than any other planet. The effect is very personal, very intimate, and if we are not aware of how it works it can make us quite unstable in our ideas. And the annoying thing is that at these times we often see our own instability but can do nothing about it. A knowledge of what can be expected may help considerably. We can then be prepared to stand strong against the moon's negative influences and use its positive ones to help us to get ahead. Who has not heard of going with the tide?

Moon reflects, has no light of its own. It reflects the sun—the life giver—in the form of vital movement. Moon controls the tides, the blood rhythm, the movement of sap in trees and plants. Its nature is inconstancy and change so it signifies our moods, our superficial behavior—walking, talking and especially thinking. Being a true reflector of other forces, moon is cold, watery like the surface of a still lake, brilliant and scintillating at times, but easily ruffled and disturbed by the winds of change.

The moon takes 28½ days to circle the earth and the Zodiac. It spends just over 2¼ days in each sign. During that time it reflects the qualities, energies and characteristics of the sign and, to a degree, the planet which rules the sign. While the moon in its transit occupies a sign incompatible with our own birth sign, we can expect to feel a vague uneasiness, perhaps a touch of irritableness. We should not be discouraged nor let the feeling get us down, or, worse still, allow ourselves to take the discomfort out on others. Try to remember that the moon has to change signs within 55 hours and, provided you are not physically ill, your mood will probably change with it. It is amazing how frequently depression lifts with the shift in the moon's position. And, of course, when the moon is transiting a sign compatible or sympathetic to yours you will probably feel some sort of stimulation or just plain happy to be alive.

In the horoscope, the moon is such a powerful indicator that competent astrologers often use the sign it occupied at birth as the birth sign of the person. This is done particularly when the sun is on the cusp, or edge, of two signs. Most experienced astrologers, however, coordinate both sun and moon signs by reading and confirming from one to the other and secure a far more accurate and personalized analysis.

For these reasons, the moon tables which follow this section (see pages 28–35) are of great importance to the individual. They show the days and the exact times the moon will enter each sign of the Zodiac for the year. Remember, you have to adjust the indicated times to local time. The corrections, already calculated for most of the main cities, are at the beginning of the tables. What follows now is a guide to the influences that will be reflected to the earth by the moon while it transits each of the twelve signs. The influence is at its peak about 26 hours after the moon enters a sign.

MOON IN ARIES

This is a time for action, for reaching out beyond the usual self-imposed limitations and faint-hearted cautions. If you have plans in your head or on your desk, put them into practice. New ventures, applications, new jobs, new starts of any kind—all have a good chance of success. This is the period when original and dynamic impulses are being reflected onto the earth. The energies are extremely vital and favor the pursuit of pleasure and adventure in practically every form. Sick people should feel an improvement. Those who are well will probably find themselves exuding confidence and optimism. People fond of physical exercise should find their bodies growing with tone and well-being. Boldness, strength, determination should characterize most of your activities with a readiness to face up to old challenges. Yesterday's problems may seem petty and exaggerated—so deal with them. Strike out alone. Self-reliance will attract others to you. This is a good time for making friends. Business and marriage partners are more likely to be impressed with the man and woman of action. Opposition will be overcome or thrown aside with much less effort than usual. CAUTION: Be dominant but not domineering.

MOON IN TAURUS

The spontaneous, action-packed person of yesterday gives way to the cautious, diligent, hardworking "thinker." In this period ideas will probably be concentrated on ways of improving finances. A great deal of time may be spent figuring out and going over schemes and plans. It is the right time to be careful with detail. People will find themselves working longer than usual at their desks. Or devoting more time to serious thought about the future. A strong desire to put order into business and financial arrangements may cause extra work. Loved ones may complain of being neglected and may fail to appreciate that your efforts are for their ultimate benefit. Your desire for system may extend to criticism of arrangements in the home and lead to minor upsets. Health may be affected through overwork. Try to secure a reasonable amount of rest and relaxation, although the tendency will be to "keep going" despite good advice. Work done conscientiously in this period should result in a solid contribution to your future security. CAUTION: Try not to be as serious with people as the work you are engaged in.

MOON IN GEMINI

The humdrum of routine and too much work should suddenly end. You are likely to find yourself in an expansive, quicksilver world of change and self-expression. Urges to write, to paint, to experience the freedom of some sort of artistic outpouring, may be very strong. Take full advantage of them. You may find yourself finishing something you began and put aside long ago. Or embarking on something new which could easily be prompted by a chance meeting, a new acquaintance, or even an advertisement. There may be a yearning for a change of scenery, the feeling to visit another country (not too far away), or at least to get away for a few days. This may result in short, quick journeys. Or, if you are planning a single visit, there may be some unexpected changes or detours on the way. Familiar activities will seem to give little satisfaction unless they contain a fresh element of excitement or expectation. The inclination will be towards untried pursuits, particularly those that allow you to express your inner nature. The accent is on new faces, new places. CAUTION: Do not be too quick to commit yourself emotionally.

MOON IN CANCER

Feelings of uncertainty and vague insecurity are likely to cause problems while the moon is in Cancer. Thoughts may turn frequently to the warmth of the home and the comfort of loved ones. Nostalgic impulses could cause you to bring out old photographs and letters and reflect on the days when your life seemed to be much more rewarding and less demanding. The love and understanding of parents and family may be important, and, if it is not forthcoming you may have to fight against a bit of self-pity. The cordiality of friends and the thought of good times with them that are sure to be repeated will help to restore you to a happier frame of mind. The feeling to be alone may follow minor setbacks or rebuffs at this time, but solitude is unlikely to help. Better to get on the telephone or visit someone. This period often causes peculiar dreams and upsurges of imaginative thinking which can be very helpful to authors of occult and mystical works. Preoccupation with the more personal world of simple human needs should overshadow any material strivings. CAUTION: Do not spend too much time thinking—seek the company of loved ones or close friends.

MOON IN LEO

New horizons of exciting and rather extravagant activity open up. This is the time for exhilarating entertainment, glamorous and lavish parties, and expensive shopping sprees. Any merrymaking that relies upon your generosity as a host has every chance of being a spectacular success. You should find yourself right in the center of the fun, either as the life of the party or simply as a person whom happy people like to be with. Romance thrives in this heady atmosphere and friendships are likely to explode unexpectedly into serious attachments. Children and younger people should be attracted to you and you may find yourself organizing a picnic or a visit to a fun-fair, the cinema or the seaside. The sunny company and vitality of youthful companions should help you to find some unsuspected energy. In career, you could find an opening for promotion or advancement. This should be the time to make a direct approach. The period favors those engaged in original research. CAUTION: Bask in popularity but not in flattery.

MOON IN VIRGO

Off comes the party cap and out steps the busy, practical worker. He wants to get his personal affairs straight, to rearrange them, if necessary, for more efficiency, so he will have more time for more work. He clears up his correspondence, pays outstanding bills, makes numerous phone calls. He is likely to make inquiries, or sign up for some new insurance and put money into gilt-edged investment. Thoughts probably revolve around the need for future security—to tie up loose ends and clear the decks. There may be a tendency to be "finicky," to interfere in the routine of others, particularly friends and family members. The motive may be a genuine desire to help with suggestions for updating or streamlining their affairs, but these will probably not be welcomed. Sympathy may be felt for less fortunate sections of the community and a flurry of some sort of voluntary service is likely. This may be accompanied by strong feelings of responsibility on several fronts and health may suffer from extra efforts made. CAUTION: Everyone may not want your help or advice.

MOON IN LIBRA

These are days of harmony and agreement and you should find yourself at peace with most others. Relationships tend to be smooth and sweet-flowing. Friends may become closer and bonds deepen in mutual understanding. Hopes will be shared. Progress by cooperation could be the secret of success in every sphere. In business, established partnerships may flourish and new ones get off to a good start. Acquaintances could discover similar interests that lead to congenial discussions and rewarding exchanges of some sort. Love, as a unifying force, reaches its optimum. Marriage partners should find accord. Those who wed at this time face the prospect of a happy union. Cooperation and tolerance are felt to be stronger than dissension and impatience. The argumentative are not quite so loud in their bellowings, nor as inflexible in their attitudes. In the home, there should be a greater recognition of the other point of view and a readiness to put the wishes of the group before selfish insistence. This is a favorable time to join an art group. CAUTION: Do not be too independent—let others help you if they want to.

MOON IN SCORPIO

Driving impulses to make money and to economize are likely to cause upsets all round. No area of expenditure is likely to be spared the axe, including the household budget. This is a time when the desire to cut down on extravagance can become near fanatical. Care must be exercised to try to keep the aim in reasonable perspective. Others may not feel the same urgent need to save and may retaliate. There is a danger that possessions of sentimental value will be sold to realize cash for investment. Buying and selling of stock for quick profit is also likely. The attention may turn to having a good clean up round the home and at the office. Neglected jobs could suddenly be done with great bursts of energy. The desire for solitude may intervene. Self-searching thoughts could disturb. The sense of invisible and mysterious energies at work could cause some excitability. The reassurance of loves ones may help. CAUTION: Be kind to the people you love.

MOON IN SAGITTARIUS

These are days when you are likely to be stirred and elevated by discussions and reflections of a religious and philosophical nature. Ideas of far-away places may cause unusual response and excitement. A decision may be made to visit someone overseas, perhaps a person whose influence was important to your earlier character development. There could be a strong resolution to get away from present intellectual patterns, to learn new subjects and to meet more interesting people. The superficial may be rejected in all its forms. An impatience with old ideas and unimaginative contacts could lead to a change of companions and interests. There may be an upsurge of religious feeling and metaphysical inquiry. Even a new insight into the significance of astrology and other occult studies is likely under the curious stimulus of the moon in Sagittarius. Physically, you may express this need for fundamental change by spending more time outdoors: sports, gardening or going for long walks. CAUTION: Try to channel any restlessness into worthwhile study.

MOON IN CAPRICORN

Life in these hours may seem to pivot around the importance of gaining prestige and honor in the career, as well as maintaining a spotless reputation. Ambitious urges may be excessive and could be accompanied by quite acquisitive drives for money. Effort should be directed along strictly ethical lines where there is no possibility of reproach or scandal. All endeavors are likely to be characterized by great earnestness, and an air of authority and purpose which should impress those who are looking for leadership or reliability. The desire to conform to accepted standards may extend to sharp criticism of family members. Frivolity and unconventional actions are unlikely to amuse while the moon is in Capricorn. Moderation and seriousness are the orders of the day. Achievement and recognition in this period could come through community work or organizing for the benefit of some amateur group. CAUTION: Dignity and esteem are not always self-awarded.

MOON IN AQUARIUS

Moon in Aquarius is in the second last sign of the Zodiac where ideas can become disturbingly fine and subtle. The result is often a mental "no-man's land" where imagination cannot be trusted with the same certitude as other times. The dangers for the individual are the extremes of optimism and pessimism. Unless the imgination is held in check, situations are likely to be misread, and rosy conclusions drawn where they do not exist. Consequences for the unwary can be costly in career and business. Best to think twice and not speak or act until you think again. Pessimism can be a cruel self-inflicted penalty for delusion at this time. Between the two extremes are strange areas of self-deception which, for example, can make the selfish person think he is actually being generous. Eerie dreams which resemble the reality and even seem to continue into the waking state are also possible. CAUTION: Look for the fact and not just for the image in your mind.

MOON IN PISCES

Everything seems to come to the surface now. Memory may be crystal clear, throwing up long-forgotten information which could be valuable in the career or business. Flashes of clairvoyance and intuition are possible along with sudden realizations of one's own nature, which may be used for self-improvement. A talent, never before suspected, may be discovered. Qualities not evident before in friends and marriage partners are likely to be noticed. As this is a period in which the truth seems to emerge, the discovery of false characteristics is likely to lead to disenchantment or a shift in attachments. However, where qualities are realized it should lead to happiness and deeper feeling. Surprise solutions could bob up for old problems. There may be a public announcement of the solving of a crime or mystery. People with secrets may find someone has "guessed" correctly. The secrets of the soul or the inner self also tend to reveal themselves. Religious and philosophical groups may make some interesting discoveries. CAUTION: Not a time for activities that depend on secrecy.

MOON TABLES

TIME CORRECTIONS FOR GREENWICH MOON TABLES

London, Glasgow, Dublin, Dakar..Same time

Vienna, Prague, Rome, Kinshasa, Frankfurt,
    Stockholm, Brussels, Amsterdam, Warsaw,
    Zurich...Add 1 hour

Bucharest, Istanbul, Beirut, Cairo, Johannesburg,
    Athens, Cape Town, Helsinki, Tel Aviv............................Add 2 hours

Dhahran, Baghdad, Moscow, Leningrad, Nairobi,
    Addis Ababa, Zanzibar...Add 3 hours

Delhi, Calcutta, Bombay, Colombo....................................Add 5½ hours

Rangoon...Add 6½ hours

Saigon, Bangkok, Chungking...Add 7 hours

Canton, Manila, Hong Kong, Shanghai, Peking....................Add 8 hours

Tokyo, Pusan, Seoul, Vladivostok, Yokohama......................Add 9 hours

Sydney, Melbourne, Guam, Port Moresby............................Add 10 hours

Azores, Reykjavik...Deduct 1 hour

Rio de Janeiro, Montevideo, Buenos Aires,
    Sao Paulo, Recife...Deduct 3 hours

LaPaz, San Juan, Santiago, Bermuda, Caracas,
    Halifax...Deduct 4 hours

New York, Washington, Boston, Detroit, Lima,
    Havana, Miami, Bogota...Deduct 5 hours

Mexico, Chicago, New Orleans, Houston............................Deduct 6 hours

San Francisco, Seattle, Los Angeles, Hollywood,
    Ketchikan, Juneau...Deduct 8 hours

Honolulu, Fairbanks, Anchorage, Papeete........................Deduct 10 hours

1988 MOON TABLES—GREENWICH TIME

JANUARY		FEBRUARY		MARCH	
Day Moon Enters		**Day Moon Enters**		**Day Moon Enters**	
1. Gemini		1. Leo	6:31 pm	1. Leo	
2. Gemini		2. Leo		2. Virgo	1:26 pm
3. Cancer	0:30 am	3. Leo		3. Virgo	
4. Cancer		4. Virgo	7:10 am	4. Virgo	
5. Leo	Noon	5. Virgo		5. Libra	1:29 am
6. Leo		6. Libra	7:27 pm	6. Libra	
7. Leo		7. Libra		7. Scorpio	0:35 pm
8. Virgo	0:37 am	8. Libra		8. Scorpio	
9. Virgo		9. Scorpio	6:38 am	9. Sagitt.	8:59 pm
10. Libra	1:12 pm	10. Scorpio		10. Sagitt.	
11. Libra		11. Sagitt.	2:19 pm	11. Sagitt.	
12. Scorpio	11:21 pm	12. Sagitt.		12. Capric.	2:35 am
13. Scorpio		13. Capric.	6:20 pm	13. Capric.	
14. Scorpio		14. Capric.		14. Aquar.	5:06 am
15. Sagitt.	5:28 am	15. Aquar.	7:22 pm	15. Aquar.	
16. Sagitt.		16. Aquar.		16. Pisces	5:30 am
17. Capric.	8:20 am	17. Pisces	6:43 pm	17. Pisces	
18. Capric.		18. Pisces		18. Aries	5:30 am
19. Aquar.	8:08 am	19. Aries	6:39 pm	19. Aries	
20. Aquar.		20. Aries		20. Taurus	6:56 am
21. Pisces	7:58 am	21. Taurus	8:56 pm	21. Taurus	
22. Pisces		22. Taurus		22. Gemini	10:58 am
23. Aries	8:32 am	23. Taurus		23. Gemini	
24. Aries		24. Gemini	2:42 am	24. Cancer	7:36 pm
25. Taurus	0:54 pm	25. Gemini		25. Cancer	
26. Taurus		26. Cancer	0:36 pm	26. Cancer	
27. Gemini	7:53 pm	27. Cancer		27. Leo	7:23 am
28. Gemini		28. Cancer		28. Leo	
29. Gemini		29. Leo	0:50 am	29. Virgo	8:13 pm
30. Cancer	6:39 am			30. Virgo	
31. Cancer				31. Virgo	

Summer time to be considered where applicable.

1988 MOON TABLES—GREENWICH TIME

APRIL		MAY		JUNE	
Day Moon Enters		**Day Moon Enters**		**Day Moon Enters**	
1. Libra	8:12 am	1. Scorpio	1:24 am	1. Capric.	8:51 pm
2. Libra		2. Scorpio		2. Capric.	
3. Scorpio	6:28 pm	3. Sagitt.	8:40 am	3. Aquar.	11:48 pm
4. Scorpio		4. Sagitt.		4. Aquar.	
5. Scorpio		5. Capric.	1:55 pm	5. Aquar.	
6. Sagitt.	2:28 am	6. Capric.		6. Pisces	2:16 am
7. Sagitt.		7. Aquar.	6:08 pm	7. Pisces	
8. Capric.	8:38 am	8. Aquar.		8. Aries	5:16 am
9. Capric.		9. Pisces	8:50 pm	9. Aries	
10. Aquar.	0:41 pm	10. Pisces		10. Taurus	9:12 am
11. Aquar.		11. Aries	11:20 pm	11. Taurus	
12. Pisces	2:46 pm	12. Aries		12. Gemini	2:22 pm
13. Pisces		13. Aries		13. Gemini	
14. Aries	3:39 pm	14. Taurus	2:22 am	14. Cancer	9:42 pm
15. Aries		15. Taurus		15. Cancer	
16. Taurus	5:26 pm	16. Gemini	6:24 am	16. Cancer	
17. Taurus		17. Gemini		17. Leo	7:10 am
18. Gemini	8:48 pm	18. Cancer	0:46 pm	18. Leo	
19. Gemini		19. Cancer		19. Virgo	7:04 pm
20. Gemini		20. Leo	10:54 pm	20. Virgo	
21. Cancer	4:04 am	21. Leo		21. Virgo	
22. Cancer		22. Leo		22. Libra	7:59 am
23. Leo	2:51 pm	23. Virgo	11:12 am	23. Libra	
24. Leo		24. Virgo		24. Scorpio	6:59 pm
25. Leo		25. Libra	11:55 pm	25. Scorpio	
26. Virgo	3:44 am	26. Libra		26. Scorpio	
27. Virgo		27. Libra		27. Sagitt.	2:21 am
28. Libra	3:55 pm	28. Scorpio	10:03 am	28. Sagitt.	
29. Libra		29. Scorpio		29. Capric.	6:06 am
30. Libra		30. Sagitt.	4:44 pm	30. Capric.	
		31. Sagitt.			

Summer time to be considered where applicable.

1988 MOON TABLES—GREENWICH TIME

JULY	AUGUST	SEPTEMBER
Day Moon Enters	**Day Moon Enters**	**Day Moon Enters**
1. Aquar. 7:38 am	1. Aries 5:48 pm	1. Taurus
2. Aquar.	2. Aries	2. Gemini 8:08 am
3. Pisces 8:52 am	3. Taurus 8:12 pm	3. Gemini
4. Pisces	4. Taurus	4. Cancer 3:50 pm
5. Aries 10:41 am	5. Taurus	5. Cancer
6. Aries	6. Gemini 1:34 am	6. Cancer
7. Taurus 2:31 pm	7. Gemini	7. Leo 2:32 am
8. Taurus	8. Cancer 10:07 am	8. Leo
9. Gemini 8:17 pm	9. Cancer	9. Virgo 3:02 pm
10. Gemini	10. Leo 8:57 pm	10. Virgo
11. Gemini	11. Leo	11. Virgo
12. Cancer 4:29 am	12. Leo	12. Libra 3:32 am
13. Cancer	13. Virgo 8:37 am	13. Libra
14. Leo 2:25 pm	14. Virgo	14. Scorpio 3:25 pm
15. Leo	15. Libra 9:26 pm	15. Scorpio
16. Leo	16. Libra	16. Scorpio
17. Virgo 2:24 am	17. Libra	17. Sagitt. 2:01 am
18. Virgo	18. Scorpio 9:37 am	18. Sagitt.
19. Libra 3:04 pm	19. Scorpio	19. Capric. 9:40 am
20. Libra	20. Sagitt. 7:49 pm	20. Capric.
21. Libra	21. Sagitt.	21. Aquar. 2:09 pm
22. Scorpio 3:01 am	22. Sagitt.	22. Aquar.
23. Scorpio	23. Capric. 1:45 am	23. Pisces 2:45 pm
24. Sagitt. Noon	24. Capric.	24. Pisces
25. Sagitt.	25. Aquar. 4:20 am	25. Aries 2:33 pm
26. Capric. 4:15 pm	26. Aquar.	26. Aries
27. Capric.	27. Pisces 4:14 am	27. Taurus 2:30 pm
28. Aquar. 5:58 pm	28. Pisces	28. Taurus
29. Aquar.	29. Aries 3:45 am	29. Gemini 5:01 pm
30. Pisces 5:45 pm	30. Aries	30. Gemini
31. Pisces	31. Taurus 4:30 am	

Summer time to be considered where applicable.

1988 MOON TABLES—GREENWICH TIME

OCTOBER		NOVEMBER		DECEMBER	
Day Moon Enters		**Day Moon Enters**		**Day Moon Enters**	
1. Cancer	10:43 pm	1. Leo		1. Virgo	
2. Cancer		2. Leo		2. Virgo	
3. Cancer		3. Virgo	4:25 am	3. Libra	1:13 am
4. Leo	9:00 am	4. Virgo		4. Libra	
5. Leo		5. Libra	5:15 pm	5. Scorpio	0:47 pm
6. Virgo	9:22 pm	6. Libra		6. Scorpio	
7. Virgo		7. Libra		7. Sagitt.	10:10 pm
8. Virgo		8. Scorpio	4:39 am	8. Sagitt.	
9. Libra	10:00 am	9. Scorpio		9. Sagitt.	
10. Libra		10. Sagitt.	1:53 pm	10. Capric.	4:14 am
11. Scorpio	9:34 pm	11. Sagitt.		11. Capric.	
12. Scorpio		12. Capric.	9:23 pm	12. Aquar.	9:04 am
13. Scorpio		13. Capric.		13. Aquar.	
14. Sagitt.	7:35 am	14. Capric.		14. Pisces	0:10 pm
15. Sagitt.		15. Aquar.	2:46 am	15. Pisces	
16. Capric.	3:38 pm	16. Aquar.		16. Aries	2:53 pm
17. Capric.		17. Pisces	6:37 am	17. Aries	
18. Aquar.	9:07 pm	18. Pisces		18. Taurus	5:50 pm
19. Aquar.		19. Aries	8:50 am	19. Taurus	
20. Pisces	11:56 pm	20. Aries		20. Gemini	9:48 pm
21. Pisces		21. Taurus	10:41 am	21. Gemini	
22. Pisces		22. Taurus		22. Gemini	
23. Aries	0:49 am	23. Gemini	1:13 pm	23. Cancer	2:42 am
24. Aries		24. Gemini		24. Cancer	
25. Taurus	1:22 am	25. Cancer	5:36 pm	25. Leo	10:08 am
26. Taurus		26. Cancer		26. Leo	
27. Gemini	3:07 am	27. Cancer		27. Virgo	8:36 pm
28. Gemini		28. Leo	1:04 am	28. Virgo	
29. Cancer	7:42 am	29. Leo		29. Virgo	
30. Cancer		30. Virgo	0:12 pm	30. Libra	8:58 am
31. Leo	4:25 pm			31. Libra	

Summer time to be considered where applicable.

1988 PHASES OF THE MOON—GREENWICH TIME

New Moon	First Quarter	Full Moon	Last Quarter
(1987)	(1987)	Jan. 4	Jan. 12
Jan. 19	Jan. 25	Feb. 2	Feb. 10
Feb. 17	Feb. 24	Mar. 3	Mar. 11
Mar. 18	Mar. 25	Apr. 1	Apr. 9
Apr. 16	Apr. 23	May 1	May 9
May 15	May 23	May 31	June 7
June 14	June 22	June 29	July 6
July 13	July 22	July 29	Aug. 4
Aug. 12	Aug. 20	Aug. 27	Sep. 3
Sep. 11	Sep. 19	Sep. 25	Oct. 2
Oct. 10	Oct. 18	Oct. 25	Nov. 1
Nov. 9	Nov. 16	Nov. 23	Dec. 1
Dec. 9	Dec. 16	Dec. 23	Dec. 31

1988 PLANTING GUIDE

	Aboveground Crops	Root Crops	Pruning	Weeds Pests
January	3-21-22-26-30-31	4-11-12-13-14-17-18	4-13-14	6-7-8-9-15-16
February	18-22-23-27-28	7-8-9-10-14	9-10	3-4-5-12-16
March	20-21-25-26	5-6-7-8-12-13-16-17	8-16-17	4-10-11-14-15
April	1-17-21-22-29-30	2-3-4-5-8-9-13	4-5-13	6-7-11-15
May	1-19-20-26-27-28-29	2-6-10-11-14-15	2-10-11	3-4-8-12-13
June	15-16-22-23-24-25-26	2-3-6-7-10-11-30	6-7	4-5-8-9-13
July	20-21-22-23-27	3-4-8-12-13-31	3-4-12-13-31	1-2-6-10-11-29
August	16-17-18-19-23-24	4-5-9-28-31	9-28	2-6-7-11-29-30
September	12-13-14-15-16-19-20-24	1-5-6-28	5-6	2-3-7-8-9-10-26-30
October	11-12-13-17-21-22	2-3-9-25-26-29-30	2-3-29-30	1-4-5-6-7-27-28
November	13-14-17-18-21-22	6-7-8-26-27	8-26-27	1-2-3-4-24-28-29-30
December	10-11-15-19	3-4-5-6-7-23-24-30-31	6-7-23-24	1-2-8-26-27-28-29

1988 FISHING GUIDE

	Good	Best
January	1-2-5-6-7-19-25	3-4-12-30-31
February	1-2-3-4-5-17-24-29	10
March	1-2-3-4-11-18-30-31	5-6-25
April	16-23-28	1-2-3-4-5-9-29-30
May	3-4-9-23-30-31	1-2-15-28-29
June	1-14-27-28	2-3-7-22-26-29-30
July	1-2-6-26-28-29-30	13-22-27-31
August	1-12-20-25-26-29-30	4-24-27-28
September	3-11-22-23-25-26-27	19-24-28
October	18-23-24-27-28	2-10-22-25-26
November	1-16-20-21-23-24-25	9-22-26
December	1-9-16-20-21-22-25-26	23-24-31

MOON'S INFLUENCE OVER DAILY AFFAIRS

The Moon makes a complete transit of the Zodiac every 27 days 7 hours and 43 minutes. In making this transit the Moon forms different aspects with the planets and consequently has favorable or unfavorable bearings on affairs and events for persons according to the sign of the Zodiac under which they were born.

Whereas the Sun exclusively represents fire, the Moon rules water. The action of the Moon may be described as fluctuating, variable, absorbent and receptive. It is well known that the attraction to the Moon in combination with the movement of the Earth is responsible for the tides. The Moon has a similar effect on men. A clever navigator will make use of the tides to bring his ship to the intended destination. You also can reach your "destination" better by making use of your tides.

When the Moon is in conjunction with the Sun it is called a New Moon; when the Moon and Sun are in opposition it is called a Full Moon. From New Moon to Full Moon, first and second quarter—which takes about two weeks—the Moon is increasing or waxing. From Full Moon to New Moon, third and fourth quarter, the Moon is said to be decreasing or waning. The Moon Table indicates the New Moon and Full Moon and the quarters.

ACTIVITY	MOON IN
Business	
buying and selling	Sagittarius, Aries, Gemini, Virgo
new, requiring public support	1st and 2nd quarter
meant to be kept quiet	3rd and 4th quarter
Investigation	3rd and 4th quarter
Signing documents	1st & 2nd quarter, Cancer, Scorpio, Pisces
Advertising	2nd quarter, Sagittarius
Journeys and trips	1st & 2nd quarter, Gemini, Virgo
Renting offices, etc.	Taurus, Leo, Scorpio, Aquarius
Painting of house/apartment	3rd & 4th quarter, Taurus, Scorpio, Aquarius
Decorating	Gemini, Libra, Aquarius
Buying clothes and accessories	Taurus, Virgo
Beauty salon or barber shop visit	1st & 2nd quarter, Taurus, Leo, Libra, Scorpio, Aquarius
Weddings	1st & 2nd quarter

MOON'S INFLUENCE OVER YOUR HEALTH

ARIES	Head, brain, face, upper jaw
TAURUS	Throat, neck, lower jaw
GEMINI	Hands, arms, lungs, shoulders, nervous system
CANCER	Esophagus, stomach, breasts, womb, liver
LEO	Heart, spine
VIRGO	Intestines, liver
LIBRA	Kidneys, lower back
SCORPIO	Sex and eliminative organs
SAGITTARIUS	Hips, thighs, liver
CAPRICORN	Skin, bones, beeth, knees
AQUARIUS	Circulatory system, lower legs
PISCES	Feet, tone of being

Try to avoid work being done on that part of the body when the Moon is in the sign governing that part.

MOON'S INFLUENCE OVER PLANTS

Centuries ago it was established that seeds planted when the Moon is in certain signs and phases called "fruitful" will produce more than seeds planted when the Moon is in a Barren sign.

FRUITFUL SIGNS	*BARREN SIGNS*	*DRY SIGNS*
Taurus	Aries	Aries
Cancer	Gemini	Gemini
Libra	Leo	Sagittarius
Scorpio	Virgo	Aquarius
Capricorn	Sagittarius	
Pisces	Aquarius	

ACTIVITY	MOON IN
Mow lawn, trim plans	Fruitful sign, 1st & 2nd quarter
Plant flowers	Fruitful sign, 2nd quarter; best in Cancer and Libra
Prune	Fruitful sign, 3rd & 4th quarter
Destroy pests; spray	Barren sign, 4th quarter
Harvest potatoes, root crops	Dry sign, 3rd & 4th quarter; Taurus, Leo, and Aquarius

THE SIGNS: DOMINANT CHARACTERISTICS

March 21–April 20

The Positive Side of Aries

The Arien has many positive points to his character. People born under this first sign of the Zodiac are often quite strong and enthusiastic. On the whole, they are forward-looking people who are not easily discouraged by temporary setbacks. They know what they want out of life and they go out after it. Their personalities are strong. Others are usually quite impressed by the Arien's way of doing things. Quite often they are sources of inspiration for others traveling the same route. Aries men and women have a special zest for life that is often contagious; for others, they are often the example of how life should be lived.

The Aries person usually has a quick and active mind. He is imaginative and inventive. He enjoys keeping busy and active. He generally gets along well with all kinds of people. He is interested in mankind, as a whole. He likes to be challenged. Some would say he thrives on opposition, for it is when he is set against that he often does his best. Getting over or around obstacles is a challenge he generally enjoys. All in all, the Arien is quite positive and young-thinking. He likes to keep abreast of new things that are happening in the world. Ariens are often fond of speed. They like things to be done quickly and this sometimes aggravates their slower colleagues and associates.

The Aries man or woman always seems to remain young. Their whole approach to life is youthful and optimistic. They never say die, no matter what the odds. They may have an occasional setback, but it is not long before they are back on their feet again.

The Negative Side of Aries

Everybody has his less positive qualities—and Aries is no exception. Sometimes the Aries man or woman is not very tactful in communicating with others; in his hurry to get things done he is apt to

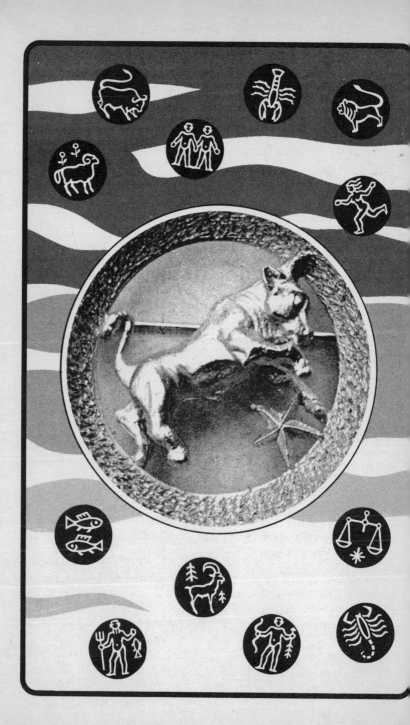

be a little callous or inconsiderate. Sensitive people are likely to find him somewhat sharp-tongued in some situations. Often in his eagerness to achieve his aims, he misses the mark altogether. At times the Arien is too impulsive. He can occasionally be stubborn and refuse to listen to reason. If things do not move quickly enough to suit the Aries man or woman, he or she is apt to become rather nervous or irritable. The uncultivated Arien is not unfamiliar with moments of doubt and fear. He is capable of being destructive if he does not get his way. He can overcome some of his emotional problems by steadily trying to express himself as he really is, but this requires effort.

April 21–May 20

The Positive Side of Taurus

The Taurus person is known for his ability to concentrate and for his tenacity. These are perhaps his strongest qualities. The Taurus man or woman generally has very little trouble in getting along with others; it's his nature to be helpful toward people in need. He can always be depended on by his friends, especially those in trouble.

The Taurean generally achieves what he wants through his ability to persevere. He never leaves anything unfinished but works on something until it has been completed. People can usually take him at his word; he is honest and forthright in most of his dealings. The Taurus person has a good chance to make a success of his life because of his many positive qualities. The Taurean who aims high seldom falls short of his mark. He learns well by experience. He is thorough and does not believe in short-cuts of any kind. The Taurean's thoroughness pays off in the end, for through his deliberateness he learns how to rely on himself and what he has learned. The Taurus person tries to get along with others, as a rule. He is not overly critical and likes people to be themselves. He is a tolerant person and enjoys peace and harmony—especially in his home life.

The Taurean is usually cautious in all that he does. He is not a person who believes in taking unnecessary risks. Before adopting any one line of action, he will weigh all of the pros and cons. The

Taurus person is steadfast. Once his mind is made up it seldom changes. The person born under this sign usually is a good family person—reliable and loving.

The Negative Side of Taurus

Sometimes the Taurus man or woman is a bit too stubborn. He won't listen to other points of view if his mind is set on something. To others, this can be quite annoying. The Taurean also does not like to be told what to do. He becomes rather angry if others think him not too bright. He does not like to be told he is wrong, even when he is. He dislikes being contradicted.

Some people who are born under this sign are very suspicious of others—even of those persons close to them. They find it difficult to trust people fully. They are often afraid of being deceived or taken advantage of. The Taurean often finds it difficult to forget or forgive. His love of material things sometimes makes him rather avaricious and petty.

May 21–June 20

The Positive Side of Gemini

The person born under this sign of the Heavenly Twins is usually quite bright and quick-witted. Some of them are capable of doing many different things. The Gemini person very often has many different interests. He keeps an open mind and is always anxious to learn new things.

The Geminian is often an analytical person. He is a person who enjoys making use of his intellect. He is governed more by his mind than by his emotions. He is a person who is not confined to one view; he can often understand both sides to a problem or question. He knows how to reason; how to make rapid decisions if need be.

He is an adaptable person and can make himself at home almost anywhere. There are all kinds of situations he can adapt to. He is a person who seldom doubts himself; he is sure of his talents and his

ability to think and reason. The Geminian is generally most satisfied when he is in a situation where he can make use of his intellect. Never short of imagination, he often has strong talents for invention. He is rather a modern person when it comes to life; the Geminian almost always moves along with the times—perhaps that is why he remains so youthful throughout most of his life.

Literature and art appeal to the person born under this sign. Creativity in almost any form will interest and intrigue the Gemini man or woman.

The Geminian is often quite charming. A good talker, he often is the center of attraction at any gathering. People find it easy to like a person born under this sign because he can appear easygoing and usually has a good sense of humor.

The Negative Side of Gemini

Sometimes the Gemini person tries to do too many things at one time—and as a result, winds up finishing nothing. Some Geminians are easily distracted and find it rather difficult to concentrate on one thing for too long a time. Sometimes they give in to trifling fancies and find it rather boring to become too serious about any one thing. Some of them are never dependable, no matter what they promise.

Although the Gemini man or woman often appears to be well-versed on many subjects, this is sometimes just a veneer. His knowledge may be only superficial, but because he speaks so well he gives people the impression of erudition. Some Geminians are sharp-tongued and inconsiderate; they think only of themselves and their own pleasure.

June 21–July 20

The Positive Side of Cancer

The Cancerians's most positive point is his understanding nature. On the whole, he is a loving and sympathetic person. He would never go out of his way to hurt anyone. The Cancer man or woman

is often very kind and tender; they give what they can to others. They hate to see others suffering and will do what they can to help someone in less fortunate circumstances than themselves. They are often very concerned about the world. Their interest in people generally goes beyond that of just their own families and close friends; they have a deep sense of brotherhood and respect humanitarian values. The Cancerian means what he says, as a rule; he is honest about his feelings.

The Cancer man or woman is a person who knows the art of patience. When something seems difficult, he is willing to wait until the situation becomes manageable again. He is a person who knows how to bide his time. The Cancerian knows how to concentrate on one thing at a time. When he has made his mind up he generally sticks with what he does, seeing it through to the end.

The Cancerian is a person who loves his home. He enjoys being surrounded by familiar things and the people he loves. Of all the signs, Cancer is the most maternal. Even the men born under this sign often have a motherly or protective quality about them. They like to take care of people in their family—to see that they are well loved and well provided for. They are usually loyal and faithful. Family ties mean a lot to the Cancer man or woman. Parents and in-laws are respected and loved. The Cancerian has a strong sense of tradition. He is very sensitive to the moods of others.

The Negative Side of Cancer

Sometimes the Cancerian finds it rather hard to face life. It becomes too much for him. He can be a little timid and retiring, when things don't go too well. When unfortunate things happen, he is apt to just shrug and say, "Whatever will be will be." He can be fatalistic to a fault. The uncultivated Cancerian is a bit lazy. He doesn't have very much ambition. Anything that seems a bit difficult he'll gladly leave to others. He may be lacking in initiative. Too sensitive, when he feels he's been injured, he'll crawl back into his shell and nurse his imaginary wounds. The Cancer woman often is given to crying when the smallest thing goes wrong.

Some Cancerians find it difficult to enjoy themselves in environments outside their homes. They make heavy demands on others, and need to be constantly reassured that they are loved.

July 21–August 21

The Positive Side of Leo

Often Leos make good leaders. They seem to be good organizers and administrators. Usually they are quite popular with others. Whatever group it is that he belongs to, the Leo man is almost sure to be or become the leader.

The Leo person is generous most of the time. It is his best characteristic. He or she likes to give gifts and presents. In making others happy, the Leo person becomes happy himself. He likes to splurge when spending money on others. In some instances it may seem that the Leo's generosity knows no boundaries. A hospitable person, the Leo man or woman is very fond of welcoming people to his house and entertaining them. He is never short of company.

The Leo person has plenty of energy and drive. He enjoys working toward some specific goal. When he applies himself correctly, he gets what he wants most often. The Leo person is almost never unsure of himself. He has plenty of confidence and aplomb. He is a person who is direct in almost everything he does. He has a quick mind and can make a decision in a very short time.

He usually sets a good example for others because of his ambitious manner and positive ways. He knows how to stick to something once he's started. Although the Leo person may be good at making a joke, he is not superficial or glib. He is a loving person, kind and thoughtful.

There is generally nothing small or petty about the Leo man or woman. He does what he can for those who are deserving. He is a person others can rely upon at all times. He means what he says. An honest person, generally speaking, he is a friend that others value.

The Negative Side of Leo

Leo, however, does have his faults. At times, he can be just a bit too arrogant. He thinks that no one deserves a leadership position except him. Only he is capable of doing things well. His opinion of himself is often much too high. Because of his conceit, he is sometimes rather unpopular with a good many people. Some Leos are too materialistic; they can only think in terms of money and profit.

Some Leos enjoy lording it over others—at home or at their place of business. What is more, they feel they have the right to. Egocentric to an impossible degree, this sort of Leo cares little about how others think or feel. He can be rude and cutting.

August 22–September 22

The Positive Side of Virgo

The person born under the sign of Virgo is generally a busy person. He knows how to arrange and organize things. He is a good planner. Above all, he is practical and is not afraid of hard work.

The person born under this sign, Virgo, knows how to attain what he desires. He sticks with something until it is finished. He never shirks his duties, and can always be depended upon. The Virgo person can be thoroughly trusted at all times.

The man or woman born under this sign tries to do everything to perfection. He doesn't believe in doing anything half-way. He always aims for the top. He is the sort of a person who is constantly striving to better himself—not because he wants more money or glory, but because it gives him a feeling of accomplishment.

The Virgo man or woman is a very observant person. He is sensitive to how others feel, and can see things below the surface of a situation. He usually puts this talent to constructive use.

It is not difficult for the Virgoan to be open and earnest. He believes in putting his cards on the table. He is never secretive or under-handed. He's as good as his word. The Virgo person is generally plain-spoken and down-to-earth. He has no trouble in expressing himself.

The Virgo person likes to keep up to date on new developments in his particular field. Well-informed, generally, he sometimes has a keen interest in the arts or literature. What he knows, he knows well. His ability to use his critical faculties is well-developed and sometimes startles others because of its accuracy.

The Virgoan adheres to a moderate way of life; he avoids excesses. He is a responsible person and enjoys being of service.

The Negative Side of Virgo

Sometimes a Virgo person is too critical. He thinks that only he can do something the way it should be done. Whatever anyone else does is inferior. He can be rather annoying in the way he quibbles over insignificant details. In telling others how things should be done, he can be rather tactless and mean.

Some Virgos seem rather emotionless and cool. They feel emo-

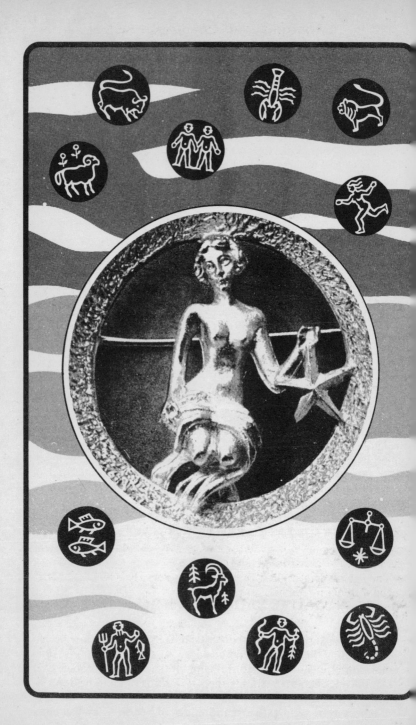

tional involvement is beneath them. They are sometimes too tidy, too neat. With money they can be rather miserly. Some try to force their opinions and ideas on others.

September 23–October 22

The Positive Side of Libra

Librans love harmony. It is one of their most outstanding character traits. They are interested in achieving balance; they admire beauty and grace in things as well as in people. Generally speaking, they are kind and considerate people. Librans are usually very sympathetic. They go out of their way not to hurt another person's feelings. They are outgoing and do what they can to help those in need.

People born under the sign of Libra almost always make good friends. They are loyal and amiable. They enjoy the company of others. Many of them are rather moderate in their views; they believe in keeping an open mind, however, and weighing both sides of an issue fairly before making a decision.

Alert and often intelligent, the Libran, always fair-minded, tries to put himself in the position of the other person. They are against injustice; quite often they take up for the underdog. In most of their social dealings, they try to be tactful and kind. They dislike discord and bickering, and most Libras strive for peace and harmony in all their relationships.

The Libra man or woman has a keen sense of beauty. They appreciate handsome furnishings and clothes. Many of them are artistically inclined. Their taste is usually impeccable. They know how to use color. Their homes are almost always attractively arranged and inviting. They enjoy entertaining people and see to it that their guests always feel at home and welcome.

The Libran gets along with almost everyone. He is well-liked and socially much in demand.

The Negative Side of Libra

Some people born under this sign tend to be rather insincere. So eager are they to achieve harmony in all relationships that they will even go so far as to lie. Many of them are escapists. They find facing

the truth an ordeal and prefer living in a world of make-believe.

In a serious argument, some Librans give in rather easily even when they know they are right. Arguing, even about something they believe in, is too unsettling for some of them.

Librans sometimes care too much for material things. They enjoy possessions and luxuries. Some are vain and tend to be jealous.

October 23–November 22

The Positive Side of Scorpio

The Scorpio man or woman generally knows what he or she wants out of life. He is a determined person. He sees something through to the end. The Scorpion is quite sincere, and seldom says anything he doesn't mean. When he sets a goal for himself he tries to go about achieving it in a very direct way.

The Scorpion is brave and courageous. They are not afraid of hard work. Obstacles do not frighten them. They forge ahead until they achieve what they set out for. The Scorpio man or woman has a strong will.

Although the Scorpion may seem rather fixed and determined, inside he is often quite tender and loving. He can care very much for others. He believes in sincerity in all relationships. His feelings about someone tend to last; they are profound and not superficial.

The Scorpio person is someone who adheres to his principles no matter what happens. He will not be deterred from a path he believes to be right.

Because of his many positive strengths, the Scorpion can often achieve happiness for himself and for those that he loves.

He is a constructive person by nature. He often has a deep understanding of people and of life, in general. He is perceptive and unafraid. Obstacles often seem to spur him on. He is a positive person who enjoys winning. He has many strengths and resources; challenge of any sort often brings out the best in him.

The Negative Side of Scorpio

The Scorpio person is sometimes hypersensitive. Often he imagines injury when there is none. He feels that others do not bother to

recognize him for his true worth. Sometimes he is given to excessive boasting in order to compensate for what he feels is neglect

The Scorpio person can be rather proud and arrogant. They can be rather sly when they put their minds to it and they enjoy outwitting persons or institutions noted for their cleverness.

Their tactics for getting what they want are sometimes devious and ruthless. They don't care too much about what others may think. If they feel others have done them an injustice, they will do their best to seek revenge. The Scorpion often has a sudden, violent temper; and this person's interest in sex is sometimes quite unbalanced or excessive.

November 23–December 20

The Positive Side of Sagittarius

People born under this sign are often honest and forthright. Their approach to life is earnest and open. The Sagittarian is often quite adult in his way of seeing things. They are broadminded and tolerant people. When dealing with others the person born under the sign of Sagittarius is almost always open and forthright. He doesn't believe in deceit or pretension. His standards are high. People who associate with the Sagittarian, generally admire and respect him.

The Sagittarian trusts others easily and expects them to trust him. He is never suspicious or envious and almost always thinks well of others. People always enjoy his company because he is so friendly and easy-going. The Sagittarius man or woman is often good-humored. He can always be depended upon by his friends, family, and co-workers.

The person born under this sign of the Zodiac likes a good joke every now and then; he is keen on fun and this makes him very popular with others.

A lively person, he enjoys sports and outdoor life. The Sagittarian is fond of animals. Intelligent and interesting, he can begin an animated conversation with ease. He likes exchanging ideas and discussing various views.

He is not selfish or proud. If someone proposes an idea or plan that is better than his, he will immediately adopt it. Imaginative yet practical, he knows how to put ideas into practice.

He enjoys sport and game, and it doesn't matter if he wins or loses. He is a forgiving person, and never sulks over something that has not worked out in his favor.

He is seldom critical, and is almost always generous.

The Negative Side of Sagittarius

Some Sagittarians are restless. They take foolish risks and seldom learn from the mistakes they make. They don't have heads for money and are often mismanaging their finances. Some of them devote much of their time to gambling.

Some are too outspoken and tactless, always putting their feet in their mouths. They hurt others carelessly by being honest at the wrong time. Sometimes they make promises which they don't keep. They don't stick close enough to their plans and go from one failure to another. They are undisciplined and waste a lot of energy.

December 21–January 19

The Positive Side of Capricorn

The person born under the sign of Capricorn is usually very stable and patient. He sticks to whatever tasks he has and sees them through. He can always be relied upon and he is not averse to work.

An honest person, the Capricornian is generally serious about whatever he does. He does not take his duties lightly. He is a practical person and believes in keeping his feet on the ground.

Quite often the person born under this sign is ambitious and knows how to get what he wants out of life. He forges ahead and never gives up his goal. When he is determined about something, he almost always wins. He is a good worker—a hard worker. Although things may not come easy to him, he will not complain, but continue working until his chores are finished.

He is usually good at business matters and knows the value of money. He is not a spendthrift and knows how to put something away for a rainy day; he dislikes waste and unnecessary loss.

The Capricornian knows how to make use of his self-control. He

can apply himself to almost anything once he puts his mind to it. His ability to concentrate sometimes astounds others. He is diligent and does well when involved in detail work.

The Capricorn man or woman is charitable, generally speaking, and will do what is possible to help others less fortunate. As a friend, he is loyal and trustworthy. He never shirks his duties or responsibilities. He is self-reliant and never expects too much of the other fellow. He does what he can on his own. If someone does him a good turn, then he will do his best to return the favor.

The Negative Side of Capricorn

Like everyone, the Capricornian, too, has his faults. At times, he can be over-critical of others. He expects others to live up to his own high standards. He thinks highly of himself and tends to look down on others.

His interest in material things may be exaggerated. The Capricorn man or woman thinks too much about getting on in the world and having something to show for it. He may even be a little greedy.

He sometimes thinks he knows what's best for everyone. He is too bossy. He is always trying to organize and correct others. He may be a little narrow in his thinking.

January 20–February 18

The Positive Side of Aquarius

The Aquarius man or woman is usually very honest and forthright. These are his two greatest qualities. His standards for himself are generally very high. He can always be relied upon by others. His word is his bond.

The Aquarian is perhaps the most tolerant of all the Zodiac personalities. He respects other people's beliefs and feels that everyone is entitled to his own approach to life.

He would never do anything to injure another's feelings. He is never unkind or cruel. Always considerate of others, the Aquarian is always willing to help a person in need. He feels a very strong tie between himself and all the other members of mankind.

The person born under this sign is almost always an individualist. He does not believe in teaming up with the masses, but prefers going his own way. His ideas about life and mankind are often quite advanced. There is a saying to the effect that the average Aquarian is fifty years ahead of his time.

He is broadminded. The problems of the world concern him greatly. He is interested in helping others no matter what part of the globe they live in. He is truly a humanitarian sort. He likes to be of service to others.

Giving, considerate, and without prejudice, Aquarians have no trouble getting along with others.

The Negative Side of Aquarius

The Aquarian may be too much of a dreamer. He makes plans but seldom carries them out. He is rather unrealistic. His imagination has a tendency to run away with him. Because many of his plans are impractical, he is always in some sort of a dither.

Others may not approve of him at all times because of his unconventional behavior. He may be a bit eccentric. Sometimes he is so busy with his own thoughts, that he loses touch with the realities of existence.

Some Aquarians feel they are more clever and intelligent than others. They seldom admit to their own faults, even when they are quite apparent. Some become rather fanatic in their views. Their criticism of others is sometimes destructive and negative.

February 19–March 20

The Positive Side of Pisces

The Piscean can often understand the problems of others quite easily. He has a sympathetic nature. Kindly, he is often dedicated in the way he goes about helping others. The sick and the troubled often turn to him for advice and assistance.

He is very broadminded and does not criticize others for their faults. He knows how to accept people for what they are. On the whole, he is a trustworthy and earnest person. He is loyal to his

friends and will do what he can to help them in time of need. Generous and good-natured, he is a lover of peace; he is often willing to help others solve their differences. People who have taken a wrong turn in life often interest him and he will do what he can to persuade them to rehabilitate themselves.

He has a strong intuitive sense and most of the time he knows how to make it work for him; the Piscean is unusually perceptive and often knows what is bothering someone before that person, himself, is aware of it. The Pisces man or woman is an idealistic person, basically, and is interested in making the world a better place in which to live. The Piscean believes that everyone should help each other. He is willing to do more than his share in order to achieve cooperation with others.

The person born under this sign often is talented in music or art. He is a receptive person; he is able to take the ups and downs of life with philosophic calm.

The Negative Side of Pisces

Some Pisceans are often depressed; their outlook on life is rather glum. They may feel that they have been given a bad deal in life and that others are always taking unfair advantage of them. The Piscean sometimes feel that the world is a cold and cruel place. He is easily discouraged. He may even withdraw from the harshness of reality into a secret shell of his own where he dreams and idles away a good deal of his time.

The Piscean can be rather lazy. He lets things happen without giving the least bit of resistance. He drifts along, whether on the high road or on the low. He is rather short on willpower.

Some Pisces people seek escape through drugs or alcohol. When temptation comes along they find it hard to resist. In matters of sex, they can be rather permissive.

THE SIGNS AND
THEIR KEY WORDS

		POSITIVE	NEGATIVE
ARIES	self	courage, initiative, pioneer instinct	brash rudeness, selfish impetuosity
TAURUS	money	endurance, loyalty, wealth	obstinacy, gluttony
GEMINI	mind	versatility	capriciousness, unreliability
CANCER	family	sympathy, homing instinct	clannishness, childishness
LEO	children	love, authority, integrity	egotism, force
VIRGO	work	purity, industry, analysis	fault-finding, cynicism
LIBRA	marriage	harmony, justice	vacillation, superficiality
SCORPIO	sex	survival, regeneration	vengeance, discord
SAGITTARIUS	travel	optimism, higher learning	lawlessness
CAPRICORN	career	depth	narrowness, gloom
AQUARIUS	friends	human fellowship, genius	perverse unpredictability
PISCES	confine-ment	spiritual love, universality	diffusion, escapism

THE ELEMENTS AND QUALITIES OF THE SIGNS

ELEMENT	SIGN	QUALITY	SIGN
FIRE...............	ARIES LEO SAGITTARIUS	CARDINAL........	ARIES LIBRA CANCER CAPRICORN
EARTH............	TAURUS VIRGO CAPRICORN	FIXED...............	TAURUS LEO SCORPIO AQUARIUS
AIR...................	GEMINI LIBRA AQUARIUS		
WATER............	CANCER SCORPIO PISCES	MUTABLE.........	GEMINI VIRGO SAGITTARIUS PISCES

Every sign has both an element and a quality associated with it. The element indicates the basic makeup of the sign, and the quality describes the kind of activity associated with each.

Signs can be grouped together according to their *element* and *quality*. Signs of the same element share many basic traits in common. They tend to form stable configurations and ultimately harmonious relationships. Signs of the same quality are often less harmonious, but they share many dynamic potentials for growth as well as profound fulfillment.

THE FIRE SIGNS

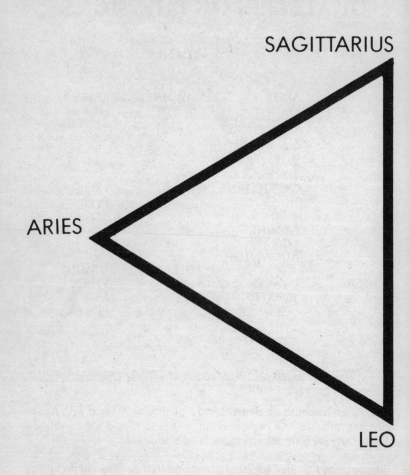

SAGITTARIUS

ARIES

LEO

This is the fire group. On the whole these are emotional, volatile types, quick to anger, quick to forgive. They are adventurous, powerful people and.act as a source of inspiration for everyone. They spark into action with immediate exuberant impulses. They are intelligent, self-involved, creative and idealistic. They all share a certain vibrancy and glow that outwardly reflects an inner flame and passion for living.

THE EARTH SIGNS

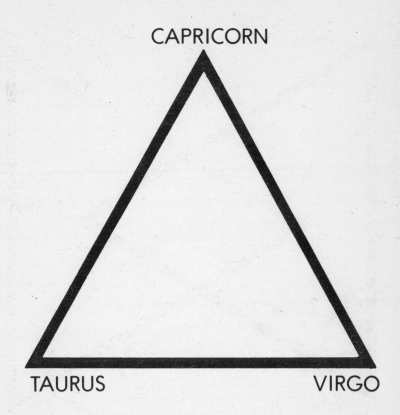

This is the earth group. They are in constant touch with the material world and tend to be conservative. Although they are all capable of spartan self-discipline, they are earthy, sensual people who are stimulated by the tangible, elegant and luxurious. The thread of their lives is always practical, but they do fantasize and are often attracted to dark, mysterious, emotional people. They are like great cliffs overhanging the sea, forever married to the ocean but always resisting erosion from the dark, emotional forces that thunder at their feet.

THE AIR SIGNS

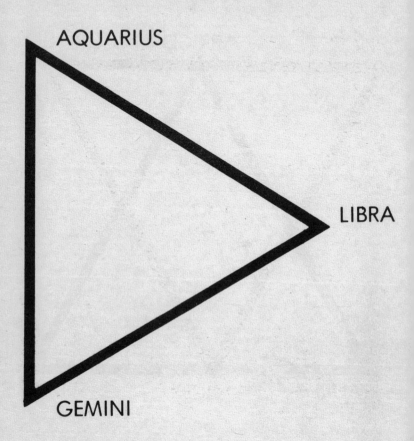

This is the air group. They are light, mental creatures desirous of contact, communication and relationship. They are involved with people and the forming of ties on many levels. Original thinkers, they are the bearers of human news. Their language is their sense of word, color, style and beauty. They provide an atmosphere suitable and pleasant for living. They add change and versatility to the scene, and it is through them that we can explore new territory of human intelligence and experience.

THE WATER SIGNS

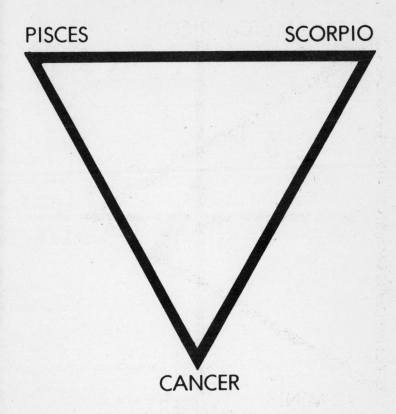

PISCES

SCORPIO

CANCER

This is the water group. Through the water people, we are all joined together on emotional, non-verbal levels. They are silent, mysterious types whose magic hypnotizes even the most determined realist. They have uncanny perceptions about people and are as rich as the oceans when it comes to feeling, emotion or imagination. They are sensitive, mystical creatures with memories that go back beyond time. Through water, life is sustained. These people have the potential for the depths of darkness or the heights of mysticism and art.

THE CARDINAL SIGNS

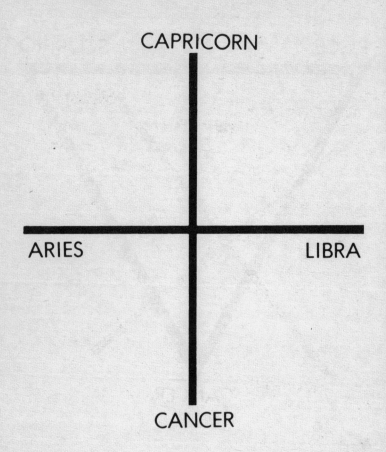

Put together, this is a clear-cut picture of dynamism, activity, tremendous stress and remarkable achievement. These people know the meaning of great change since their lives are often characterized by significant crises and major successes. This combination is like a simultaneous storm of summer, fall, winter and spring. The danger is chaotic diffusion of energy; the potential is irrepressible growth and victory.

THE FIXED SIGNS

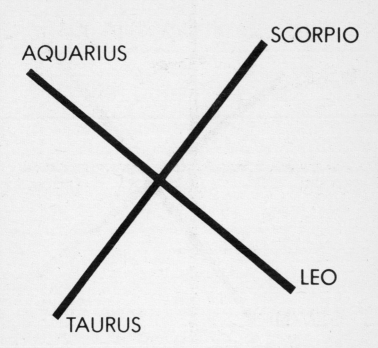

Fixed signs are always establishing themselves in a given place or area of experience. Like explorers who arrive and plant a flag, these people claim a position from which they do not enjoy being deposed. They are staunch, stalwart, upright, trusty, honorable people, although their obstinacy is well-known. Their contribution is fixity, and they are the angels who support our visible world.

THE MUTABLE SIGNS

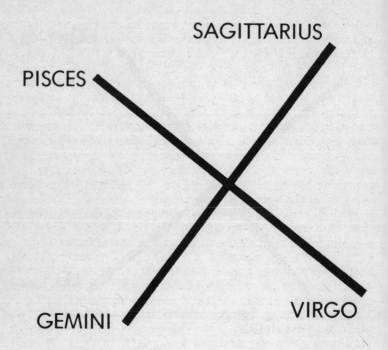

Mutable people are versatile, sensitive, intelligent, nervous and deeply curious about life. They are the translators of all energy. They often carry out or complete tasks initiated by others. Combinations of these signs have highly developed minds; they are imaginative and jumpy and think and talk a lot. At worst their lives are a Tower of Babel. At best they are adaptable and ready creatures who can assimilate one kind of experience and enjoy it while anticipating coming changes.

HOW TO APPROXIMATE YOUR RISING SIGN

Apart from the month and day of birth, the exact *time* of birth is another vital factor in the determination of an accurate horoscope. Not only do the planets move with great speed, but one must know how far the Earth has turned during the day. That way you can determine exactly where the planets are located with respect to the precise birthplace of an individual. This makes *your* horoscope *your* horoscope. In addition to these factors, another grid is laid upon that of the Zodiac and the planets: the houses. After all three have been considered, specific planetary relationships can be measured and analyzed in accordance with certain ordered procedures. It is the skillful translation of all this complex astrological language that a serious astrologer strives for in his attempt at coherent astrological synthesis. Keep this in mind.

The horoscope sets up a kind of framework around which the life of an individual grows like wild ivy, this way and that, weaving its way around the trellis of the natal positions of the planets. The year of birth tells us the positions of the distant, slow-moving planets like Jupiter, Saturn, Uranus and Pluto. The month of birth indicates the Sun sign, or birth sign as it is commonly called, as well as indicating the positions of the rapidly moving planets like Venus, Mercury and Mars. The day of birth locates the position of our Moon, and the moment of birth determines the houses through what is called the Ascendant, or Rising Sign.

As the Earth rotates on its axis once every 24 hours, each one of the twelve signs of the Zodiac appears to be "rising" on the horizon, with a new one appearing about every two hours. Actually it is the turning of the Earth that exposes each sign to view, but you will remember that in much of our astrological work we are discussing "apparent" motion. This *Rising Sign* marks the Ascendant and it colors the whole orientation of a horoscope. It indicates the sign governing the first house of the chart, and will thus determine which signs will govern all the other houses. The idea is a bit complicated at first, and we needn't dwell on complications in this introduction, but if you can imagine two color wheels with twelve divisions superimposed upon each other, one moving slowly and the other remaining still, you will have some idea of how the signs keep shifting the "color" of the houses as the Rising Sign continues to change every two hours.

The important point is that the birth chart, or horoscope, actually does define specific factors of a person's makeup. It contains a picture of being, much the way the nucleus of a tiny cell contains the potential for an entire elephant, or a packet of seeds contains a rosebush. If there were no order or continuity to the world, we could plant roses and get elephants. This same order that gives continuous flow to our lives often annoys people if it threatens to determine too much of their lives. We must grow from what we were planted, and there's no reason why we can't do that magnificently. It's all there in the horoscope. Where there is limitation, there is breakthrough; where there is crisis, there is transformation. Accurate analysis of a horoscope can help you find these points of breakthrough and transformation, and it requires knowledge of subtleties and distinctions that demand skillful judgment in order to solve even the simplest kind of personal question.

It is still quite possible, however, to draw some conclusions based upon the sign occupied by the Sun alone. In fact, if you're just being introduced to this vast subject, you're better off keeping it simple. Otherwise it seems like an impossible jumble, much like trying to read a novel in a foreign language without knowing the basic vocabulary. As with anything else, you can progress in your appreciation and understanding of astrology in direct proportion to your interest. To become really good at it requires study, experience, patience and above all—and maybe simplest of all—a fundamental understanding of what is actually going on right up there in the sky over your head. It is a vital living process you can observe, contemplate and ultimately understand. You can start by observing sunrise, or sunset, or even the full Moon.

In fact you can do a simple experiment after reading this introduction. You can erect a rough chart by following the simple procedure below:

1. Draw a circle with twelve equal segments.

2. Starting at what would be the nine o'clock position on a clock, number the segments, or houses, from 1 to 12 in a *counterclockwise direction*.

3. Label house number 1 in the following way: 4 A.M.-6 A.M.

4. In a counterclockwise direction, label the rest of the houses: 2 A.M.-4 A.M., MIDNIGHT-2 A.M., 10 P.M-MIDNIGHT, 8 P.M.-10 P.M., 6 P.M.-8 P.M., 4 P.M.-6 P.M., 2 P.M.-4 P.M., NOON-2 P.M., 10 A.M.-NOON, 8 A.M.-10 A.M., and 6 A.M.-8 A.M.

5. Now find out what time you were born and place the sun in the appropriate house.

6. Label the edge of that house with your Sun sign. You now have a description of your basic character and your fundamental drives. You can also see in what areas of life on Earth you will be most likely to focus your constant energy and center your activity.

7. If you are really feeling ambitious, label the rest of the houses with the signs, starting with your Sun sign, in order, still in a *counterclockwise direction.* When you get to Pisces, start over with Aries and keep going until you reach the house behind the Sun.

8. Look to house number 1. The sign that you have now labeled and attached to house number 1 is your Rising sign. It will color your self-image, outlook, physical constitution, early life and whole orientation to life. Of course this is a mere approximation, since there are many complicated calculations that must be made with respect to adjustments for birth time, but if you read descriptions of the sign preceding and the sign following the one you have calculated in the above manner, you may be able to identify yourself better. In any case, when you get through labeling all the houses, your drawing should look something like this:

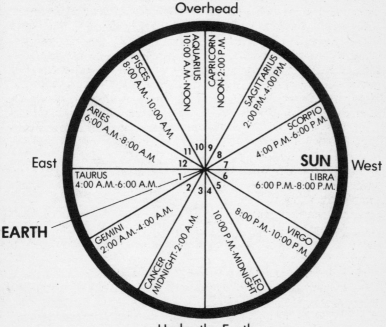

Overhead

Under the Earth

Basic chart illustrating the position of the Sun in Scorpio,
with the Ascendant Taurus as the Rising Sign.

This individual was born at 5:15 P.M. on October 31 in New York City. The Sun is in Scorpio and is found in the 7th house. The Rising sign, or the sign governing house number 1, is Taurus, so this person is a blend of Scorpio and Taurus.

Any further calculation would necessitate that you look in an ephemeris, or table of planetary motion, for the positions of the rest of the planets for your particular birth year. But we will take the time to define briefly all the known planets of our Solar System and the Sun to acquaint you with some more of the astrological vocabulary that you will be meeting again and again. (See page 21 for a full explanation of the Moon in all the Signs.)

THE PLANETS AND SIGNS THEY RULE

The signs of the Zodiac are linked to the planets in the following way. Each sign is governed or ruled by one or more planets. No matter where the planets are located in the sky at any given moment, they still rule their respective signs, and when they travel through the signs they rule, they have special dignity and their effects are stronger.

Following is a list of the planets and the signs they rule. After looking at the list, go back over the definitions of the planets and see if you can determine how the planet ruling *your* Sun sign has affected your life.

SIGNS	RULING PLANETS
Aries	Mars, Pluto
Taurus	Venus
Gemini	Mercury
Cancer	Moon
Leo	Sun
Virgo	Mercury
Libra	Venus
Scorpio	Mars, Pluto
Sagittarius	Jupiter
Capricorn	Saturn
Aquarius	Saturn, Uranus
Pisces	Jupiter, Neptune

THE PLANETS
OF THE
SOLAR SYSTEM

Here are the planets of the Solar System. They all travel around the Sun at different speeds and different distances. Taken with the Sun, they all distribute individual intelligence and ability throughout the entire chart.

The planets modify the influence of the Sun in a chart according to their own particular natures, strengths and positions. Their positions must be calculated for each year and day, and their function and expression in a horoscope will change as they move from one area of the Zodiac to another.

Following, you will find brief statements of their pure meanings.

THE SUN

SUN

This is the center of existence. Around this flaming sphere all the planets revolve in endless orbits. Our star is constantly sending out its beams of light and energy without which no life on Earth would be possible. In astrology it symbolizes everything we are trying to become, the center around which all of our activity in life will always revolve. It is the symbol of our basic nature and describes the natural and constant thread that runs through everything that we do from birth to death on this planet.

To early astrologers, the sun seemed to be another planet because it crossed the heavens every day, just like the rest of the bodies in the sky.

It is the only star near enough to be seen well—it is, in fact, a dwarf star. Approximately 860,000 miles in diameter, it is about ten times as wide as the giant planet Jupiter. The next nearest star is nearly 300,000 times as far away, and if the Sun were located as far away as most of the bright stars, it would be too faint to be seen without a telescope.

Everything in the horoscope ultimately revolves around this singular body. Although other forces may be prominent in the charts of some individuals, still the Sun is the total nucleus of being and symbolizes the complete potential of every human being alive. It is vitality and the life force. Your whole essence comes from the position of the Sun.

You are always trying to express the Sun according to its position by house and sign. Possibility for all development is found in the Sun, and it marks the fundamental character of your personal radiations all around you.

It is the symbol of strength, vigor, wisdom, dignity, ardor and generosity, and the ability for a person to function as a mature individual. It is also a creative force in society. It is consciousness of the gift of life.

The underdeveloped solar nature is arrogant, pushy, undependable and proud, and is constantly using force.

MERCURY

Mercury is the planet closest to the Sun. It races around our star, gathering information and translating it to the rest of the system. Mercury represents your capacity to understand the desires of your own will and to translate those desires into action.

In other words it is the planet of Mind and the power of communication. Through Mercury we develop an ability to think, write, speak and observe—to become aware of the world around us. It colors our attitudes and vision of the world, as well as our capacity to communicate our inner responses to the outside world. Some people who have serious disabilities in their power of verbal communication have often wrongly been described as people lacking intelligence.

Although this planet (and its position in the horoscope) indicates your power to communicate your thoughts and perceptions to the world, intelligence is something deeper. Intelligence is distributed throughout all the planets. It is the relationship of the planets to each other that truly describes what we call intelligence. Mercury rules speaking, language, mathematics, draft and design, students, messengers, young people, offices, teachers and any pursuits where the mind of man has wings.

VENUS

Venus is beauty. It symbolizes the harmony and radiance of a rare and elusive quality: beauty itself. It is refinement and delicacy, softness and charm. In astrology it indicates grace, balance and the aesthetic sense. Where Venus is we see beauty, a gentle drawing in of energy and the need for satisfaction and completion. It is a special touch that finishes off rough edges. It is sensitivity, and affection, and it is always the place for that other elusive phenomenon: love. Venus describes our sense of what is beautiful and loving. Poorly developed, it is vulgar, tasteless and self-indulgent. But its ideal is the flame of spiritual love—Aphrodite, goddess of love, and the sweetness and power of personal beauty.

MARS

This is raw, crude energy. The planet next to Earth but outward from the Sun is a fiery red sphere that charges through the horoscope with force and fury. It represents the way you reach out for new adventure and new experience. It is energy and drive, initiative, courage and daring. The power to start something and see it through. It can be thoughtless, cruel and wild, angry and hostile, causing cuts, burns, scalds and wounds. It can stab its way through a chart, or it can be the symbol of healthy spirited adventure, well-channeled constructive power to begin and keep up the drive. If you have trouble starting things, if you lack the get-up-and-go to start the ball rolling, if you lack aggressiveness and self-confidence, chances are there's another planet influencing your Mars. Mars rules soldiers, butchers, surgeons, salesmen—any field that requires daring, bold skill, operational technique or self-promotion.

JUPITER

This is the largest planet of the Solar System. Scientists have recent-ly learned that Jupiter reflects more light than it receives from the Sun. In a sense it is like a star itself. In astrology it rules good luck and good cheer, health, wealth, optimism, happiness, success and joy. It is the symbol of opportunity and always opens the way for new possibilities in your life. It rules exuberance, enthusiasm, wis-dom, knowledge, generosity and all forms of expansion in general. It rules actors, statesmen, clerics, professional people, religion, pub-lishing and the distribution of many people over large areas.

Sometimes Jupiter makes you think you deserve everything, and you become sloppy, wasteful, careless and rude, prodigal and lawless, in the illusion that nothing can ever go wrong. Then there is the danger of over-confidence, exaggeration, undependability and over-indulgence.

Jupiter is the minimization of limitation and the emphasis on spirituality and potential. It is the thirst for knowledge and higher learning.

SATURN

Saturn circles our system in dark splendor with its mysterious rings, forcing us to be awakened to whatever we have neglected in the past. It will present real puzzles and problems to be solved, causing delays, obstacles and hindrances. By doing so, Saturn stirs our own sensitivity to those areas where we are laziest.

Here we must patiently develop *method,* and only through painstaking effort can our ends be achieved. It brings order to a horoscope and imposes reason just where we are feeling least reasonable. By creating limitations and boundary, Saturn shows the consequences of being human and demands that we accept the changing cycles inevitable in human life. Saturn rules time, old age and sobriety. It can bring depression, gloom, jealousy and greed, or serious acceptance of responsibilities out of which success will develop. With Saturn there is nothing to do but face facts. It rules laborers, stones, granite, rocks and crystals of all kinds.

The Outer Planets

The following three are the outer planets. They liberate human beings from cultural conditioning, and in that sense are the law breakers. In early times it was thought that Saturn was the last planet of the system—the outer limit beyond which we could never go. The discovery of the next three planets ushered in new phases of human history, revolution and technology.

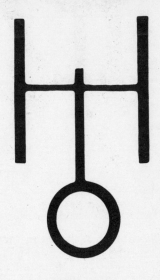

URANUS

Uranus rules unexpected change, upheaval, revolution. It is the symbol of total independence and asserts the freedom of an individual from all restriction and restraint. It is a breakthrough planet and indicates talent, originality and genius in a horoscope. It usually causes last-minute reversals and changes of plan, unwanted separations, accidents, catastrophes and eccentric behavior. It can add irrational rebelliousness and perverse bohemianism to a personality or a streak of unaffected brilliance in science and art. It rules technology, aviation and all forms of electrical and electronic advancement. It governs great leaps forward and topsy-turvy situations, and *always* turns things around at the last minute. Its effects are difficult to ever really predict, since it rules sudden last-minute decisions and events that come like lightning out of the blue.

NEPTUNE

Neptune dissolves existing reality the way the sea erodes the cliffs beside it. Its effects are subtle like the ringing of a buoy's bell in the fog. It suggests a reality higher than definition can usually describe. It awakens a sense of higher responsibility often causing guilt, worry, anxieties or delusions. Neptune is associated with all forms of escape and can make things seem a certain way so convincingly that you are absolutely sure of something that eventually turns out to be quite different.

It is the planet of illusion and therefore governs the invisible realms that lie beyond our ordinary minds, beyond our simple factual ability to prove what is "real." Treachery, deceit, disillusionment and disappointment are linked to Neptune. It describes a vague reality that promises eternity and the divine, yet in a manner so complex that we cannot really fathom it at all. At its worst Neptune is a cheap intoxicant; at its best it is the poetry, music and inspiration of the higher planes of spiritual love. It has dominion over movies, photographs and much of the arts.

PLUTO

Pluto lies at the outpost of our system and therefore rules finality in a horoscope—the final closing of chapters in your life, the passing of major milestones and points of development from which there is no return. It is a final wipeout, a closeout, an evacuation. It is a distant, subtle but powerful catalyst in all transformations that occur. It creates, destroys, then recreates. Sometimes Pluto starts its influence with a minor event or insignificant incident that might even go unnoticed. Slowly but surely, little by little, everything changes, until at last there has been a total transformation in the area of your life where Pluto has been operating. It rules mass thinking and the trends that society first rejects, then adopts and finally outgrows.

Pluto rules the dead and the underworld—all the powerful forces of creation and destruction that go on all the time beneath, around and above us. It can bring a lust for power with strong obsessions.

It is the planet that rules the metamorphoses of the caterpillar into a butterfly, for it symbolizes the capacity to change totally and forever a person's life style, way of thought and behavior.

FAMOUS PERSONALITIES

ARIES: Hans Christian Andersen, Pearl Bailey, Marlon Brando, Wernher Von Braun, Charlie Chaplin, Joan Crawford, Da Vinci, Bette Davis, Doris Day, W. C. Fields, Alec Guinness, Adolf Hitler, Billie Holiday, Thomas Jefferson, Nikita Khrushchev, Elton John, Arturo Toscanini, J. P. Morgan, Paul Robeson, Gloria Steinem, Lowell Thomas, Vincent van Gogh, Tennessee Williams

TAURUS: Fred Astaire, Charlote Brontë, Carol Burnett, Irving Berlin, Bing Crosby, Salvador Dali, Tchaikovsky, Queen Elizabeth II, Duke Ellington, Ella Fitzgerald, Henry Fonda, Sigmund Freud, Orson Welles, Joe Louis, Lenin, Karl Marx, Golda Meir, Eva Peron, Bertrand Russell, Shakespeare, Kate Smith, Benjamin Spock, Barbra Streisand, Shirley Temple, Harry Truman

GEMINI: Mikhail Baryshnikov, Boy George, Igor Stravinsky, Carlos Chavez, Walt Whitman, Bob Dylan, Ralph Waldo Emerson, Judy Garland, Paul Gauguin, Allen Ginsberg, Benny Goodman, Bob Hope, Burl Ives, John F. Kennedy, Peggy Lee, Marilyn Monroe, Joe Namath, Cole Porter, Laurence Olivier, Harriet Beecher Stowe, Queen Victoria, John Wayne, Frank Lloyd Wright

CANCER: "Dear Abby," David Brinkley, Yul Brynner, Pearl Buck, Marc Chagall, Jack Dempsey, Mildred (Babe) Zaharias, Mary Baker Eddy, Henry VIII, John Glenn, Ernest Hemingway, Lena Horne, Oscar Hammerstein, Helen Keller, Ann Landers, George Orwell, Nancy Reagan, Rembrandt, Richard Rodgers, Ginger Rogers, Rubens, Jean-Paul Sartre, O. J. Simpson

LEO: Neil Armstrong, Russell Baker, James Baldwin, Emily Brontë, Wilt Chamberlain, Julia Child, Cecil B. De Mille, Ogden Nash, Amelia Earhart, Edna Ferber, Arthur Goldberg, Dag Hammarskjöld, Alfred Hitchcock, Mick Jagger, George Meany, George Bernard Shaw, Napoleon, Jacqueline Onassis, Henry Ford, Francis Scott Key, Andy Warhol, Mae West, Orville Wright

VIRGO: Ingrid Bergman, Warren Burger, Maurice Chevalier, Agatha Christie, Sean Connery, Lafayette, Peter Falk, Greta Garbo, Althea Gibson, Arthur Godfrey, Goethe, Buddy Hackett, Michael Jackson, Lyndon Johnson, D. H. Lawrence, Sophia Loren, Grandma Moses, Arnold Palmer, Queen Elizabeth I, Walter Reuther, Peter Sellers, Lily Tomlin, George Wallace

LIBRA: Brigitte Bardot, Art Buchwald, Truman Capote, Dwight D. Eisenhower, William Faulkner, F. Scott Fitzgerald, Gandhi, George Gershwin, Micky Mantle, Helen Hayes, Vladimir Horowitz, Doris Lessing, Martina Navratalova, Eugene O'Neill, Luciano Pavarotti, Emily Post, Eleanor Roosevelt, Bruce Springsteen, Margaret Thatcher, Gore Vidal, Barbara Walters, Oscar Wilde

SCORPIO: Vivien Leigh, Richard Burton, Art Carney, Johnny Carson, Billy Graham, Grace Kelly, Walter Cronkite, Marie Curie, Charles de Gaulle, Linda Evans, Indira Gandhi, Theodore Roosevelt, Rock Hudson, Katherine Hepburn, Robert F. Kennedy, Billie Jean King, Martin Luther, Georgia O'Keeffe, Pablo Picasso, Jonas Salk, Alan Shepard, Robert Louis Stevenson

SAGITTARIUS: Jane Austen, Louisa May Alcott, Woody Allen, Beethoven, Willy Brandt, Mary Martin, William F. Buckley, Maria Callas, Winston Churchill, Noel Coward, Emily Dickinson, Walt Disney, Benjamin Disraeli, James Doolittle, Kirk Douglas, Chet Huntley, Jane Fonda, Chris Evert Lloyd, Margaret Mead, Charles Schulz, John Milton, Frank Sinatra, Steven Spielberg

CAPRICORN: Muhammad Ali, Isaac Asimov, Pablo Casals, Dizzy Dean, Marlene Dietrich, James Farmer, Ava Gardner, Barry Goldwater, Cary Grant, J. Edgar Hoover, Howard Hughes, Joan of Arc, Gypsy Rose Lee, Martin Luther King, Jr., Rudyard Kipling, Mao Tse-tung, Richard Nixon, Gamal Nasser, Louis Pasteur, Albert Schweitzer, Stalin, Benjamin Franklin, Elvis Presley

AQUARIUS: Marian Anderson, Susan B. Anthony, Jack Benny, Charles Darwin, Charles Dickens, Thomas Edison, John Barrymore, Clark Gable, Jascha Heifetz, Abraham Lincoln, John McEnroe, Yehudi Menuhin, Mozart, Jack Nicklaus, Ronald Reagan, Jackie Robinson, Norman Rockwell, Franklin D. Roosevelt, Gertrude Stein, Charles Lindbergh, Margaret Truman

PISCES: Edward Albee, Harry Belafonte, Alexander Graham Bell, Frank Borman, Chopin, Adelle Davis, Albert Einstein, Jackie Gleason, Winslow Homer, Edward M. Kennedy, Victor Hugo, Mike Mansfield, Michelangelo, Edna St. Vincent Millay, Liza Minelli, John Steinbeck, Linus Pauling, Ravel, Diana Ross, William Shirer, Elizabeth Taylor, George Washington

SCORPIO

CHARACTER ANALYSIS

Of all the signs of the Zodiac, Taureans are perhaps the most diligent and determined. They are hardworkers and stick with something once it's begun. They are generally thorough people and are careful to avoid making mistakes. Patient, the Taurean knows how to bide his time. If something doesn't work out as scheduled, he will wait until the appropriate moment comes along, then forge ahead.

The person born under this sign is far from lazy. He will work hard to achieve whatever it is he desires. He is so determined that others often think of him as being unreasonably stubborn. He'll stick to a point he believes is right—nothing can force him to give up his chosen path once his mind is made up.

The Taurean takes his time in whatever he does. He wants to make sure everything is done right. At times this may exasperate people who are rather quick about things. Still and all, a job done by a Taurean is generally a job well done. Careful, steady, and reliable, the Taurus person is just the opposite of high-strung. This person can generally take a lot upon himself. Sometimes his burdens or worries are of such proportions that others would find them impossible to carry, but somehow the Taurean manages in his silent way.

The Taurean may be even-tempered, but he puts up with nonsense from no one. Others had better not take advantage of his balanced disposition. If they do, they are apt to rue the day.

The Taurus man or woman plans well before taking any one line of action. He believes in being well-prepared before embarking on any one project. Others may see him as a sort of slow-poke, but he is not being slow—just sure. He is not the sort of person who would act on a whim or fancy. He wants to be certain of the ground he is standing on.

Scorpios tend to be consistent in all that they do. They never do things halfway. They are not afraid of conflict situations or emergencies. Under duress they can be relied upon to handle things in a calm manner. He is generally constructive and positive in the way he channels his forces. He is against waste and feels committed to make every gesture—every action—count.

In spite of his good sense of purpose and direction, the person born under the sign of Scorpio is sometimes the victim of his conflicting moods. He may contradict himself several times a day without feeling that he is being untrue to himself and his beliefs. He believes that every moment has its own truth. He feels his moods strongly and believes that it is necessary to obey them in order to remain the person he is. The Scorpio is an organizer. He likes to have things his own way or not at all. On the whole, he is what you would call a principled person. He holds fast to his ideals.

His understanding of life is sometimes remarkable. He is not short on insight and often can analyze a human situation accurately long before others. His knowledge of things in general is often superior to that of others. In spite of the intelligence he has at his disposal he is not the kind of person to take the easy way toward a goal. He seems to have a penchant for argumentation. In some instances, he seems to bring about quarrels just for the enjoyment he derives from crossing swords.

The Scorpio's ability to fly into a rage is considerable. People sometimes wind up disliking him intensely after having witnessed one of his fits of temper. This does not bother him, however. If he loses a friend or two along his way in life he is not apt to let it upset him. He keeps moving on—his ultimate goal always in sight. He is capable of being angry at someone quite abruptly but it never lasts very long. He has more important things to do in life besides holding grudges.

He does not believe in using fancy or complicated language; he is to the point—not really caring how blunt he may sound to sensitive ears. Power—and how to get it—is what is most important to him in life; he does not try to hide this fact.

In spite of him being straight-off-the-shoulder in most of his dealings, the Scorpio man or woman is capable of holding back a fact or two—especially if it is to his or her advantage.

Health

On the whole, the person born under this sign is quite healthy. His constitution is generally strong; he seldom has to worry about common ailments. He is capable of great spurts of energy. He can apply himself to a strenuous task for a long period of time without tiring. The Scorpio person rather enjoys stress and strain; it proves his mettle. As has already been mentioned, the Scorpio man or woman is seldom bothered by illnesses; their resistance is remarkably strong. When, however, he does become ill—really ill—he has to give in in order to recuperate. Illness is a sort of weakness or frailty to him. He is ashamed of himself when he is sick and does all he can to quickly recover. If he tries to fight it—that is, act as if he weren't incapacitated—he often winds up worse off than when he began. It is difficult at times for the Scorpio to realize that even he has limits.

In spite of the fact that he can take on a lot, it is also important that the person born under the sign of Scorpio learn how to relax. Often, Scorpio people push themselves to the limit—and sometimes there are serious consequences to pay. Overworked Scorpios are highly susceptible to breakdowns of various sorts. It is the cultivated Scorpio man or woman who knows when and how to relax. Because of their serious attitude toward most things, the Scorpio when young often seems much older than what he really is.

The Scorpio man or woman is often sturdily built. There is usually something massive about them—they are often largeboned and have deep set interesting eyes. In general, they could best be described as sensuous in their appearance and behavior. Scorpio women are often beautiful in a seductive way. Their voices are sometimes husky and rather sexy.

The weakest part of the Scorpio's anatomy is his digestive system. Whenever he becomes ill this is the area usually affected. The sensible person born under this sign pays attention to minor warnings of an oncoming illness and does something about it while there is still time. Some people born under this sign pick up infections rather easily.

Occupation

The Scorpio man or woman is a very industrious person. He enjoys keeping busy and he always finishes what he starts. He does not believe in turning out slipshod work; he's a professional. The Scorpio is not a person lacking in push or energy. He takes his work seriously and does what he can to be recognized for his deeds.

Quite often the person born under the sign of Scorpio dislikes heavy work. He would much rather leave that to someone else. He is goal-directed. It is important for him to achieve what he desires . . . in some instances, it does not matter how. When he sets his mind to it—and he usually does—he can accomplish almost anything he wishes. Obstacles do not frighten him; in fact, the threat of opposition seems to spur him on. He is no quitter. He'll hang on until the bitter end. His never-say-die attitude helps him to scan heights that would frighten others. He's confident of himself and of the moves he makes.

The Scorpio person is ambitious. He can make work even when there isn't any—just to keep busy. Idleness tends to bore him and make him disagreeable. He is fascinated by difficult tasks. He enjoys figuring out ways of how to attack a project or a chore. He doesn't always choose the easiest route—but the most challenging. In short he's a fighter.

His intellectual ability is quite superior. There is almost no subject that would stump him. He is not afraid of learning something new and is quite capable of applying himself to new or different trains of thought if he feels they will help him achieve his ends.

Generally speaking Scorpio people prefer to work for themselves—they don't like to share tasks, but will if it is absolutely necessary. People who work with them are not apt to find this relationship an enjoyable one, for the Scorpio is always ready to bring about a quarrel or argument if things are not going exactly the way he likes.

Often people born under this sign do extremely well in the field of medicine or science. They have a deep interest in exploration of all sorts and are willing to devote their whole lives to something that is somewhat elusive and mysterious. The Scorpio has an open mind and this helps him to succeed in the things he does. He likes to make tests; to prove things through experimentation. He isn't afraid of taking risks. He is always sure of himself—sure that he'll come out a winner. Some people born under the sign of Scorpio make good detectives and lawyers.

The Scorpio person feels deeply whenever he is engaged socially. He can either hate someone or love them; there is no middle of the road. He cannot afford to be indifferent. He'll admire someone if he feels that person deserves to be admired. He makes a strong leader. The people working under him may dislike him rather intensely but they will not try to usurp his authority. He won't put up with any nonsense from his subordinates and he lets them know that right from the start.

In whatever he undertakes, he forges ahead with no thought of quitting until the goal has been reached. His powers of concentration are amazingly strong. He seldom allows himself to be distracted from the path he has chosen. He expects the people working under him to have the same sort of devotion to purpose that he has. He can be quite a driver at times. If others are not up to his standards, he won't waste time by pampering them—he'll simply discard them and take on new people.

Some Scorpios have a bit of the genius in them. They are quite perceptive and often can accurately guess what someone else is thinking—particularly in a conflict situation.

People born under this sign are basically materialists. They are quite fond of money and what it can do and make no effort to disguise their interest. They are extremely power-oriented. Money seldom presents a problem to them. One way or another, they almost always come by the finances they feel they need or deserve. They are fond of luxuries as well, of course; and are sometimes deeply involved in such power-games as "keeping up with the Joneses;" in most instances the Joneses wind up trying to keep up with them.

The Scorpio person is careful in the way he handles his finances. He doesn't believe in waste, although at times he is given to being extravagent. When he is wealthy, he can be a bit of a show-off about it. He can easily detect a false friend—someone who associates with him for the gain he is likely to derive from the relationship.

Home and Family

In general, the person born under the sign of Scorpio is not terribly interested in an intense domestic life. He does not like to feel tied down by home and family. However, he is adaptable and will be willing to sacrifice some of his freedoms for the comforts and conveniences a home life can provide. Routine, though, bores him and is apt to put him in a bad mood. He enjoys a home life that has a surprise in it now and again. Day-in day-out monotony is something he refuses to tolerate.

He is as efficient and forceful in his homemaking as he is in other things. He likes to see to it that everything runs well. His home may be quite glamorous in an ostentatious way. He is fond of a show of luxury. His tastes in furnishings is likely to be somewhat outspoken. It is likely to offend someone who has refined or cultivated taste.

The Scorpio man is proud. He enjoys showing off his possessions. His family is important to him. He likes his wife and children to support him in his interests and attitudes. Keeping his home attractive and luxurious is a full-time activity for many

Scorpios. They are interested in having the latest appliances and the best trademark.

The Scorpio person likes to rule his own roost. His mate had better not try to take the head position. He wears the pants in the family and is apt to make that unmistakably clear before the marriage has taken place. All of the major decisions must be made by him. He'll listen to another's point of view but will hardly take it into consideration when making up his mind.

Luxury helps the Scorpio man or woman to feel successful. It has definite psychological influence. The Scorpio in shabby surroundings is apt to be quite difficult to get along with. A show of affluence brightens his spirits and helps him to feel that he is on the right road.

The Scorpio person is often fond of large families. He may not be as responsible as he should be in caring for them. Quite often he is a strict parent and tolerates no misbehavior from his offspring. The children may resent his iron hand—especially when they are young—but as they reach adulthood they are likely to be thankful for his firmness. The Scorpio is only concerned with instilling those values in his children which will help them to go far in the battlefield of life. He can be quite a disciplinarian. Some of them are quite possessive of their children.

Scorpios as children are often very affectionate. As a rule, they are sensitive children and should be handled in a considerate and loving way. Emotionally, they may not be as strong as children born under other signs. The observant and sensitive parent should have no trouble in bringing him up in such a way that he is able to develop his personality along natural lines as he reaches a stage of independence.

At times the Scorpio child may be difficult to manage. He may be delinquent at times and cause some trouble at school. In spite of this, he is apt to show strong creative or artistic talent during his growing-up period. The wise parent or guardian will do what he can to foster this interest in such a way that it develops along satisfactory lines.

Social Relationships

Scorpio people are deeply interested in sex. They enjoy being physically involved with the people they feel themselves attracted to. They are often given to experimentation in sex; they are curious and want to know all there is to discover. They are, by and large, intensely passionate and intensely emotional. Life without love is difficult for them to imagine. It is important to them that their sex life is well arranged and interesting. They may spend a great deal of time getting involved sexually with all kinds of people before they are satisfied and can concentrate their attention on just one person.

LOVE AND MARRIAGE

The Scorpio can be quite a flirt. He may have quite a number of affairs before he thinks about settling down. In every romantic adventure he is quite sincere. He does not believe in being false or untrue when involved with someone. However, his interest may dissolve after he feels he has discovered everything there was to find out about a particular person. He is not very interested in light romances. He means business when it comes to love. He expects his lover to be as honest in his affections as he is.

The Scorpio is in need of someone who is as passionate and understanding as he is. His romances may be rather violent at times; an element of struggle may be quite definite in them—in fact, it is this quality that will perhaps keep his interest alive in a love affair. He likes to be admired and complimented by his partner. He hates criticism and is apt to become rather difficult if his lover finds fault with him.

He does what he can to make his loved one comfortable and happy. He can be rather generous when in love and is never without a gift or some token of his affection. He likes to impress his loved one with a show of luxury. Often his gifts are quite expensive.

It is important to the Scorpio person that the object of his affections be true during the relationship. He is very jealous and possessive. If he suspects deceit, he can be violent.

The best partner for a Scorpio person is one who can compliment his character. Someone who does not mind being agreeable and supportive. Someone who does not mind letting him make all of the decisions both large and small. A quiet, retiring sort of person sometimes makes the ideal mate for the man or woman born under Scorpio. Two Scorpios often clash; however, if they are cultivated and understand themselves well, they can go far together—helping each other out in various ways.

When the Scorpio man or woman sets his sights on someone he generally wins them. He can be quite demonstrative when dealing with someone who tries to stand between him and his loved one. He will do everything in his power to win the person who interests him. Some people born under this sign will stop at nothing in order to eliminate competition. Others are rather jealous and suspicious when they really have no cause to be.

In married life, the Scorpio person seldom gives himself completely—even though he may expect this of his partner. There is always a corner of himself which he does not give away. In general, the person born under this sign is faithful to his mate. However, if home life is rather dull, he will do what he can not to spend too much time there. He'll see to it that outside interests keep him occupied as much as possible.

The Scorpio person marries for keeps. He is not the kind of person who shouts "divorce!" as soon as something goes wrong. Marriage is important to him and he is willing to do whatever is necessary to keep the relationship alive and fruitful.

Romance and the Scorpio Woman

The Scorpio woman is generally quite attractive and is often sought after by the opposite sex. Her attractiveness is sometimes more suggestive than real. Her voice is rather rough and mellow— her mannerisms not without charm. She can be quite passionate when in love. She may be too much to handle for the man of moderate romantic interests. She does what she can to make a success of her love life. When in love, she does not hold back her affections. She expects the same honesty from her partner.

She is always serious when in love. She may have a great number of affairs before actually settling down. Romance is important to her. But more important is that she find a man that is compatible to her interests and needs. The man she desires, she usually wins. She is sure of herself in matters of the heart and can be very persuasive when necessary. Men find her difficult to ignore or resist. She may be rather jealous and possessive. If she suspects her lover of not being true, she can become quite angry and vindictive.

She is usually accurate when sizing up someone who interests her. She seldom choses the wrong man. She is usually very faithful when married. She does all she can to help her man get ahead in his career. She supports him in all his interests and often is able to supply him with some very good advice. She will never let her husband down even in difficult times. She will fight for her husband if it is necessary.

The Scorpio woman is a bit old-fashioned when it comes to attitudes about marriage. She is often contented with her role as housewife and mother. She does everything she can to keep the household in order.

Although others may not think her suitable material for a mother because of her emotional and sometimes explosive outbursts, she does what she can to bring up her children correctly. She is rather strict, especially when they are young. They understand her better though, as they grow older.

Romance and the Scorpio Man

The Scorpio man is often popular with women. There is something magnetic about his charm. He is protective and adventurous. His passionate way in love often sweeps women off their feet. Love—in each affair—is a matter of life and death. He does not believe in being lighthearted.

As a rule, he is warm and generous. He knows how to make a woman feel loved and wanted. He expects his loved one to be as demonstrative as he is in expressing her love. By nature, he is possessive and resents another's interest in his woman. He can easily become jealous. His anger can be quite frightening to a sensitive woman.

The Scorpio man makes a good husband and father. He is a good provider, most often, and sees to it that his family has everything it needs. His married life is apt to be full of ups and downs. He is affectionate though and true in his desire to be a good husband; this sometimes makes it easier for his wife to accept his changeable nature. He is faithful. Once settled down he is apt to stay true to his wife. The cultivated Scorpio man is often successful in marriage. He knows how to withhold his negative traits so that they do not seriously affect the relationship.

He is fond of large families. Even though he may father one himself, he may not have enough interest in his offspring—especially when they are young—to make them feel secure and well loved. As the children grow older, however, and reach an adult stage, his interest is likely to increase considerably. At any rate, he will always see to it that they never want for anything.

Woman—Man

SCORPIO WOMAN
ARIES MAN

Although it's possible that you could find happiness with a man born under the sign of the Ram, it's uncertain as to how long that happiness would last.

An Aries who has made his mark in the world and is somewhat

steadfast in his outlooks and attitudes could be quite a catch for you. On the other hand, men under this sign are often swift-footed and quick-minded; their industrious mannerisms may fail to impress you, especially if you feel that much of their get-up-and-go often leads nowhere.

When it comes to a fine romance, you want someone with a nice, broad shoulder to lean on. You are likely to find a relationship with someone who doesn't like to stay put for too long somewhat upsetting.

The Aries man may have a little trouble in understanding you, too . . . at least, in the beginning of the relationship. He may find you a bit too shy and moody. Aries men tend to speak their minds; he's liable to criticize you at the drop of a hat.

You may find a man born under this sign too demanding. He may give you the impression that he expects you to be at his beck and call. You have a lot of patience at your disposal and he may try every last bit of it. He is apt to be not as thorough as you in everything he does. In order to achieve success or a goal quickly, he is liable to overlook small but important details—and regret it when it is too late.

Being married to an Aries does not mean that you'll have a secure and safe life as far as finances are concerned. Not all Aries are rash with cash, but they lack the sound head you perhaps have for putting away something for that inevitable rainy day. He'll do his best, however, to see that you're adequately provided for—even though his efforts may leave something to be desired as far as you're concerned.

With an Aries man for a mate, you'll find yourself constantly among people. Aries people generally have many friends—and you may not heartily approve of them all. People born under this sign are often more interested in "interesting" people than they are in influential ones. Although there may be a family squabble from time to time, you are stable enough to be able to take it in your stride.

Aries men love children. They make wonderful fathers. Kids take to them like ducks to water. Their quick minds and behavior appeal to the young.

SCORPIO WOMAN
TAURUS MAN

If you've got your heart set on a man born under the sign of Taurus, you'll have to learn the art of being patient. Taureans take their time about everything—even love.

The steady and deliberate Taurus man is a little slow on the draw; it may take him quite a while before he gets around to popping that question. For the woman who doesn't mind twiddling her thumbs, the waiting and anticipating almost always pays off. Taurus men want to make sure that every step they take is a good one —particularly, if they feel that the path they're on leads to the altar.

If you are in the mood for a whirlwind romance, you had better cast your net in shallower waters. Moreover, most Taureans prefer to do the angling themselves. They are not keen on women taking the lead; once she does, he's liable to drop her like a dead fish. If you let yourself get caught on his terms, you'll find that he's fallen for you—hook, line, and sinker.

The Taurus man is fond of a comfortable homelife. It is very important to him. If you keep those home fires burning you will have no trouble keeping that flame in your Taurean's heart aglow. You have a talent for homemaking; use it. Your taste in furnishings is excellent. You know how to make a house come to life with colors and decorations.

Taurus, the strong, steady, and protective Bull may not be your idea of a man on the move, still he's reliable. Perhaps he could be the anchor for your dreams and plans. He could help you to acquire a more balanced outlook and approach to your life. If you're given to impulsiveness, he could help you to curb it. He's the man who is always there when you need him.

When you tie the knot with a man born under Taurus, you can put away fears about creditors pounding on the door. Taureans are practical about everything including bill-paying. When he carries you over that threshold, you can be certain that the entire house is paid for, not only the doorsill.

As a housewife, you won't have to worry about putting aside your many interests for the sake of back-breaking house chores. Your Taurus hubby will see to it that you have all the latest time-saving appliances and comforts.

Your children will be obedient and orderly. Your Taurus husband will see to that.

SCORPIO WOMAN
GEMINI MAN

Gemini men, in spite of their charm and dashing manner, may make your skin crawl. They may seem to lack the sort of common sense you set so much store in. Their tendency to start something then, out of boredom, never finish it, may do nothing more than exasperate you.

You may be inclined to interpret a Gemini's jumping around

from here to there as childish if not downright neurotic. A man born under this sign will seldom stay put and if you should take it upon yourself to try and make him sit still, he's liable to resent it strongly.

On the other hand, the Gemini man is liable to think you're an old slowpoke—someone far too interested in security and material things. He's attracted to things that sparkle and dazzle; you, with your practical way of looking at things most of the time, are likely to seem a little dull and uninteresting to this gadabout. If you're looking for a life of security and permanence, you'd better look elsewhere for your Mr. Right.

Chances are you'll be taken by his charming ways and facile wit—few women can resist Gemini magic—but after you've seen through his live-for-today, gossamer facade, you'll most likely be very happy to turn your attention to someone more stable, even if he is not as interesting. You want a man who is there when you need him. You need someone on whom you can fully rely. Keeping track of a Gemini's movements will make you dizzy. Still, if you are a patient woman, you should be able to put up with someone contrary—especially if you feel the experience may be well worth the effort.

A successful and serious Gemini could make you a very happy woman, perhaps if you gave him half a chance. Although you may think he's got bats in his belfry, the Gemini man generally has a good brain and can make good use of it when he wants. Some Geminis who have learned the importance of being diligent have risen to great heights, professionally. President Kennedy was a Gemini as was Thomas Mann and William Butler Yeats. Once you can convince yourself that not all people born under the sign of the Twins are witless grasshoppers, you'll find that you've come a long way in trying to understand them.

Life with a Gemini man can be more fun than a barrel of clowns. You'll never experience a dull moment. He's always the life of the party. He's a little scatterbrained when it comes to handling money most of the time. You'd better handle the budgeting and bookkeeping.

In ways, he's like a child and perhaps that is why he can get along so well with the younger generation.

SCORPIO WOMAN
CANCER MAN

The man born under the sign of Cancer may very well be the man after your own heart. Generally, Cancer people are steady. They are interested in security and practicality. Despite their seemingly grouchy exterior, men born under the sign of the Crab are rather sensitive and kind individuals. They are amost always hard workers and are very interested in becoming successful in business as well as in society. You'll find that his conservative outlook on many things often agrees with yours. He'll be a man on whom you can depend come rain or shine. He'll never shirk his responsibilities as a provider and he'll always see to it that his wife and family never want.

Your patience will come in handy if you decide it's a Cancer may you want for a mate. He isn't the type that rushes headlong into romance. He wants to be sure about love as you do. If after the first couple of months of dating, he suggests that you take a walk with him down lovers' lane, don't jump to the conclusion that he's about to make his "great play." Chances are he'll only hold your hand and seriously observe the stars. Don't let his coolness fool you, though. Beneath his starched reserve lies a very warm heart. He's just not interested in showing off as far as affection is concerned. Don't think his interest is wandering if he doesn't kiss you goodnight at the front door; that just isn't his style. For him, affection should only be displayed for two sets of eyes—yours and his. He's passionate only in private.

He will never step out of line. He's too much of a gentleman for that. When you're alone with him and there's no chance of you being disturbed or spied upon, he'll pull out an engagement ring (that used to belong to his grandmother) and slip it on your trembling finger.

Speaking of relatives, you'll have to get pretty much used to the fact that Cancer men are overly fond of their mothers. When he says his mother is the most wonderful woman in the world, you'd better agree with him—that is, if you want to become his wife.

He'll always be a faithful husband; Cancer men never play around after they've taken that marriage vow. They don't take marriage responsibilities lightly. He'll see to it that everything in the house runs smoothly and that bills are paid promptly—never put aside. He's liable to take all kinds of insurance policies out on his family and property. He'll arrange it so that when retirement time rolls around, you'll both be very well off.

Men under this sign make patient and understanding fathers.

SCORPIO WOMAN
LEO MAN

To know a man born under the sign of the Lion is not necessarily to love him—even though the temptation may be great. When he fixes most girls with his leonine double-whammy, it causes their hearts to pitter-pat and their minds to cloud over.

You are a little too sensible to allow yourself to be bowled over by a regal strut and a roar. Still, there's no denying that Leo has a way with women—even sensible women like yourself. Once he's swept a girl off her feet, it may be hard for her to scramble upright again. However, you are no pushover for romantic charm—especially if you feel it's all show.

He'll wine you and dine you in the fanciest places. He'll croon to you under the moon and shower you with diamonds if he can get a hold of them . . . but, it would be wise to find out just how long that shower is going to last before consenting to be his wife.

Lions in love are hard to ignore, let alone brush off. Your no's will have a way of nudging him on until he feels he has you completely under his spell. Once mesmerized by this romantic powerhouse, you will most likely find yourself doing things you never dreamed of. Leos can be like vain pussycats when involved romantically. They like to be cuddled, curried, and tickled under the chin. This may not be your cup of tea exactly, still when you're romantically dealing with a man born under the sign of Leo, you'll find yourself doing all kinds of things to make him purr.

Although he may be big and magnanimous while trying to win you, he'll let out a blood-curdling roar if he thinks he's not getting the tender love and care he feels is his due. If you keep him well supplied with affection, you can be sure his eyes will never look for someone else and his heart will never wander.

Leo men often tend to be authoritarian—they are born to lord it over others in one way or another, it seems. If he is the top banana at his firm, he'll most likely do everything he can to stay on top. If he's not number one, he's most likely working on it and will be sitting on the throne before long.

You'll have more security than you can use if he is in a position to support you in the manner to which he feels you should be accustomed. He is apt to be too lavish, at least by your standards.

You'll always have plenty of friends when you have a Leo for a mate. He's a natural-born friend-maker and entertainer. He loves to kick up his heels at a party.

As fathers, Leos tend to spoil their children no end.

SCORPIO WOMAN
VIRGO MAN

Although the Virgo man may be a bit of a fuss-budget at times, his seriousness and dedication to common sense may help you to overlook his tendency to sometimes be overcritical about minor things.

Virgo men are often quiet, respectable types who set great store in conservative behavior and level-headedness. He'll admire you for your practicality and tenacity—perhaps even more than for your good looks. He's seldom bowled over by a glamour-puss. When he gets his courage up, he turns to a serious and reliable girl for romance. He'll be far from a Valentino while dating. In fact, you may wind up making all the passes. Once he does get his motor running, however, he can be a warm and wonderful fellow—to the right girl.

He's gradual about love. Chances are your romance with him will most likely start out looking like an ordinary friendship. Once he's sure you're no fly-by-night flirt and have no plans of taking him for a ride, he'll open up and rain sunshine all over your heart.

Virgo men tend to marry late in life. He believes in holding out until he's met the right girl. He may not have many names in his little black book; in fact, he may not even have a black book. He's not interested in playing the field; leave that to men of the more flamboyant signs. The Virgo man is so particular that he may remain romantically inactive for a long period. His girl has to be perfect or it's no go. If you find yourself feeling weak-kneed for a Virgo man, do your best to convince him that perfect is not so important when it comes to love; help him to realize that he's missing out on a great deal by not considering the near-perfect or whatever it is you consider yourself to be. With your sure-fire perseverance, you will most likely be able to make him listen to reason and he'll wind up reciprocating your romantic interests.

The Virgo man is no block of ice. He'll respond to what he feels to be the right feminine flame. Once your love-life with a Virgo man starts to bubble, don't give it a chance to fall flat. You may never have a second chance at winning his heart.

If you should ever have a falling out with him, forget about patching up. He'd prefer to let the pieces lie scattered. Once married, though, he'll stay that way—even if it hurts. He's too conscientious to try to back out of a legal deal of any sort.

The Virgo man is as neat as a pin. He's thumbs down on sloppy housekeeping. Keep everything bright, neat, and shiny . . . and that goes for the children, too, at least by the time he gets home from work. Chocolate-coated kisses from Daddy's little girl go over like a lead balloon with him.

SCORPIO WOMAN
LIBRA MAN

You are apt to find men born under the sign of Libra too wrapped up in their own private dreams to be really interesting as far as love and romance are concerned. Quite often, he is a difficult person to bring back down to earth; it is hard for him to face reality at times. Although he may be very cautious about weighing both sides of an argument, he may never really come to a reasonable decision about anything. Decision-making is something that often makes the Libra man uncomfortable; he'd rather leave that job to someone else. Don't ask him why for he probably doesn't know himself.

Qualities such as permanance and constancy are important to you in a love relationship. The Libra man may be quite a puzzle for you. One moment he comes on hard and strong with declarations of his love; the next moment you find he's left you like yesterday's mashed potatoes. It does no good to wonder what went wrong. Chances are: nothing, really. It's just one of Libra's strange ways.

He is not exactly what you would call an ambitious person; you are perhaps looking for a mate or friend with more drive and fidelity. You are the sort of person who is interested in getting ahead—in making some headway in the areas that interest you; the Libran is often contented just to drift along. He does have drive, however, but it's not the long-range kind. It is not that he's shiftless or lazy. He's interested in material things; he appreciates luxuries and the like, but he may not be willing to work hard enough to obtain them. Beauty and harmony interest him. He'll dedicate a lot of time arranging things so that they are aesthetically pleasing. It would be difficult to accuse the Libra man of being practical; nine times out of ten, he isn't.

If you do begin a relationship with a man born under this sign, you will have to coax him now and again to face various situations in a realistic manner. You'll have your hands full, that's for sure. But if you love him, you'll undoubtedly do your best to understand him—no matter how difficult this may be.

If you take up with a Libra man, either temporarily or permanently, you'd better take over the task of managing his money. Often he has little understanding of financial matters; he tends to spend without thinking, following his whims.

SCORPIO WOMAN
SCORPIO MAN

Many find the Scorpio's sting a fate worse than death. When his anger breaks loose, you had better clear out of the vicinity.

The average Scorpio may strike you as a brute. He'll stick pins into the balloons of your plans and dreams if they don't line up with what he thinks is right. If you do anything to irritate him—

just anything—you'll wish you hadn't. He'll give you a sounding out that would make you pack your bags and go back to Mother— if you were that kind of a girl.

The Scorpio man hates being tied down to home life—he would rather be out on the battlefield of life, belting away at whatever he feels is a just and worthy cause, instead of staying home nestled in a comfortable armchair with the evening paper. If you are a girl who has a homemaking streak—don't keep those home fires burning too brightly too long; you may just run out of firewood.

As passionate as he is in business affairs and politics, the Scorpio man still has plenty of pep and ginger stored away for lovemaking.

Most women are easily attracted to him—perhaps you are no exception. Those who allow a man born under this sign to sweep them off their feet, shortly find that they're dealing with a pepper pot of seething excitement. The Scorpio man is passionate with a capital P, you can be sure of that. But he's capable of dishing out as much pain as pleasure. Damsels with fluttering hearts who, when in the embrace of a Scorpio, think "This is it," had better be in a position moments later to realize that "Perhaps this isn't it."

Scorpios are blunt. An insult is likely to whiz out of his mouth quicker than a compliment.

If you're the kind of woman who can keep a stiff upper lip, take it on the chin, turn a deaf ear, and all of that, because you feel you are still under his love spell in spite of everything: lots of luck.

If you have decided to take the bitter with the sweet, prepare yourself for a lot of ups and downs. Chances are you won't have as much time for your own affairs and interests as you'd like. The Scorpio's love of power may cause you to be at his constant beck and call.

Scorpios like fathering large families. They love children but quite often they fail to live up to their responsibilities as a parent.

SCORPIO WOMAN
SAGITTARIUS MAN

Sagittarius men are not easy to catch. They get cold feet whenever visions of the altar enter the romance. You'll most likely be attracted to the Sagittarian because of his sunny nature. He's lots of laughs and easy to get along with, but as soon as the relationship begins to take on a serious hue, you may feel yourself a little letdown.

Sagittarians are full of bounce; perhaps too much bounce to suit you. They are often hard to pin down; they dislike staying put. If he ever has a chance to be on-the-move, he'll latch onto it without so much as a how-do-you-do. Sagittarians are quick people—both in mind and spirit. If ever they do make mistakes, it's because of their zip; they leap before they look.

If you offer him good advice, he most likely won't follow it. Saigittarians like to rely on their own wits and ways.

His up-and-at-'em manner about most things is likely to drive you up the wall. He's likely to find you a little too slow and deliberate. "Get the lead out of your shoes," he's liable to tease when you're accompanying him on a stroll or jogging through the park with him on Sunday morning. He can't abide a slowpoke.

At times you'll find him too much like a kid—too breezy. Don't mistake his youthful zest for premature senility. Sagittarians are equipped with first-class brain power and know how to use it. They are often full of good ideas and drive. Generally, they are very broadminded people and very much concerned with fair play and equality.

In the romance department, he's quite capable of loving you wholeheartedly while treating you like a good pal. His hail-fellow-well-met manner in the arena of love is likely to scare off a dainty damsel. However, a woman who knows that his heart is in the right place won't mind it too much if, once in a while, he slaps her (lightly) on the back instead of giving her a gentle embrace.

He's not so much of a homebody. He's got ants in his pants and enjoys being on the move. Humdrum routine—especially at home—bores him silly. At the drop of a hat, he may ask you to whip off your apron and dine out for a change. He's a past-master in the instant surprise department. He'll love to keep you guessing. His friendly, candid nature will win him many friends. He'll expect his friends to be yours, and vice-versa.

Sagittarians make good fathers when the children become older; with little shavers, they feel all thumbs.

SCORPIO WOMAN
CAPRICORN MAN

The Capricorn man is quite often not the romantic kind of lover that attracts most women. Still, with his reserve and calm, he is capable of giving his heart completely once he has found the right girl. The Capricorn man is thorough and deliberate in all that he does; he is slow and sure.

He doesn't believe in flirting and would never lead a heart on a merry chase just for the game of it. If you win his trust, he'll give you his heart on a platter. Quite often, it is the woman who has to take the lead when romance is in the air. As long as he knows you're making the advances in earnest, he won't mind—in fact, he'll probably be grateful. Don't get to thinking he's all cold fish; he isn't. While some Capricorns are indeed quite capable of expressing passion, others often have difficulty in trying to display affection. He should have no trouble in this area, however, once he has found a patient and understanding girl.

The Capricorn man is very interested in getting ahead. He's quite ambitious and usually knows how to apply himself well to whatever task he undertakes. He's far from being a spendthrift. Like you, he knows how to handle money with extreme care. You, with your knack for putting away pennies for that rainy day, should have no difficulty understanding his way with money. The Capricorn man thinks in terms of future security. He wants to make sure that he and his wife have something to fall back on when they reach retirement. There's nothing wrong with that; in fact, it's a plus quality.

The Capricorn man will want you to handle household matters efficiently. Most Capricorn-oriented women will have no trouble in doing this. If he should check up on you from time to time, don't let it irritate you. Once you assure him that you can handle it all to his liking, he'll leave you alone.

The Capricorn man likes to be liked. He may seem dull to some, but underneath his reserve there is sometimes an adventurous streak that has never had a chance to express itself. He may be a real daredevil in his heart of hearts. The right woman—the affectionate, adoring woman can bring out that hidden zest in his nature.

He makes a loving, dutiful father, even though he may not understand his children completely.

SCORPIO WOMAN
AQUARIUS MAN

You are liable to find the Aquarius man the most broadminded man you have ever met; on the other hand, you are also liable to find him the most impractical. Oftentimes, he's more of a dreamer than a doer. If you don't mind putting up with a man whose heart and mind are as wide as the Missouri but whose head is almost always up in the clouds, then start dating that Aquarian who has somehow captured your fancy.

He's no dumbbell; make no mistake about that. He can be busy making some very complicated and idealistic plans when he's got that out-to-lunch look in his eyes. But more than likely, he'll never execute them. After he's shared one or two of his progressive ideas with you, you are liable to ask yourself, "Who is this nut?" But don't go jumping to conclusions. There's a saying that Aquarians are a half-century ahead of everybody else in the thinking department.

If you decide to answer "Yes" to his "Will you marry me?", you'll find out how right his zany whims are on or about your 50th anniversary. Maybe the waiting will be worth it. Could be that you have an Einstein on your hands—and heart.

Life with an Aquarian won't be one of total dispair if you can learn to temper his airiness. The Aquarian always maintains an open mind; he'll entertain the ideas and opinions of everybody although he may not agree with all of them.

His broadmindedness doesn't stop when it comes to you and your personal freedom. You won't have to give up any of your hobbies or projects after you're married; he'll encourage you to continue in your interests.

He'll be a kind and generous husband. He'll never quibble over petty things. Keep track of the money you both spend. He can't. Money burns a hole in his pockets.

At times, you may feel like calling it quits because he fails to satisfy your intense feelings. Chances are, though, that you'll always give him another chance.

He's a good family man. He understands children as much as he loves them.

SCORPIO WOMAN
PISCES MAN

The Pisces man could be the man you've looked for high and low and thought never existed. He's terribly sensitive and terribly romantic. Still, he has a very strong individual character and is well aware that the moon is not made of green cheese. He'll be very considerate of your every wish and will do his best to see to it that your relationship is a happy one.

The Pisces man is great for showering the object of his affection with all kinds of little gifts and tokens of his love.

He's just the right mixture of dreamer and realist; he's capable of pleasing most women's hearts. When it comes to earning bread and butter, the strong Pisces will do all right in the world. Quite often they are capable of rising to the very top. Some do extremely well as writers or psychiatrists. He'll be as patient and understanding with you as you will undoubtedly be with him. One thing a Pisces man dislikes is pettiness; anyone who delights in running another into the ground is almost immediately crossed off his list of possible mates. If you have any small grievances with your girl-friends, don't tell him. He couldn't care less and will think less of you if you do.

If you fall in love with a weak kind of Piscean, don't give up your job at the office before you get married. Better hang onto it until a good time after the honeymoon; you may still need it. A funny thing about the man born under this sign is that he can be content almost anywhere. This is perhaps because he is quite inner-directed and places little value on material things. In a shack or a palace, the Pisces man is capable of making the best of all possible adjustments. He won't kick up a fuss if the roof leaks and if the fence is in sad need of repair, he's liable just to shrug his shoulders. He's got more important things on his mind, he'll tell you. At this point, you'll most likely feel like giving him a piece of your mind. Still and all, the Pisces man is not shiftless or aimless; it is important to understand that material gain is never a direct goal for someone born under this sign.

Pisces men have a way with the sick and troubled. He can listen to one hard-luck story after another without seeming to tire. He often knows what's bothering someone before that someone knows it himself.

As a lover, he'll be quite attentive. You'll never have cause to doubt his intentions or sincerity. Everything will be above-board in his romantic dealings with you.

Children are delighted with Pisces men because of their permissiveness.

Man—Woman

SCORPIO MAN
ARIES WOMAN

The Aries woman may be a little too bossy and busy for you. Generally speaking, Aries are ambitious creatures. They can become a little impatient with people who are more thorough and deliberate than they are—especially if they feel they're taking too much time. The Aries woman is a fast worker. Sometimes she's so fast she forgets to look where she's going. When she stumbles or falls, it would be nice if you were there to catch her. Aries are proud women. They don't like to be told "I told you so" when they err. Tongue lashings can turn them into blocks of ice. Don't begin to think that the Aries woman frequently gets tripped up in her plans. Quite often they are capable of taking aim and hitting the bull's-eye. You'll be flabbergasted at times by their accuracy as well as by their ambition. On the other hand, you're apt to spot a flaw in the Aries woman's plans before she does.

You are perhaps somewhat slower than the Aries in attaining your goals. Still, you are not apt to make mistakes along the way; you're almost always well prepared.

The Aries woman is rather sensitive. She likes to be handled with gentleness and respect. Let her know that you love her for her brains as well as for her good looks. Never give her cause to become jealous. Handle her with tender love and care and she's yours.

The Aries woman can be giving if she feels her partner is deserving. She is no iceberg; she responds to the proper masculine flame. She needs a man she can look up to and feel proud of. If the shoe fits, put it on. If not, better put your sneakers back on and quietly tiptoe out of her sight. She can cause you plenty of heartache if you've made up your mind about her but she hasn't made up hers about you. Aries women are at times very demanding. Some of them tend to be high-strung; they can be difficult if they feel their independence is being hampered.

The cultivated Aries woman makes a wonderful homemaker and hostess. You'll find she's very clever in decorating and using color. Your house will be tastefully furnished; she'll see to it that it radiates harmony. The Aries wife knows how to make guests feel at home.

Although the Aries woman may not be keen on burdensome responsibilities, she is fond of children and the joy they bring.

SCORPIO MAN
TAURUS WOMAN

The woman born under the sign of Taurus may lack a little of the sparkle and bubble you often like to find in a woman. The Taurus woman is generally down-to-earth and never flighty. It's important to her that she keep both feet flat on the ground. She is not fond of bounding all over the place, especially if she's under the impression that there's no profit in it.

On the other hand, if you hit it off with a Taurus woman, you won't be disappointed in romance. The Taurus woman is all woman and proud of it too. She can be very devoted and loving once she decides that her relationship with you is no fly-by-night romance. Basically, she's a passionate person. In sex, she's direct and to-the-point. If she really loves you, she'll let you know she's yours—and without reservations. Better not flirt with other women once you've committed yourself to her. She is capable of being jealous and possessive.

She'll stick by you through thick and thin. It's almost certain that if the going ever gets rough, she'll not go running home to her mother. She can adjust to hard times just as graciously as she can to the good times.

Taureans are, on the whole, even-tempered. They like to be treated with kindness. Pretty things and soft things make them purr like kittens.

You may find her a little slow and deliberate. She likes to be safe and sure about everything. Let her plod along if she likes; don't coax her but just let her take her own sweet time. Everything she does is done thoroughly and, generally, without mistakes. Don't ride her for being a slowpoke. It could lead to flying pots and pans and a fireworks display that would put Bastille Day to shame. The Taurus woman doesn't anger readily but when prodded enough, she's capable of letting loose with a cyclone of anger. If you treat her with kindness and consideration, you'll have no cause for complaint.

The Taurean loves doing things for her man. She's a whiz in the kitchen and can whip up feasts fit for a king if she thinks they'll be royally appreciated. She may not fully understand you, but she'll adore you and be faithful to you if she feels you're worthy of it.

The woman born under Taurus will make a wonderful mother. She knows how to keep her children well-loved, cuddled, and warm. She may find them difficult to manage, however, when they are teen-agers.

SCORPIO MAN
GEMINI WOMAN

The Gemini woman may be too much of a flirt to ever strike your heart seriously. Then again, it depends on what kind of mood she's in. Gemini women can change from hot to cold quicker than a cat can wink it's eye. Chances are her fluctuations will tire you, and you'll pick up your heart—if it's not already broken into small pieces—and go elsewhere. Women born under the sign of the Twins have the talent of being able to change their moods and attitudes as frequently as they change their party dresses.

Sometimes, Gemini girls like to whoop it up. Some of them are good-time girls who love burning the candle at both ends. You'll see them at parties and gatherings, surrounded by men of all types, laughing gaily and kicking up their heels. Wallflowers, they're not. The next day you may bump into the same girl at the neighborhood library and you'll hardly recognize her for her "sensible" attire. She'll probably have five or six books under her arm—on five or six different subjects. In fact, she may even work there. If you think you've met the twin sister of Dr. Jekyll and Mr. Hyde, you're most likely right.

You'll probably find her a dazzling and fascinating creature—for a time, at any rate. Most men do. But when it comes to being serious about love you may find that that sparkling Eve leaves quite a bit to be desired. It's not that she has anything against being serious, it's just that she might find it difficult trying to be serious with you.

At one moment, she'll be capable of praising you for your steadfast and patient ways; the next moment she'll tell you in a cutting way that you're an impossible stick in the mud.

Don't even begin to fathom the depths of her mercurial soul—it's full of false bottoms. She'll resent close investigation, anyway, and will make you rue the day you ever took it into your head to try to learn more about her than she feels is necessary. Better keep the relationship full of fun and fancy free until she gives you the go-ahead. Take as much of her as she is willing to give; don't ask for more. If she does take a serious interest in you, then she'll come across with the goods.

There will come a time when the Gemini girl will realize that she can't spend her entire life at the ball and that the security and warmth you have to offer is just what she needs to be a happy, complete woman.

As a mother, she's easy-going with her children. She likes to spoil them as much as she can.

SCORPIO MAN
CANCER WOMAN

The girl born under Cancer needs to be protected from the cold, cruel world. She'll love you for your masculine yet gentle manner; you make her feel safe and secure. You don't have to pull any he-man or heroic stunts to win her heart; that's not what interests her. She's more likely to be impressed by your sure, steady ways—that way you have of putting your arm around her and making her feel that she's the only girl in the world. When she's feeling glum and tears begin to well up in her eyes, you have that knack of saying just the right thing—you know how to calm her fears, no matter how silly some of them may seem.

The girl born under this sign is inclined to have her ups and downs. You have that talent for smoothing out the ruffles in her sea of life. She'll most likely worship the ground you walk on or put you on a terribly high pedestal. Don't disappoint her if you can help it. She'll never disappoint you. This is the kind of woman who will take great pleasure in devoting the rest of her natural life to you. She'll darn your socks, mend your overalls, scrub floors, wash windows, shop, cook, and do just about anything short of murder in order to please you and to let you know that she loves you. Sounds like that legendary good old-fashioned girl, doesn't it? Contrary to popular belief, there are still a good number of them around—and many of them are Cancer people.

Of all the signs of the Zodiac, the women under the Cancer sign are the most maternal. In caring for and bringing up children, they know just how to combine the right amount of tenderness with the proper dash of discipline. A child couldn't ask for a better mother. Cancer women are sympathetic, affectionate, and patient with their children.

While we're on the subject of motherhood, there's one thing you should be warned about: never be unkind to your mother-in-law. It will be the only golden rule your Cancer wife will probably expect you to live up to. No mother-in-law jokes in the presence of your wife, please. With her, they'll go over like a lead balloon. Mother is something pretty special for her. She may be the crankiest, noisiest old bat this side of the Great Divide, still she's your wife's mother; you'd better treat her like she's one of the landed gentry. Sometimes this may be difficult to swallow, but if you want to keep your home together and your wife happy, you'd better learn to grin and bear it.

Treat your Cancer wife like a queen and she'll treat you royally.

SCORPIO MAN
LEO WOMAN

If you can manage a girl who likes to kick up her heels every now and again, then the Leo woman was made for you. You'll have to learn to put away jealous fears—or at least forget about them—when you take up with a woman born under this sign, because she's often the kind that makes heads turn and tongues wag. You don't necessarily have to believe any of what you hear—it's most likely just jealous gossip or wishful thinking. Take up with a Leo woman and you'll be taking off on a romance full of fire and ice; be prepared to take the good things with the bad—the bitter with the sweet.

The Leo girl has more than a fair share of grace and glamor. She is aware of her charms and knows how to put them to good use. Needless to say, other women in her vicinity turn green with envy and will try anything short of shoving her into the nearest lake, in order to put her out of commission.

If she's captured your heart and fancy, woo her intensely if your intention is to eventually win her. Shower her with expensive gifts and promise her the moon—if you're in a position to go that far—then you'll find her resistance beginning to weaken. It's not that she's difficult, she'll probably make a fuss over you once she's decided you're the man for her, but she does enjoy a lot of attention. What's more: she feels she's entitled to it. Her mild arrogance, though, is becoming. The Leo woman knows how to transform the crime of excessive pride into a very charming misdemeanor. It sweeps most men right off their feet. Those who do not succumb to her leonine charm are few and far between.

If you've got an important business deal to clinch and you have doubts as to whether or not it will go over well, bring your Leo girl along to that business luncheon and it's a cinch that that contract will be yours. She won't have to do or say anything—just be there, at your side. The grouchiest oil magnate can be transformed into a gushing, obedient schoolboy if there's a Leo woman in the room.

If you're rich and want to stay that way, don't give your Leo mate a free hand with the charge accounts and credit cards. If you're poor, the luxury-loving Leo will most likely never enter your life.

She makes a strict yet easy-going mother. She loves to pal around with her children.

SCORPIO MAN
VIRGO WOMAN

The Virgo woman may be a little too difficult for you to understand at first. Her waters run deep. Even when you think you know her, don't take any bets on it. She's capable of keeping things hidden in the deep recesses of her womanly soul—things she'll only release when she's sure that you're the man she's been looking for. It may take her some time to come around to this decision. Virgo girls are finicky about almost everything; everything has to be letter-perfect before they're satisfied. Many of them have the idea that the only people who can do things right are Virgos.

Nothing offends a Virgo woman more than slovenly dress, sloppy character, or a careless display of affection. Make sure your tie is not crooked and your shoes sport a bright shine before you go calling on this lady. Keep your off-color jokes for the locker-room, she'll have none of that. Take her arm when crossing the street. Don't rush the romance. Trying to corner her in the back of a cab may be one way of striking out. Never criticize the way she looks—in fact, the best policy would be to agree with her as much as possible. Still, there's just so much a man can take; all those dos and don'ts you'll have to follow if you want to get to first base. After a few dates, you may come to the conclusion that she just isn't worth all that trouble. However, the Virgo woman is mysterious enough generally speaking, to keep her men running back for more. Chances are you'll be intrigued by her airs and graces.

If love-making means a lot to you, you'll be disappointed at first in the cool ways of your Virgo woman. However, under her glacial facade there lies a caldron of seething excitement. If you're patient and artful in your romantic approach, you'll find that all that caution was well worth the trouble. When Virgos love, they don't stint. It's all or nothing as far as they're concerned. Once they're convinced that they love you, they go all the way, right off the bat—tossing caution to the wind.

One thing a Virgo woman can't stand in love is hypocrisy. They don't give a hoot about what the neighbors say, if their hearts tell them "Go ahead!" They're very concerned with human truths . . . so much so that if their hearts stumble upon another fancy, they're liable to be true to that new heart-throb and leave you standing in the rain. She's honest to her heart and will be as true to you as you are with her, generally. Do her wrong once, however, and it's farewell.

Both strict and tender, she tries to bring out the best in her children.

SCORPIO MAN
LIBRA WOMAN

As the old saying goes: It's a woman's prerogative to change her mind. Whoever said it must have had the Libra woman in mind. Her changeability, in spite of its undeniable charm (sometimes) could actually drive even a man of your patience up the wall. She's capable of smothering you with love and kisses one day and on the next, avoid you like the plague. If you think you're a man of steel nerves then perhaps you can tolerate her sometime-ness without suffering too much. However, if you own up to the fact that you're only a mere mortal who can only take so much, then you'd better fasten your attention on a girl who's somewhat more constant.

But don't get the wrong idea: a love affair with a Libra is not bad at all. In fact, it can have an awful lot of plusses to it. Libra women are soft, very feminine, and warm. She doesn't have to vamp all over the place in order to gain a man's attention. Her delicate presence is enough to warm the cockles of any man's heart. One smile and you're like a piece of putty in the palm of her hand.

She can be fluffy and affectionate—things you like in a girl. On the other hand, her indecision about which dress to wear, what to cook for dinner, or whether to redo the rumpus room or not could make you tear your hair out. What will perhaps be more exasperating is her flat denial to the accusation that she cannot make even the simplest decision. The trouble is that she wants to be fair or just in all matters; she'll spend hours weighing pros and cons. Don't make her rush into a decision; that will only irritate her.

The Libra woman likes to be surrounded by beautiful things. Money is not object where beauty is concerned. There will always be plenty of flowers in the house. She'll know how to arrange them tastefully, too. Women under this sign are fond of beautiful clothes and furnishings. They will run up bills without batting an eye—if given the chance.

Once she's cottoned to you, the Libra woman will do everything in her power to make you happy. She'll wait on you hand and foot when you're sick and bring you breakfast in bed on Sundays. She'll be very thoughtful and devoted. If anyone dares suggest you're not the grandest man in the world, your Libra wife will give that person a piece of her mind.

Libras work wonders with children. Gentle persuasion and affection are all she uses in bringing them up. It works.

SCORPIO MAN
SCORPIO WOMAN

The Scorpio woman can be a whirlwind of passion—perhaps too much passion to really suit you. When her temper flies, you'd better lock up the family heirlooms and take cover. When she chooses to be sweet, you're apt to think that butter wouldn't melt in her mouth—but, of course, it would.

The Scorpio woman can be as hot as a tamale or as cool as a cucumber, but whatever mood she's in, she's in it for real. She does not believe in posing or putting on airs.

The Scorpio woman is often sultry and seductive—her femme fatale charm can pierce through the hardest of hearts like a laser ray. She may not look like Mata Hari (quite often Scorpios resemble the tomboy next door) but once she's fixed you with her tantalizing eyes, you're a goner.

Life with the Scorpio woman will not be all smiles and smooth-sailing; when prompted, she can unleash a gale of venom. Generally, she'll have the good grace to keep family battles within the walls of your home. When company visits, she's apt to give the impression that married life with you is one great big joyride. It's just one of her ways of expressing her loyalty to you—at least in front of others. She may fight you tooth and nail in the confines of your living room, but at a ball or during an evening out, she'll hang onto your arm and have stars in her eyes.

Scorpio women are good at keeping secrets. She may even keep a few buried from you.

Never cross her on even the smallest thing. When it comes to revenge, she's an eye-for-an-eye woman. She's not too keen on forgiveness—especially if she feels she's been wronged unfairly. You'd be well advised not to give her any cause to be jealous, either. When the Scorpio woman sees green, your life will be made far from rosy. Once she's put you in the doghouse, you can be sure that you're going to stay there a while.

You may find life with a Scorpio woman too draining. Although she may be full of the old paprika, it's quite likely that she's not the kind of girl you'd like to spend the rest of your natural life with. You'd prefer someone gentler and not so hot-tempered . . . someone who can take the highs with the lows and not bellyache . . . someone who is flexible and understanding. A woman born under Socrpio can be heavenly, but she can also be the very devil when she chooses.

As a mother, a Scorpio is protective and encouraging.

SCORPIO MAN
SAGITTARIUS WOMAN

The Sagittarius woman is hard to keep track of: first she's here, then she's there. She's a woman with a severe case of itchy feet. She's got to keep on the move.

People generally like her because of her hail-fellow-well-met manner and breezy charm. She is constantly good-natured and almost never cross. She is the kind of girl you're likely to strike up a palsy-walsy relationship with; you might not be interested in letting it go any farther. She probably won't sulk if you leave it on a friendly basis, either. Treat her like a kid sister and she'll eat it up like candy.

She'll probably be attracted to you because of your restful, self-assured manner. She'll need a friend like you to help her over the rough spots in her life; she'll most likely turn to you for advice.

There is nothing malicious about a girl born under this sign. She is full of bounce and good cheer. Her sunshiny disposition can be relied upon on even the rainiest of days. No matter what she says or does, you'll always know that she means well. Sagittarians are sometimes short on tact. Some of them say anything that comes into their pretty little heads, no matter what the occasion. Sometimes the words that tumble out of their mouths seem downright cutting and cruel; they mean well but often everything they say comes out wrong. She's quite capable of losing her friends—and perhaps even yours—through a careless slip of the lip. Always remember that she is full of good intentions. Stick with her if you like her and try to help her mend her ways.

She's not a girl that you'd most likely be interested in marrying, but she'll certainly be lots of fun to pal around with. Quite often, Sagittarius women are outdoor types. They're crazy about things like fishing, camping, and mountain climbing. They love the wide open spaces. They are fond of all kinds of animals. Make no mistake about it: this busy little lady is no slouch. She's full of pep and ginger.

She's great company most of the time; she's more fun than a three-ring circus when she's in the right company. You'll like her for her candid and direct manner. On the whole, Sagittarians are very kind and sympathetic women.

If you do wind up marrying this girl-next-door type, you'd better see to it that you handle all of the financial matters. Sagittarians often let money run through their fingers like sand.

As a mother, she'll smother her children with love and give them all of the freedom *they* think they need.

SCORPIO MAN
CAPRICORN WOMAN

The Capricorn may not be the most romantic woman of the Zodiac, but she's far from frigid when she meets the right man. She believes in true love; she doesn't appreciate getting involved in flings. To her, they're just a waste of time. She's looking for a man who means "business'—in life as well as in love. Although she can be very affectionate with her boyfriend or mate, she tends to let her head govern her heart. That is not to say she is a cool, calculating cucumber. On the contrary, she just feels she can be more honest about love if she consults her brains first. She wants to size-up the situation before throwing her heart in the ring. She wants to make sure it won't get stepped on.

The Capricorn woman is faithful, dependable, and systematic in just about everything she undertakes. She is quite concerned with security and sees to it that every penny she spends is spent wisely. She is very economical about using her time, too. She does not believe in whittling away her energy on a scheme that is not going to pay off.

Ambitious themselves, they are quite often attracted to ambitious men—men who are interested in getting somewhere in life. If a man of this sort wins her heart, she'll stick by him and do all she can to help him get to the top.

The Capricorn woman is almost always diplomatic. She makes an excellent hostess. She can be very influential when your business acquaintances come to dinner.

The Capricorn woman is likely to be very concerned, if not downright proud, about her family tree. Relatives are pretty important to her, particularly if they're socially prominent. Never say a cross word about one of her family. That can really go against her grain and she'll punish you by not talking to you for days.

She's generally thorough in whatever she does. Capricorn women are well-mannered and gracious, no matter what their backgrounds. They seem to have it in their natures to always behave properly.

If you should marry a woman born under this sign, you need never worry about her going on a wild shopping spree. They understand the value of money better than most women. If you turn over your paycheck to her at the end of the week, you can be sure that a good hunk of it will wind up in the bank.

The Capricorn mother is loving and correct.

SCORPIO MAN
AQUARIUS WOMAN

If you find that you've fallen head over heels for a woman born under the sign of the Water Bearer, you'd better fasten your safety belt. It may take you quite a while to actually discover what this girl is like—and even then, you may have nothing to go on but a string of vague hunches. The Aquarian is like a rainbow, full of bright and shining hues; she's like no other girl you've ever known. There is something elusive about her—something delightfully mysterious. You'll most likely never be able to put your finger on it. It's nothing calculated, either; Aquarians don't believe in phony charm.

There will never be a dull moment in your life with this Water Bearing woman; she seems to radiate adventure and magic. She'll most likely be the most open-minded and tolerant woman you've ever met. She has a strong dislike for injustice and prejudice. Narrow-mindedness runs against her grain.

She is very independent by nature and quite capable of shifting for herself if necessary. She may receive many proposals for marriage from all sorts of people without ever really taking them seriously. Marriage is a very big step for her; she wants to be sure she knows what she's getting into. If she thinks that it will seriously curb her independence and love of freedom, she's liable to shake her head and give the man his engagement ring back—if indeed she's let the romance get that far.

The line between friendship and romance is a pretty fuzzy one for an Aquarian. It's not difficult for her to remain buddy-buddy with an ex-lover. She's tolerant, remember? So, if you should see her on the arm of an old love, don't jump to any hasty conclusions.

She's not a jealous person herself and doesn't expect you to be, either. You'll find her pretty much of a free spirit most of the time. Just when you think you know her inside-out, you'll discover that you don't really know her at all.

She's a very sympathetic and warm person; she can be helpful to people in need of assistance and advice.

She'll seldom be suspicious even if she has every right to be. If the man she loves slips and allows himself a little fling, chances are she'll just turn her head the other way. Her tolerance does have its limits, however, and her man should never press his luck at hanky-panky.

She makes a big-hearted mother; her good qualities rub off on her children.

SCORPIO MAN
PISCES WOMAN

The Pisces woman places great value on love and romance. She's gentle, kind, and romantic. Perhaps she's that girl you've been dreaming about all these years. Like you, she has very high ideals; she will only give her heart to a man who she feels can live up to her expectations.

She will never try to wear the pants in the family. She's a staunch believer in the man being the head of the house. Quite often Pisces women are soft and cuddly. They have a feminine, domestic charm that can win the heart of just about any man.

Generally, there's a lot more to her than just a pretty exterior and womanly ways. There's a brain ticking behind that gentle face. You may not become aware of it—that is, until you've married her. It's no cause for alarm, however; she'll most likely never use it against you. But if she feels you're botching up your married life through careless behavior or if she feels you could be earning more money than you do, she'll tell you about it. But any wife would, really. She'll never try to usurp your position as head and bread-winner of the family. She'll admire you for your ambition and drive. If anyone says anything against you in her presence, she'll probably break out into tears. Pisces women are usually very sensitive and their reaction to frustration or anger is often just a plain good old-fashioned cry. They can weep buckets when inclined.

She'll prepare an extra-special dinner for you when you've made a new conquest in your profession. Don't bother to go into the details though at the dinner table; she doesn't have much of a head for business matters, usually, and is only too happy to leave that up to you.

She is a wizard in decorating a home. She's fond of soft and beautiful things. There will always be a vase of fresh flowers on the dining room table. She'll see to it that you always have plenty of socks and underwear in the top dresser drawer.

Treat her with tenderness and your relationship will be an enjoyable one. Pisces women are generally fond of sweets, so keep her in chocolates (and flowers, of course) and you'll have a happy wife. Never forget birthdays or anniversaries; she won't.

If you have a talent for patience and gentleness, it will certainly pay off in your relationship with a Pisces woman. Chances are she'll never make you regret that you placed that band of gold on her finger.

There is usually a strong bond between a Pisces mother and her children. She'll try to give them things she never had as a child and is apt to spoil them as a result.

SCORPIO

SCORPIO

YEARLY FORECAST: 1988

*Forecast for 1988 Concerning Business and
Financial Matters, Job Prospects,
Travel, Health, Romance and Marriage
for Those Born with the Sun
in the Zodiacal Sign of Scorpio.
October 23—November 22*

Look ahead to a year of promise. Your indomitable ruling planet, Pluto, continues to give you a strong sense of personal purpose to which is added the desire to expand and develop far beyond your usual capacity. For many this will mean an extension of self into marriage or business partnership for you may soon appreciate that there is more to be gained by willing cooperation than aggression. Preparations can be completed if you feel you are not quite ready for full development, but this will not take long. By later in the year, you will feel you have achieved something worthwhile and will be already planning for the future of the family or the further development of business. You could benefit financially through no particular effort on your part, some of you because of your partners' efforts and others through a legacy or windfall. While you are looking for increased productivity and personal development through your opportunity to share, the main pressure seems to be on a subjective level. Your natural determination will be stimulated. You will apply yourself to building a sound structure for the future. Many will come to realize the importance of study, communication and your need to understand everyday routine of bread and butter neighborliness. Traveling, especially when it comes to short trips, will play an important part in your year. As ever, you will travel with a purpose. Health can at times be tested, but this is nothing new and you will soon appreciate your natural limitations. Overexertion is likely to be your worst enemy. Hard practicalities and a determination to get as far as you can in the time available may give you little time or inclination to let your hair down. In this respect you can be brought out of your shell through close personal relationships and active sharing. It is a year to be generous. You will find your generosity is amply returned. It is the major areas of life that will call for your attention, so you should expect to grow in a meaningful way. There are always dangers of losing perspective when you are seeking expansion. Provided you do not lose sight of the needs of others on whom you may have to depend, you should have a really good year. If you become selfish, however, you could suffer in the long term.

You will feel you have a good deal to tidy up or get into shape in the first nine or ten weeks of the year. Thoughts of expansion can be stirring you. See to it that you have everything organized before the initial assault. Attend to labor matters. See that employees are happy with their conditions. It is better to be a little out of pocket yourself in order to avoid problems later on when you will have little time to spare for details. You are likely to see a profit from your sensible preparation between July 22 and November 29. Other envious concerns may become interested in your progress and there could be an opportunity to widen your scope even further in the take-over field. The period between March 8 and July 21, and again during December, will be the main time of expansion. During this time you will need all the cooperation you can get and should make hay while the sun shines. Partnership is very much in the cards and should be taken up with due consideration to the small print as well as the main objectives. You may have little time to consider publicity and run-of-the-mill ties or communications, especially between February 14 and June 9, and again after November 12. Nevertheless, despite the pressure, you should see to it that your information on what is going on around you as well as your impact on the community is up to date. Strengthen your basic structure by making yourself known as a reliable and trustworthy business person. This may mean you have to work harder than you thought and have less time for leisure. Think of the future. Between July 22 and August 21 you may find it suits you to take note of what the big boys in business have to say. Development needs support and recognition.

Up to March 7 your income may come most easily from your daily work. There is a possibility of promotion or opportunity to make more of your chances. It will pay to hang on to any gains or bonuses you make up to the middle of February. Be hard if necessary because you must be in good shape financially if you are to increase your potential during this year of expansion. Use your capital wisely. There could be extra expense between February 14 and June 9 and possibly again after November 12. It could be necessary to lay out money on travel or keep in touch with essential contacts. Provided you are practical, you should spend your money wisely, but be prepared to have some minor worries. Adjust when and where necessary. From July 22 to November 29 you could feel more settled financially. There could be increased income, or tax rebates or even good news about an inheritance. Provided you have applied yourself, there seems every hope of increasing joint funds during this period. The desire to expand may tempt some to speculate during the year. This is not particularly wise, and is most chancy in the periods May 22 to July 12 and again between October 23 and 31. Putting your energy into more creative activities will bring in money, while speculation could easily lose it.

Work should give you pleasure up to about March 7. You could be developing your own techniques or getting yourself into good trim for the year to follow. There could be promotion or extra responsibility that allows you some latitude rather than imposing a restriction on your day. There could be extra work or long hours between February 14 and June 9, and possibly again after November 12. This may be caused through expansion of business, problems of communications or ill-health of work colleagues. Be prepared to persevere. There seems less scope for the artistically motivated worker than the craftsman. And there will be ups and downs for all. Many skills can be developed in a year when much depends on your sense of application and subjective development. Between July 22 and November 29 try to make your position secure for the future.

For many, widening horizons will mean romantic developments. You may feel that this is the year when you must test your individuality to the full and come to terms with life. Marriage will be the natural outlet. It could be a great spiritual and emotional year. As you have a need to keep your feet on the ground, there are good practical reasons for sharing in order to make the future more satisfying. From January 15 to February 8 you may feel lighthearted and dip your toe in the waters of love. Married couples may think of increasing the family. It is a time to be relaxed and enjoy your love life. Between November 23 and December 16 you could be attracted to someone and be pleased to find this is mutual. The period between March 6 to July 21 should be promising for those who contemplate marriage, with special emphasis in the dates between March 8 and April 2. You do not usually treat relationships lightly. This year you will be more than usually sure of what you are doing, since this could be the big year. For late starters the last month of the year may suit your book if you intend to wed.

A busy year will mean you are obliged to keep yourself in good condition. You are likely to be fully extended for most of the year and subjecting yourself to a lot of pressure, using up a lot of energy. Your natural resilience will see you through and you will need to start the year off looking after your diet and building up a store of energy. You are one of the best when it comes to appreciation of good food and can get a little carried away when enthused. So exercise judgment without losing the pleasure. There could be some extra stress or unexpected pressure on you, and you do not want to carry superfluous weight which has to be shed in difficult circumstances. Between February 15 and May 26 you may feel things are not going as you would like and can get a bit strung up. You may be inclined to act or react hastily or take on more than you should. It will be difficult, but you should try to keep some sort of control, or seek some form of relaxation that will relieve tension. You could be careless if under pressure and accidents can happen in a moment of stress. Minor irritations will only make you more up-tight, so do take things in their true perspective and slow down occasionally. Minor cuts and burns between July 13 and October 22 can slow your progress. There is some possibility of infection if you do not have early attention. November and December seem lively months. Use your energy constructively. Have a checkup between March 20 and April 18.

Traveling seems to be of a local nature for most of the year. You could have a hectic time keeping pace with all that is going on around you, both at work and in the local community. It may be necessary to visit relatives quite frequently. A holiday overseas may be best arranged between June 21 and July 21 when things are a little easy after the pressure of events. Journey with a purpose in the first nineteen days of the year. You could have an important engagement. The last ten days of the year, also, should not be wasted. You are getting somewhere so you should see you get there on time.

DAILY FORECAST
January–December: 1988
JANUARY

1. FRIDAY. Good. Enjoy a happy reunion. Love springs eternal in the human breast. Meeting long-lost friends at the beginning of the year should put you in a good mood. Home comforts mean a great deal. It will be a lazy sort of day with all thoughts of work far from your mind. There could be news of a property coming up for sale. The younger members of the family give pleasure. Parents think of what they can do to make their children's future more secure. There can be some nostalgia, a common experience when families get together once in a while. Looking at family photographs and other momentoes is sure to bring back memories. It will also add to the fun and probably create a lot of laughter.

2. SATURDAY. Disquieting. A review of the expenses for the end-of-year festivities can give you a shock. You will need to do something extra to make up your family bank balance. Parting with dear friends and loved ones can leave you feeling miserable. Someone cannot stand farewells and leaves in a hurry. A long journey lies ahead and you are not in the mood to enjoy it. Thoughts of going back to intensive studies can make you feel unhappy. An older person can make heavy demands on your time. Try to find out all you can about some bit of family history resurrected over the holidays. Look after your money and keep an eye open for anyone who is likely to sell you short or try to rob you.

3. SUNDAY. Deceptive. Someone could break a promise. You are not in the mood to accept excuses, so you may mark another pal off your list. A journey can be canceled. This could be a blessing in disguise. An important local personage seems to be rather mixed up. There could be good reason. Do not take everything or everyone at face value. You should be determined to do your own thing whatever the inconvenience. You may find later that your important personage turns out to be a friend who sees your point of view. Relatives can make you think of the past. A trip down memory lane can be more satisfying than a routine flight or some sort of general get-together.

4. MONDAY. Disquieting. Work can be delayed due to late arrivals. A careless mistake can cost you time and money. It may be necessary to go on a long journey because a work colleague has let you down. Communications in general are confused. Mail and commuter services could be disorganized. News is not very encouraging, anyway. Students returning to college can find there is some misunderstanding that will slow down their efforts. Personal plans can be activated. Do what you think is right and rely on no one else. Initiative can pay off. Let everyone know that you can cope, despite local problems. Relatives can let you down, but you should be resilient enough to fall back on your own resources.

5. TUESDAY. Quiet. Keep out of the limelight. You could be in a position of control today and will need time to collect your wits. Don't seek out trouble with any work staff or others who will look to you for guidance and instruction. Take it all in your stride. Be careful that you are not putting your reputation at risk. It could be wiser to let others do all the donkey work while you stay aloof and observe. Make preparations for a move forward. This may be a little frustrating. An earlier expectation of progress may not be realized. Settle down to take the day as it comes. Those at home will not miss you too much as long as they feel that you are happy in your work.

6. WEDNESDAY. Disturbing. Personal plans can be badly upset. Be determined if you mean to succeed. Business activities are likely to cause rearrangement. It may be necessary to move to another location. Something out of your control can make you cancel an appointment. A loved one may leave you. Home can feel strange without one of its younger members. You could be oversensitive to the remarks made by someone. You have to make your way in the world and should not worry about those who envy you. A promotion is possible. Productivity is up and you could be making progress. It is entirely possible that you could have a stroke of luck later in the day.

7. THURSDAY. Variable. Someone could make a last-ditch attempt to balk you. Do not get upset or worry about your prospects. If you jump to conclusions you could be quite wrong. Use your head. You have sound financial backing for anything you attempt, so why should you rise to the bait? A loan can be repaid or a debt settled.

Your reputation is strengthened. You feel better when a banker shows confidence in your collateral. A worry over money can be cleared up. Take sound advice about home décor from a fellow worker who knows. A romantic appointment should be just right. Let this help you forget your problems, at least for a short time.

8. FRIDAY. Good. Enjoy meeting a romantic friend. Relatives may take a lively interest in your social life. There could be rumors of an impending wedding in the family. Attend to business with an open mind. You may receive some unusual advice from a perfectionist. Do not discard this before you have investigated its merits. Imaginative people are hard to come by, but you cannot always pin them down. Meet someone with charitable ideas and try to do a good turn for another. Money matters at business seem to be unusually orderly. Perhaps you have some hidden helpers? Go about your affairs gently. Be gracious to others and you will reap benefits too. A great day to meditate or use your intuition which is so seldom wrong.

9. SATURDAY. Buoyant. Make the most of your friends. Local activities can keep you on the go all day. You could be happily surprised to meet someone you admire. Some important people are quite human and understanding after all. Get things into perspective with a partner. It is a good time to make agreements. A business arrangement can lead to increased trade at the local level. This will cut costs and provide a reliable fallback if things get less busy. A shopping expedition with parents can be really enjoyable. Get around amongst your relatives while you have the time. Some important document may need attention. Do not put off dealing with whatever demands action.

10. SUNDAY. Good. Be prepared to move quickly. Your quick wits may be in demand today, especially if someone gets into trouble. Keep a discreet distance if you see things beginning to warm up, but respond immediately if you hear a call for help. Family security is important. There can be a lot of activity in the home. Someone may be keen to splurge on a get-together. Try to persuade them to cool it. It will be much more beneficial to do things quietly behind closed doors. A visit to someone in hospital will be appreciated. Your mind could be working overtime. Arrange a visit or a deal if you can manage it. There could be property on the market. Prices may be somewhat steep, but may still be worth pushing.

11. MONDAY. Variable. Keep your wits about you. You can pick up a bargain without too much fuss if you are on your toes.

Spend wisely on something needed in the home. Discuss any financial problem with the family. Two heads are always better than one. An arrangement affecting the young and active members of the household should be tried out. Keep in the background and make no comment till you see how it works. Someone in a responsible position is likely to let you down. A private agreement with a well-known local entrepreneur proves to be a washout. Your employer could well be in a bad mood and trust no one. It will be up to you to prove that you are reliable and can be trusted.

12. TUESDAY. Good.   Share a confidence. But if you have a private romance in progress, keep that known only to your family. An important matter close to your heart can be settled today. It is high time you got your finances into working order. Your savings should be at a high point. Think about giving someone you love a present. Seek financial backing if you have something new to market. It is not wise to leave a decision hanging fire too long. Strike while the iron is hot. A young couple could learn of a home on the market. If you have a chance, urge them to make a firm offer. Details can be straightened out later. With real estate matters, time is usually at a premium.

13. WEDNESDAY. Fair.   You could be on your own. If home comforts are short today, be happy to accept neighborly hospitality. There could be something unpleasant to do and no one can do it for you. Whatever needs to be done should be done well and in the manner you fully understand. Someone may leave home or may have difficulty getting back on time. A new arrangement regarding a home loan can get you out of a tight spot. Invite someone home who intrigues you. Time taken earlier in preparation can be well worth your while. There could be good news from a government office, despite an apparent lack of cooperation from another department.

14. THURSDAY. Rewarding.   Alterations affecting your home life can be unsettling. You have influential friends who will make your problems seem much easier. Look after personal matters, despite any other pressures. It is essential you attempt to make progress. The right approach now could mean you are in line for an increase in salary or will have a private source of income. There could be a challenge in relationships. An unusual person may attract you. There may be two sides of this friend's nature, so you could be in store for a dilemma. Have the courage of your convictions. Make your own decisions. A surprise move in a property deal could please you.

15. FRIDAY. Variable. You can throw caution to the winds today. Spending money can be a natural part of your early relaxation. It is essential to get rid of some high spirits. Someone else can benefit in the process. You may live to regret it later, but you must live for the moment. News of an increase in your savings will help you keep up appearances. This is a good time to make some arrangement about modernizing the home. Get advice on a way to increase earnings by home work. Keep in touch with someone who has a good knowledge of property business. There could be an opportunity to come to terms with a real estate agent. Conditions seem favorable for a trade, so do not haggle too much.

16. SATURDAY. Demanding. A change of routine will do you good. The weekend should be occupied with interests that allow you to spread your wings constructively. If you are obliged to work, see that you are paid extra. You will feel you are worth every penny of it. Keep a firm grip of things. Part with no money that is not productive. Some may say you are being cheap. They are entitled to their opinion but do not know what is up your sleeve. A unique opportunity to make a killing may be just around the corner. Someone with most original ideas is likely to intrigue you. You could be asked to undertake an unusual duty. Feel free and able to do whatever is asked of you.

17. SUNDAY. Deceptive. You feel you are in love. A heady morning follows an evening of entertainment. Perhaps you have met the right one this time. A day for pleasant dreams and hopes for the future is in store. Relatives who visit may comment on your faraway look. Take the opportunity to relax well away from anything remotely like work. A date with the boy or girl next door is all you need to make you happy. You could be in the mood to talk to anyone who understands your sensitive feelings. Mind you do not say too much. Someone may take you the wrong way or blow things out of all proportion. Use your intuition. When you are in top form you can read the thoughts of others. This may help you keep control. Use your magnetism.

18. MONDAY. Changeable. A local issue can come to a head. Some senior official may be called in to settle a grievance. Conditions at work are rather chaotic. You may feel things have gone beyond your capabilities. A careless attitude to starting the week could put you in a fix. Look out for anyone who is slipshod and give them a wide berth. There could be a lot of tidying up to do before you make a start on a new project. A delay could put everything out of joint, so get yourself organized early in the day. Expectations do not match up to actualities in the morning. Later on you will feel you have a grip on things. A bit of support from a senior will help.

19. TUESDAY. Tricky.   Be positive in handling a domestic issue. Get a firm grip on finances and spend wisely. A bargain should be accepted, though at the time you may think it rather expensive. Strike while the iron is hot in a property deal. Now is the time to take your courage in both hands to overcome something affecting a member of the family. Subsidize a younger person who may need money in a hurry. A dispute can be quickly settled if you are honest and don't beat about the bush. Your pride could be hurt later in the day. You could hear a remark that strikes deep. Do not be resentful. Better get things out of your system than brood and give yourself ulcers.

20. WEDNESDAY. Good.   A change is as good as a rest. There could be a new job on the horizon. Nothing seems to be upsetting so you could, perhaps, make a move that has no strings attached. Consolidate your financial position. There may be some hope of getting a post nearer home which will cut out considerable traveling. A specialist may get in touch about home improvements. Take note of advice given. This is rather out of the ordinary run of things. Real estate dealings can be at a critical stage. You can settle to your advantage after a lot of hard bargaining. Another day and you could be out of luck. Colleagues can bring you good luck.

21. THURSDAY. Variable.   The course of true love never did run smooth, but keep smiling. You have the romantics on your side, so it can't be as bad as all that. The next few days could be important in your love life. An early disagreement can upset you. Do not take a lot of notice of materialistic people who may throw cold water on your plans. A relative can be most understanding. So much depends on the close cooperation of those near you who feel as do you. Trust your deeper feelings and don't be afraid to let your emotions show. If you are in love, show that you know what it's all about. Someone with a nasty streak may be jealous.

22. FRIDAY. Sensitive.   Develop your creative talents. Look for any chance to publicize yourself in the local press. An artistic ad can do more than an expensive campaign. You could be in a most sensitive mood and receptive to imaginative suggestions. Try to make full use of these aids that come from people you know and trust. Take no notice of rumors about the love affairs of others.

There will be time enough to handle your own problems if and when they arise. A shortage of ready money can slow you down later in the day. You could have been expecting this, so should know how to cope. Avoid doing things that are totally out of your normal routine.

23. SATURDAY. Variable. Be positive. Do not be put off by rumors. A distraction can get you completely confused and you could lose valuable time from an essential job. If you are worried, the best cure is to do something constructive that will boost your morale as well as your pocket. The condition of a relative can be cause for concern. You are in a position to help in a material way, so should not spend too much time allowing your imagination to wander. Do not seek to avoid an issue. You are quite capable of managing anything that has to be done. Any inferior feelings are totally in the mind. An employer can note your determination to get ahead and give you support.

24. SUNDAY. Good. This could be your lucky day. News of a new home can give you heart. Put all your strength and good will into a service for others. After a health worry you may be assured there is nothing wrong. Share your joy with the family. You could hear of a job opening for someone close to you. Encourage them to take this opportunity. An older person can make you feel welcome. Accept any advice you receive about old-fashioned remedies. These can be more reliable than modern methods. Make plans for the future. Family arrangements should be made for a forthcoming event. A lot can be settled and a schedule agreed.

25. MONDAY. Variable. Thank your lucky stars you have someone to love. If your head is in the clouds it will help you to put up with problems down on the ground. A parent can be more than difficult. Progress will be hard to make in the face of unwilling cooperation or possibly deliberate contradiction at work. A business partnership can be threatened if your associate considers you are being over-imaginative. Try to explain the more sophisticated side of the business. A legal problem can come to the point of decision which could mean more aggravation. Any property deal with you in an inferior position should be avoided. Your love life can be a happy escape from problems around you.

26. TUESDAY. Fair. A decision may have to be made. Someone can go out of your life leaving you disoriented. Perhaps this is as well, for you have to make your true position known. Your love life remains a haven of peace. Whatever others may think you have to be honest with those who seek your cooperation. You are never one to lower standards and should stand on your dignity to make this quite clear. A legal problem or decision can make you come to terms with reality. Now you can appreciate why you have to respect yourself as well as others. Your partner could be having a rough time. Give all the love you can to improve the situation. Love will win in the end.

27. WEDNESDAY. Disquieting. Give up trying to explain if people are dumb. You may have the wrong end of the stick although you don't realize it at the moment. Traveling is likely to be difficult. Some member of the family can get under your feet all day if transport breaks down. Nerves and tempers can get a bit frayed if you are living too close to someone for too long. Look for a bit of light relief. A change will do you good, though it may upset your schedule. Discussions about home security are not helpful. There seems to be a lack of clear thinking at home. If you leave the house or apartment for any length of time, be sure it is secure. A careless word can cost you dearly.

28. THURSDAY. Variable. Difficult decisions need to be made. Do not drive too hard a bargain or jump to conclusions. A hasty word can upset someone very close to your heart. If there is a joint decision to be made, see that you take your partner or prospective mate fully into your confidence. Wagging tongues can lead you astray. The future of children or dependents can be a matter of some concern. Look ahead to the long-term situation and do not be afraid of present complications which will eventually clear. A parent or other person you respect can lend a helping hand and steady your nerves. You may realize you are never completely on your own.

29. FRIDAY. Mixed. Your partner could have a stroke of luck. Cooperation should pay off if you are careful what you undertake. Your share of a bargain can be a subject for much discussion. A disagreement can be happily solved by the intervention of a third party. Do not underestimate the versatility of someone in your family who plays the role of mother and confessor. Research should be beneficial at this time. Prepare well if you have to state your case against hardened debaters in the evening. What was so easily gained in the morning by cooperation can be lost in the evening by coldness. Be considerate. Do not waste all your hard work. Find other ways to get your point across.

30. SATURDAY. Deceptive. Weekend travel arrangements can be easily upset. An illness or unwillingness to travel on the part of someone can throw your schedule out of gear. Relatives are unreliable. A babysitter may let you down in an emergency. You could be out on a limb. Accept nothing at face value. Market traders exaggerate more than usual. You find it hard to publicize yourself in the face of doubt or ridicule. Accept the fact that some folk are just not interested in what you have to say. Try to keep romance on an even keel, even though you may have some doubts about the principles of others. Despite difficulties you can keep things in perspective if you stand on your own feet.

31. SUNDAY. Variable. You could be in need of comfort today. If your energy gives out at the last moment do not be too disappointed. Someone is likely to look after you willingly. High hopes may have to be rationalized. Look ahead and make plans for the future, but be sure, first of all, that you have the know how. You could have an exaggerated opinion of your chances in the outside world. Get down to some basic consideration of what you have to offer. Are you as careful as you would wish? An incident may show you how you can slip up through a moment's carelessness. Get away from everyday things with your loved one. Consider your future together.

FEBRUARY

1. MONDAY. Disquieting. Act with assurance. You could be in a position of some strength if you realize your full potential. Conditions may not yet be right for a complete appreciation of your success. Do not let this discourage you. In due course you will get what you are after. Parents can be at cross purposes. Do not take sides or expect to gain much from them at the moment. A business relationship can meet with some opposition from home. If there is some discord where you are living, it is better to concentrate your activities out of doors. An official can try to browbeat you. This is likely to arouse your indignation. Under the circumstances, be proud of the attention. Stand up for your rights.

2. TUESDAY. Disturbing. There is further need to assert yourself. A change of conditions or environment could do you good. First effects could be disturbing. Those who have once lived with you for some time could miss you. Parting can bring problems, but you should not be deterred. A certain amount of jealousy may be influencing people who presently oppose you. You could wield the heavy stick if you chose. It may be difficult to avoid prejudice. A business deal can give you more kudos and add to your income. Provided you act quickly, there is no one to question your ability. Temper urgency with consideration of essentials. Give credit where it is due.

3. WEDNESDAY. Fair. Productivity pays rich dividends. Be of service wherever you can. There is a great future ahead if you take your chances and show you can earn your living. Promotion can come your way. Staff or colleagues are fully in support of your aims. If you treat those beneath you with respect you are bound to get a ready response when you need support. A certain amount of gossip or verbal disagreement can sour the air. Someone may find it hard to take 'no' for an answer. It is pointless trying to explain to obstinate people. An important contract could net you considerable personal gain. This could be financial as well as social. Unorthodoxy can be rewarding.

4. THURSDAY. Good. Personal intervention in business finances will benefit all. You could feel inspired. Put forward imaginative schemes for increasing profits. They will be accepted if you press your point with your usual conviction. This is the real thing and at this stage you appear to have no opposition. Minor details can be interesting. You are not usually too taken up with the little things, but can learn a lot about everyday matters if you are gentle and understanding with a friend who wants to help you. The ball can be in your court later in the day. Why not show an interest in someone you know well and have an evening out.

5. FRIDAY. Disturbing. Excessive demands on time and money will not help you. Try to keep control of your feelings when in company. A rude or crude word could do you a lot of damage among your friends. Someone who has claimed to be a friend may be a wolf in sheep's clothing. Hide your anger if your pride is hurt. Recrimination will do no good. It may be necessary in the evening to say goodby to a loved one. Parting with a child who is off to a new school can be heartrending. Curb your anxieties. These stages of life are all part of growing up or growing older. Avoid mixing business with pleasure. You could be too irritable to tolerate company. Look for a quiet place to relax.

6. SATURDAY. Difficult. You may feel sorry for yourself today. A loved one is distant and you want to be friendly. A visit to your local club can shatter you. Prices may have increased overnight. A new management has plans that are out of sympathy with you. Do not get overexcited. This is not the end of the world. If you are not welcome in some social circles, then why bother fraternising. An unusual interlude can unsettle you. It seems time you took a more quiet role and did a bit of thinking. From time to time you will find it necessary to get away from everyone and think things out. You could envy those who have the facility to cut themselves off from the world mentally.

7. SUNDAY. Deceptive. News of an illness could make you sad. A tear shed in the privacy of your room can ease feelings considerably. You are aware it is bad for you to bottle things up but pride does not allow a public display. News received can be mischievous or deceptive. Without getting out to investigate yourself, you could remain in the dark. A shortage of energy may keep you out of circulation for the whole of the day. Do not try to be too rational. Things are happening that would confuse the best of people. If you find it difficult to trust your own judgment, how can you put too much faith in anyone else's? Don't push your luck.

8. MONDAY. Variable. Get yourself organized. There are cross currents that can lead you on to the rocks. An ability to read the signs will protect you. Make full use of your powers of communication. Relationships can become frayed when money is discussed. Do not put too much emphasis on material things if you are talking about love. There may be news from the family that will make your day. Though you are to some extent withdrawn from a lot of the domestic activity, you appreciate keeping in touch. Research should begin to show its value. A friend of the family can give discrete advice on a matter dear to your heart. You are inclined to go to extremes so cool it.

9. TUESDAY. Disquieting. Doubts about a relationship can be worrying. Half baked ideas will get you nowhere. If you have had enough of loneliness for the last few days, it is time you made a personal appearance. Decide what you want to do and do it. Undoubtedly you will tread on someone's toes. This cannot be helped. Be moderate when handling your resources. You could be tempted to overspend on your own personal comforts. Is this really necessary or are you being a bit obsessional. A promise may be made that should not be too openly accepted. People in love make strange statements. Be careful; the day of reckoning can be much more traumatic than you may realize.

10. WEDNESDAY. Variable. Face up to another challenge. Reason and logic can be all against you. Be true to yourself and use your intuition. Quick wits can get you out of a financial difficulty. A domestic failure can soon be righted if you are prepared to spend money without asking questions. Settle a property deal with a handshake. Cut out the trimmings. Parents are once more in disagreement over a personal matter. An important person is not inclined to let a property deal go through. It is hard to convince a normally sensible member of the family that your intentions are sound. Perhaps you are better off waiting until conditions improve before attempting to buy a bit of land.

11. THURSDAY. Good. Be at peace with your fellow man. Essential relationships should blossom. Look after those everyday matters that so easily go by the board. There could be good news at work. Your boss may have you lined up for a pay rise which you have obviously earned. Money can be spent on your behalf, just to make life more comfortable for you. Today is a good day for the ladies who have something in mind to buy. There should be enough stashed away to get what you want. Most folk seem to be in a happy and cooperative mood which makes life very pleasant. On days like this you don't mind helping out. It will be nice to feel that a diet is working after all.

12. FRIDAY. Variable. Take a hard line on money matters. Some may say you are being crude or unkind. Look things straight in the eye and do what you feel you have to do. This could be a once in a lifetime decision. Tension could reach a high point and you may have to react to circumstances. Be positive and you will make improvements. There is plenty of support from logical and businesslike people who understand what you are after. A parent could be particularly helpful once you have made it clear where you are going. A family arrangement is likely to pay off. You could be in the black after all the doubts and worries. Do a deal if you think you have it all sewn up.

13. SATURDAY. Uncertain. You could be feeling your responsibilities. Don't take life too seriously or you will make matters worse. A relationship may be developing where you work. You will have to decide where priorities lie or you will get at cross purposes. A loved one could be a little off color or you may not be feeling very sociable. Best to give it a miss for today. Start the day off with purpose if you are to make the right impression. Hard facts can make you consider your financial future. Hard work can also wear you out by the end of the day. You seem in need of a rest or a cuddle before tomorrow. You could be unlucky for the latter and have to console yourself.

14. SUNDAY. Good. A major family transaction may be discussed. A parent may draw your attention to some development that involves money and labor. The weekend get-together can be more important than puttering around attending to routine chores. There could be an offer of new accommodation near work and at a reasonable price. Relatives seem likely to drop in on you with up-to-the-minute reports of local events. If the weather is suitable, today is a good day to visit old haunts. Something could stir deep down if you meet someone from the past. Consult one of your parents if you want advice on an investment. Try to make a social contact with someone in the real estate world. It's a day of rest, but should not be wasted.

15. MONDAY. Variable. It could be a wasted day. If you have things to do, get on with it. Somewhere along the line there could be distractions and opportunities to forget the essentials. Fellow workers seem in no mood to concentrate. You could find yourself being moved around for no particular reason. There is a possibility that the weekend has left you feeling under the weather. In which case, you could be better off at home. An employer seems to be understanding. You receive good news about the health of a parent who has been considering giving up work. There seems plenty of life left in the very dear person, much to your relief. A domestic improvement gets the go-ahead from official planners.

16. TUESDAY. Fair. There is a choice between doing your own thing or cooperating with the family. For peace of mind sort out personal problems first. Look after a matter of home security. Do not leave valuable heirlooms or other sentimental articles unguarded. As the day progresses you should be able to get around to a variety of jobs. Attend to any outstanding business connected with property or land. There may be a bit of business you can manage for someone who has not the time or aptitude. Make arrangements for accommodation. While shopping you may spot a piece of old-fashioned furniture that intrigues you. This could be a good investment, provided the frame is undamaged.

17. WEDNESDAY. Fair. Settle an issue with parents. Something of importance can be tidied up once and for all. A property deal can now be finalized and a straightforward move made. It could be the first day in a new home. News of a relative may sadden you. The health of someone dear may be cause for concern, but there are positive outlets for your energy. Home security can depend on your ability to take chances and get on with the job of the moment. An incentive bonus should find you responsive to meet the challenge. Strike while the iron is hot if you want to get ahead. It may be necessary to cancel a date. Make up your mind on priorities and let all concerned know your schedule.

18. THURSDAY. Good. Use your imagination. Avoid doing anything that needs physical strength only. Let your mind wander a little until you feel you are on the right track. Artistic folk should be on the ball. A speculation could come off today and provide a pleasant change. Deep seated hopes can be realized if you allow your intuition to work. Sensitivity is your strong point and a hunch could be right. A child can give you great pleasure by showing off individual talents; this one could be a chip off the old block making memories come flooding back. Show biz people could have a good day, though you will have to feel your audience more than usual. Relax and let it happen.

19. FRIDAY. Variable. You could be annoyed with someone. You must allow others to be as independent as they wish, even if it does upset your schedule. It's all too easy to get on your high horse. Things may not go smoothly despite your good intentions. An argument with a neighbor can put you off for the rest of the day. It will take a kindly word from someone older and more understanding to make you feel better. Hard facts have to be faced at work. You may feel you have the cares of the world on your shoulders. It's not so bad, though, as your boss will probably appreciate you. You do make mountains out of molehills at times. Get to your meals at the proper times. It will not help matters to push yourself too far.

20. SATURDAY. Good. Make the family happy. An engagement can be announced and there will be immediate talk of dates and arrangements. Essential work should be rewarding and productive. A partnership can be struck up while you are working. Couples will look at the practical side of things, even when they are out doing the weekend shopping. You may be able to read someone's thoughts and be happy about it. A diet you've been given recently should be put into operation today. You will have support from someone who is eager to see you get the best out of life. Try your hand in the kitchen with some new recipes. Today you will enjoy working, because you do well what suits you.

21. SUNDAY. Special. You could be lucky. Essentially a day to suit yourself. Do what you want and you will offend no one. Time is not likely to be wasted. Whatever you undertake will be well done and give you and your friends considerable pleasure.

Local involvement is in the cards. Look for cooperation and you will not be disappointed. Your partner has an eye for a bargain. Without a doubt this could be a day for a breakthrough into new fields of experience. No need to look back once you have the bit in your teeth. They say that fortune favors the brave. You can take the plunge and carry all with you. So be brave and optimistic that all will work out well.

22. MONDAY. Variable.   Be considerate of your partner. You may need all the support and good will you can muster before the day is over. Approach things sensitively. Put yourself in others' shoes if you are to get the best return. There could be some aggravation at home. Difficulties can arise that slow down progress and encourage arguments or differences of opinion. You may have to stand out firmly against someone if interference gets too much. A gentle reminder that you have to consider others can help you from being too much to the point. Though you may feel like a showdown, there is a strong possibility you can overdo the strong-arm stuff and be the loser. So be sensitive as well as strong.

23. TUESDAY. Disturbing.   You could feel cut off. There may be a sort of vacuum that leaves you drifting nowhere in particular. Try to keep in touch with your partner or someone who understands your moods. If you take on too much on your own you could feel frustrated or drive yourself too hard for your own good. It is a time to come to some firm conclusion. A quiet period can help you resolve the situation in your mind. Then you can make your statement and be quite sure you are taking the correct action. Make firm your commitment in local affairs. You may cause some upset, but if you are honest will offend no one. Make your point.

24. WEDNESDAY. Variable.   Someone may stop you doing your own thing. A disagreement with a parent can make you feel unwanted. Interference by a responsible person makes your love life a little difficult. An engagement may have to be broken because a stage production is not attracting the public. Financial worries can make you think again about a family holiday. Avoid taking chances with family reserves or other people's money, even on the advice of a respected broker. There is some chance that he is being over-optimistic. You must be more in tune with family thinking. Listen to what someone in real estate has to say. There you have a better chance of a good investment.

25. THURSDAY. Good.   Make a study of the market as it affects your work and income. There should be prospects of developing through partnership or affiliation with some larger concern. A new bonus scheme at work should put you in a good frame of mind. Joint efforts seem to be paying off. Your partner could have a stroke of luck. Look around for ways of enjoying life that will involve all the family. A health problem of the past is likely to receive attention that eases a pain. You may feel you can now ease off a diet that has become too restrictive. Mind you don't go too far at once and undo all the good you have achieved. Enjoy yourself in moderation.

26. FRIDAY. Variable. No one wants to listen to you. Great plans may have to wait till you can make people understand. You may be obliged to travel far to achieve something. This could go against the grain. There may be reason to spend the night away from home because of a break down in out of town communications. Some may be glad to see your back and you could feel a little hurt. Do not be resentful. An important person in the world of entertainment will make you feel more at ease when others appear to have let you down. You can put your point of view across to someone who can help. So why waste time and energy on the clerks when you can talk to the manager.

27. SATURDAY. Good. Look after your personal interests. A trip to see someone from the past could help you unwind. Make full use of any publicity you can get to put across your own particular view. Stand up and be counted. You can never expect to get anywhere if you just drift along with the tide. In-laws can step in and help you out of a tight spot. It could be a nice change to spend the weekend away from home and the usual weekend chores. A meeting with someone in publishing could put you on to a new opening. You must look ahead and get yourself organized for future expansion. Listen to a professional who can give you a few tips. Do some meaningful research on subjects that interest you.

28. SUNDAY. Disquieting. You could be a bit homesick. Outside activities and interests may take up most of your time without giving much satisfaction. Mind you do not step out of line if you get bored. There is a chance you can bite off more than you can chew. It may be necessary to blow your trumpet or show off to a certain extent. The danger is that you can lose friends and possibly a lover by making too much noise. A health problem could develop if you do not keep some control over your diet. Someone may comment on your appearance and this will deflate you. Pay attention to detail. It can be all too easy to let things slip.

29. MONDAY. Variable. Business deals can cause some domestic upset. Make all arrangements watertight before leaving for the office. There could be basic changes during the day that will leave little time for adjustment of personal details. It may be necessary to be away from home for a day or more. You could be offered a role that will bring in quite a bit of money. Someone in control thinks highly of you. Application will get you places where taking your time will not. There is a hard day's slog ahead. You will upset some and will browbeat others to get your own way. Success is important. There is no room for half measures. So don't expect anyone to favor you while you are sitting around.

MARCH

1. TUESDAY. Rewarding. Make hay while the sun shines. You may be in luck today so should do all to boost your reputation. A pleasant manner will get you more than you may imagine. Sitting in the hotseat is not necessarily a solemn condition. Business will prosper if you are up to date with processes and see that your work force is happy. Take the opportunity to further good working relationships while everyone is in a positive mood. Make proposals for development of production if you feel you have things moving in the right direction. This seems an ideal day to get a relationship moving again. You have time, now that your business life is more organized, to enjoy a little light entertainment with someone you appreciate.

2. WEDNESDAY. Good. Today is a good day to clinch a deal. In many ways you seem to have it all buttoned up. Take positive steps. Do not hang back waiting for others to approach. A specialist may produce the key to a business problem. From now on there should be a rapid turnover and profits begin to accumulate. This could be some sort of breakthrough, an exciting day with friends who appreciate your enthusiasm. Today could be quite emotional also, though you may not wish to show your feelings in public. You could achieve something that has been a secret ambition for a long time. Be thankful. It is a day to be active yet show feeling. Be romantic with someone who understands how you feel.

3. THURSDAY. Disquieting. You may feel you are making progress towards a personal goal. Keep your eyes steadfastly ahead. You can achieve whatever is right while you are single-

minded and appreciate what friends will do to help. There will not
be an easy road if you rub some official the wrong way. A disagreement of objectives is likely to bring your schemes to a halt.
Use your humanitarian qualities to convince some important person that you are doing the right thing for society. You may be losing out on a number of personal pleasures in order to get something started. Look after the interests of children. A business
transaction may fall through because financial support is denied.

4. FRIDAY. Disquieting.   Someone could ask a favor of you.
You may have to deny yourself to oblige them. Be prepared to
keep out of the limelight while someone else is making all the
news. Be methodical. You have things to do that are not yet for
public discussion. A letter is likely to upset you if you are not practical. Hard words can be spoken and you may not be in the position to retaliate. It is best to bide your time. Keep your thoughts to
yourself for a little while; you could be disappointed at the plight
of someone in trouble. Do not be hard-hearted. Better to try to do
something practical, though you know there will be little thanks
for your efforts.

5. SATURDAY. Deceptive.   There could be trouble brewing.
You will be able to feel the undercurrents. Do not jump to conclusions. A word out of place can do great damage. Keep your ear to
the ground. Neighbors seem to be aggressive. There are rumors
that seem to have little fact to back them up. Get on with private
preparation for a future project. If some people try to distract you,
let them know exactly where to get off. Too much mental or imaginative work can get you down. Look after your own health even if
you are particularly concerned about a friend who is in the hospital. Someone is going to let you down or let the cat out of the bag if
you can't please them. Do nothing deceitful yourself.

6. SUNDAY. Good.   Someone is likely to switch on you. An
unusual encounter may have you wondering what has hit you. In
the nicest possible way, you may find you have to change your
habits. You may feel this is to be a quiet day when you can relax
and make plans for the future. Consider certain basic essentials.
The family will come into your calculations. A discussion with
those who can keep a secret should benefit all. You have a lot to
contribute and should have a fair hearing. A partnership development can catch you pleasantly by surprise. There is good news of a
relative. You could have an invitation. Throw your hat in the air if
it will please you. You have to do something or burst.

7. MONDAY. Variable. A nosey person can spoil a plan you have for the near future. You will meet extravagant people who cannot keep anything quiet, even their dress. Show you remember someone dear to you with a present. Do not expect too much from your work colleagues or people in your employ. A lot of time could be spent arguing and getting nowhere. Carelessness may lead to complications and a slowturn round that will benefit no one. Look after your health. Watch your diet or consumption if taken out to dinner. A common sense approach to a local problem will bring a satisfactory solution. Be firm if you want to have some peace. News received can make things very clear.

8. TUESDAY. Fair. Go for the gold! Half measures never do meet with your approval. Someone can come back into your life unexpectedly. A most personal desire may be granted. You may be very introspective or obsessed with something you feel has to be done. Observers may think you are being thoughtless or snobbish. Children can easily win your approval. A teacher or manager may have cause to comment on the work of your child. This will cheer you up. You may reflect on the past. Recall family ties and look forward to the future through someone else. A show biz producer can make an offer that is too good to refuse. You should feel just right to show off your best talent. A good day to ask the parents for consent.

9. WEDNESDAY. Quiet. Take a breather. Collect your thoughts and see how you stand financially. If you are expecting some heavy expense in the near future you should see what you have to play with. There may be a slight difference of opinion early in the day. This could encourage you to keep quiet and get on with your own affairs. With conditions gradually developing towards personal expansion and a widening of your responsibilities, you should be glad to have some free time to make plans. There could be a partnership development during the year. You will have to stand your corner, so be prepared. If you see any way to make extra money, do something about it.

10. THURSDAY. Quiet. Another run of the mill day. A break from work may give you time to catch up on a lot of personal matters you could well clear up. The small everyday things in life have recently become much more important. You will find you need time to look after minor details, keep in touch with neighborhood activities and generally be involved in a low key way. This could be part of an apprenticeship for greater things to come. First of all you must learn to manage the minor details. Harden yourself to communicating with people at all stages of development and in all walks of life. This is the way you learn the basics of life and business. The greater your understanding is, the better you'll do.

11. FRIDAY. Fair. You should feel happier about your prospects. This could be a lucky day if you are prepared to share your resources and are not afraid to spend some money. A concentration of effort is needed. After a break from intense activity of the recent past, you should be ready for anything. Stand your ground if asked to travel faster and further than you intend. A transaction connected with the family should turn out well. Look closely at a bit of property brought to your notice. There should be possibilities for development. Your partner can be very generous. Have an evening out with your neighbors. It is time you let your hair down a bit. You tend to drive yourself too hard.

12. SATURDAY. Deceptive. It is time you made your point. If you have anything to get off your chest this is as good a time as any. Straight speaking can get you out of difficulty, though you may be too direct for some. Do not let this bother you. Be honest with someone you care for deeply. Your love will be returned. Only the over-sensitive need protection. You are just as sensitive to what is going on as the next one. So you can feel the mood and will not make a mistake when you are with a special person. Don't get carried away in your emotional fervor. If you are out to enjoy the evening see to it that you have a sober friend at the wheel. No party is worth risking an accident.

13. SUNDAY. Good. Have a day out with relatives. It is not really the sort of day to go far. A pleasurable interest in the things children enjoy can take you to places you seldom see during the week. A meeting with someone you know as a celebrity can give you an insight not previously recognized. Your talents can be spotted by someone paying a visit to the locality. Be happy to perform, but don't expect to be on Broadway overnight. A child performer can make you proud and a bit nostalgic. Get documents into order before the week starts tomorrow. Being briefed well can put you that much ahead. Do what you feel like doing and enjoy it, no matter who happens to be watching.

14. MONDAY. Disquieting. Your arrangements can upset domestic peace. There could be a problem to solve at home before you leave for business. Look after whoever needs attention. You seem to be up against the clock most of the day, so be prepared to work hard at whatever you have to do. It will not be easy to carry support for any personal venture. Look after basics. If you have to leave accommodation, see that it is secure. Be on your guard for thieves or sweet-talking people who are trying to get something from you for nothing. A date may have to be cancelled because of pressure of work. You must make it clear without being forceful.

15. TUESDAY. Pleasant. You should know your own mind today. Being in a gentle and sensitive mood, you could be thinking of love or marriage. Dreams of a home of your own should get you thinking along positive lines. Family folk may feel they ought to do something about home decor. There can be brilliant ideas that will have to be reduced to practicality. Young lovers should be in their element. There can be talk of engagements and weddings as couples make up their minds. Parents could be sending out invitations for a family get together. There seems to be a lot to do around the house. If you can get someone special to help, that will be fine.

16. WEDNESDAY. Good. Things are going your way. Nothing is too much when you are in a happy mood. A relationship is beginning to blossom into a possible marriage. You could feel much more comfortable about supporting a family. Children appeal to you and make you think way into the future. See that you support your dreams with a firm foundation. Your talents could be in demand. This is good for morale and for your pocket. See you make the most of your chances today. Show your affection for someone dear to you. Give something that shows you care. Sports can be popular today, even if you are only a spectator. There's not a lot of fun in doing things on your own, so join in the games.

17. THURSDAY. Fair. You feel you have room for maneuver. It could be a good time to consider making changes in your routine. Someone could have planted a thought in your mind. Talk things over with your partner if you feel a change would do you both good. Holiday plans may be considered. Why not try visiting somewhere different this year? It could be less easy than you first think because you are not too happy with changes. The company you keep will be the deciding factor. You can't be very enthusiastic on your own. A legal settlement can be satisfactory. Children can prove a unifying factor. Settle a bargain with neighbors. If you are going away anywhere let someone locally know. Leave your telephone number and temporary address.

18. FRIDAY. Deceptive. Look to your long term prospects. Important ties should be strengthened for future development. This could be a most important weekend approaching when you arrive at a point of understanding joint practicalities. For married folk a possible turning point is in store. Relatives may add support to joint ventures. You may feel you have been let down in some way. Work conditions at the close of the week could be depressing. You may be dissatisfied with the return for the week. Colleagues can be uncooperative. A job could have to be bypassed through shortage of labor. Do not let this get you down. Worrying will solve nothing. There could be disturbing news of a dear one in ill health.

19. SATURDAY. Quiet. The early hours could be active. There is possibly some need to help out a neighbor in trouble. In the middle of the night you would not appreciate such disturbance of your peace. Conditions for most of the day appear to be quiet. Routine weekend chores and duties will follow automatically, giving you time to think about other things. You probably have a lot of necessary attention for jobs if your routine earlier has been upset. There could be a more helpful turn of events near the end of the day. Relatives can drop in and surprise you. This should give you quite a lift. Someone who knows your partner proves interesting company.

20. SUNDAY. Fair. Joint activities can give a lot of satisfaction. A tie can be further strengthened. Wise counsel from a relative will make you feel you are on the right track. It seems a good day to do some forward planning about vacations. Sharing a creative pleasure with someone close to you will make your day. Children can be particularly lively, adding sparkle to the company. The peace should lend itself to romance and happy dreams of the future. A fine day for watching the antics of others, but you may rather watch and relax than get involved yourself. Your partner could be in an affectionate mood. Cool yourself if someone appears to be jealous. It's much too nice a day to get upset about a difference of opinion.

21. MONDAY. Variable. Unfinished business from last week can be handled at once. A matter should be settled without fuss. Close the books on one contract now complete. Take initiative to get something going that is on your doorstep. Neighbors can be particularly active and cooperative. Officials are hard to handle. A lot is going to depend on your own approach and positive drive. People in high places are not in the mood to assist. A contact on which you have come to depend can break down. You should not put too much faith in people who hold authority. An employer can cause upset and try to pass responsibility on to his employees.

22. TUESDAY. Changeable. Employer-employee rapport may improve. Do not take too much for granted, however. There could yet be problems which can be passed on from one to the other. If you are worried about your health or the health of one of the family, see a doctor. Any doubts can be cleared up and worry discarded. There could be some delay in fixing an appointment. Accept such things and ease your mind now that you have set the ball rolling. Conditions at work can be improved with a bit of sensible bargaining. Know how far you can go, whether as employer or employee. Look into the possibility of new methods to improve efficiency. Research should be to your advantage.

23. WEDNESDAY. Good. A light-hearted approach will get you where you want to be. Use your imagination if you are stumped for a practical answer. Carry on with any research you started yesterday. You may not come up with the answer right away, but you can have some bright idea that will throw a new light on a problem. Children can surprise you with their ingenuity. Taking a child to play school for the first time is quite an experience. Try a new line of artistic expression. Local publicity will do you no harm. Get in touch with your local art group and develop your talents with those who know the ropes. A happy day for the young in love.

24. THURSDAY. Variable. Going it alone is not a good idea. There seem to be a lot of folk out to upset your plans. A partnership will help you cope with any inconvenience, but will not fully counteract the aggravation you may have to face. Professional advice can be downright disheartening. You seem faced with a no-win situation. Influential people who have some say in your working conditions are not at all cooperative. Perhaps someone is envious that you are making progress. Traveling to a distant place may cause some inconvenience or make someone unhappy. Be careful how you treat in-laws who may be seeing things differently to you. Do not bang your head against the wall. Wait a little until conditions are more easy.

25. FRIDAY. Deceptive. A prearranged trip should free you from restrictions. Traveling for pleasure seems one way to get away from everyday routine, however, there could be some sort of hitch. Accept a certain amount of inefficiency on someone's part. In the end you will probably find things turn out right. An examination can catch you unawares. Try to keep yourself from worrying about things that may never happen. When it comes to the crunch you should be on the ball. Local conditions, neighbors and work colleagues can weary you. Do your own thing if you want to get anywhere. Do not depend on anyone who is not properly qualified. Publicize your artistic talents.

26. SATURDAY. Variable. A loving partnership should prosper. Traveling should not be undertaken solo. Your partner will have better ideas than you, probably, and will know exactly the right place to visit. A relationship can be resumed with someone a long way off. Some important legal question can be resolved when you have seen a lawyer. You will be pleased you can button up something that has worried you for some time. Publicize a partnership. Announce the happy day to all. There could be some dispute with neighbors. You may be considering a move from your present locality. Some relative may feel left out, but it's just too bad if they want to make an issue out of it.

27. SUNDAY. Mixed. A wedding may be arranged. Not everyone is approving. There could be a feeling that too much is being attempted at one time. You are looking for approval and expect to be looked up to. Without question, those who have authority will see that you are the person for the job with a lot to offer. A partnership could be under some strain. One side of the equation is taking too much for granted. Parents should be extra cooperative. They have the means and the inclination to help you reach a goal. That will counteract any doubts you have. There may be a message from an employer or major supplier that boosts your ego. You feel you are on your way.

28. MONDAY. Quiet. You may be pleased to let everyone know you are in charge without getting too involved. Keep your distance if someone seeks to get you interested in a joint project. A pet theory may not yet be ready for development. Do not get too up tight if a personal obsession is ignored or overturned. You will have time to act later. You really need cooperation, and that is not forthcoming at the moment. Partners expect too much or take too much for granted. Do not waste time or effort on a business partner who insists on doing things solo. Keep an eye open but do not, as yet, interfere. Take stock and say nothing for a little while. You are at the top and can see all that goes on.

29. TUESDAY. Good. Business profits could get a boost. Develop more than one line at once. There is room for expansion and a variety of outlets which will bring a satisfactory return. Take the advice of a financial specialist. A new investment or some new technique can save you money. Time is money, so make full use of equipment that will cut labor costs and speed up production. Accounting should be attended to if you want to be more up to date. If you hear of a local organization for the first time, consider joining. You seem set to meet new faces socially. Take your partner also. There could be happy days ahead. An interest in your fellow man will be rewarding.

30. WEDNESDAY. Variable. You could have to take over for an employer. A break down at the top could put you in a position of responsibility you do not expect. If someone in authority appears to be unreliable or forgetful, be prepared to work on your own initiative until conditions improve. Friendships are likely to grow. You could begin to feel romantic about someone you met socially. Something new could move you deeply. Your interest in the welfare of others may become centered on one particular person. This is not the time to attempt too much. Concentrate on a particular interest and you will benefit. Use your imagination when handling a neighborhood problem.

31. THURSDAY. Tricky. Positive action will prove your point. Time can be wasted talking when demonstration is all that is needed. An artistic talent should not be displayed in company that does not appreciate it. Try something different or seek better company. Joint plans can be fruitful. Keep in close touch with neighbors and neighborhood activities. Today is a good day to enjoy physical recreation with your friends. Try persuasion first in order to put over a business point. You should be in the mood to please. If you want to sell something, make it obvious. Explaining to some may be difficult. Try a bit of charm, especially if you are dealing with the opposite sex.

APRIL

1. FRIDAY. Disturbing. Local conditions may be upsetting. You may be inclined to keep your troubles to yourself. This, as you know, is not good for you. Get things out of your system and let off steam. A restriction on your movement may keep you out of circulation for a little while. Try to be philosophic if you cannot organize your life as you would like. It may be impossible to put your finger on a source of trouble. Keep a low profile. Keep your eyes and ears open and you may find out who is the fly in the ointment. Traveling to see someone could be a bit of a bore. You may ask if your journey is really necessary. Private arrangements can be easily upset. You may be able to take steps to prevent this.

2. SATURDAY. Disturbing. You may hear of a medical diagnosis that upsets your routine. Your private view of some important person is not exactly complimentary. There could be a need to put yourself out in order to please your boss. You could be given a straightforward choice about a new job. You will feel you would like a little time to think things over. Your plans for the day can be thrown out because a neighbor or relative is unable to cooperate. If you must go it alone, see that there are no other snags but allow for more heavy interference from those in authority. There could be some gossip which you should not heed. Someone could be setting you up.

3. SUNDAY. Variable. Keep your cool. Someone is likely to provoke you into action you will regret later. If a relative wants to stir you up, let them believe you are in agreement with them. No sense in having a fight without a purpose. There is a danger that you can go to extremes by the end of the day. You are inclined to let things build up until there is an explosion. It is far better to let your hair down in a friendly or competitive way. Constructive thoughts can lead to constructive action. Try to concentrate on things that matter. An original neighbor can get you thinking along new lines. Traveling a little way out of town will allow you to cool down and get yourself under control.

4. MONDAY. Sensitive. Set about your business with intent. Something could be bugging you. Until it is sorted out, you will have little peace of mind. A regular monthly activity could attract all of your attention. Work colleagues and others may think you are being snobbish or inconsiderate. Be sure your partner knows what you are about. This will avoid misunderstandings. Traveling could be a bit unreliable. Your schedule may have to be adjusted. This will annoy you considerably if you have something to do that is personally most important. Use your imagination and it will help you improvise other means of getting around. Any apparent shortcoming can turn out to your advantage.

5. TUESDAY. Variable. A loving partner can help you out of a problem. Active cooperation of neighbors or colleagues can also be to your advantage. Your routine is likely to be upset considerably. There may be difficulty in getting to a job. Alternative means of transportation should be laid out beforehand. Work people seem to have views of their own, but argument can delay productivity. An arrangement is likely to break down because someone is being pedantic. A trouble-maker can get others steamed up and cause chaos. Use your talent for sweet reasonableness to talk someone around to your point of view. It will not be easy, but may come off if you persist.

6. WEDNESDAY. Quiet.   Complete any arrangements made at work. If negotiations are under way about a contract or a delivery, get them out of the way before taking up anything new. Time taken to study your financial affairs will not be wasted. Get away from pressures. You may need peace and quiet to get your thoughts in order. It has been a hectic time lately. Consider how you can improve your income. Quite soon you may be having expansionist plans. Sharing or producing with a partner could mean even more capital being laid out. You should be quite sure where you stand. Can you afford any further development at this stage? It is up to you to make a sound judgment.

7. THURSDAY. Quiet.   More time than you expected may be needed to get your future financial situation in perspective. You may be given time off from work if your employer is available early in the morning or if you made arrangements last night. Someone with authority seems to be cooperative. This may mean you have no real financial problems. You just ought to get yourself sorted out and make firm plans. A number of minor things can need your attention. This will give you a certain amount of satisfaction and you will at least have a clear conscience about something you thought would never get done. You should make the most of this quiet rest. A lot is going to happen, and you need all your strength.

8. FRIDAY. Deceptive.   You will wonder at times whether you're on your head or your heels. Concentrate on basics. There are hard and unusual problems to be resolved. Only by being downright obstinate can you meet the occasion. A lot of talk can be wasted if you try to explain things to colleagues. Problems of communication can make a difficult situation even worse. Someone you know can have a nervous breakdown if they do not ease up. Life can be unbearable when those around you are disagreeing all the time, but love will come from your partner. If you are shattered at the end of the day there will be a warm greeting from the right person. You can share your triumphs and troubles together.

9. SATURDAY. Disturbing.   You are unlikely to get everything your own way. No matter what you think, there will be a counter view. Make no plan you cannot alter at a moment's notice. Local expeditions are necessary but are unlikely to be enjoyable. There could be a breakdown which means you have to do extra work. Your boss could be in a touchy mood. Do not make matters worse by arguing. Whatever the problem, you will overcome it by hard work and common sense. A relative can come to you with a tale of woe about being unemployed. A parent may be unsympathetic if you have difficulty paying a visit. Put up with the aggravation. It will go away in time.

10. SUNDAY. Variable. You are sure you are right. Others in the family may think differently. Discuss plans for home decoration and possible alterations. Be straightforward and cut out the fancy stuff. You will feel like action today. Others may be inclined to waffle, or have ideas that you know are beyond reason. State your case quite clearly. You will charm everyone and give them confidence in your ability so long as you do not overdo it. There is a chance that you may be led astray by your own enthusiasm. There may be a lot of confused thinking around you. Do not be misled by long words and empty promises. If you are in line for a job, be sure you know what is in store.

11. MONDAY. Good. Settle a work agreement while the going is good. Having thought something out over the weekend, you should be in a positive frame of mind. Do not barter or bicker. A cut and dried solution is what you want. There seems some need early in the day to make some domestic rearrangement. Don't hesitate about it. A personal matter can blow up in your face if you leave it too long. Having got properly started, you should feel confident enough to state your case to your boss if you feel this is the right time to seek more security. Someone of consequence may wish to be shown around your home. Accept the opportunity to make a hit.

12. TUESDAY. Good. Consolidate your gains. Romance can lead to a point of no return. Your mind may be made up. All you need is the opportunity to settle future activities. A surprise encounter can put you on your toes. Someone with surprising talent can open your eyes to new possibilities of development. Have a go at something creative you had not considered before. You may have some doubts initially, but should know you have the perseverance to come through. A chance wager can come off. Look into your holiday arrangements and schedules. You should be able to make firm bookings. Later in the day you can count on the enthusiastic support of a partner or close colleague.

13. WEDNESDAY. Quiet. Take your time. Early in the morning you may realize this is a day of days. Personal fads and likes should be catered to. Today is not a day to exert yourself. Relaxation in some way that appeals to your natural talent is more essential than hard work. If you decide to have the day off from work or your usual routine, be sure to use the time in creative ways. You are not usually an idle person, so will still find you have a full day. Lovers may idle their time away and be content. More active folk always find something to do that gives them pleasure. It is not a day for magnificent gestures or great discoveries. A happy, easy, carefree time to do your own thing.

14. THURSDAY. Variable. You may have to make up lost time in the morning. There seems no easy way out. Be prepared to slog it out in order to do your usual stint. An upset could delay you. An electrical fault may cause some hitch. Transport service is not at all up to usual standards. If you happen to be late in to work, do not expect any sympathy from your employer or work mates. Be careful if handling heavy loads. You could try to take on too much and strain a muscle. There are people around who will not let sleeping dogs lie. Steer clear of such folk, they will only make a tense situation worse. Family will be excited about something in the evening. You should get willing assistance if something has to be done around the house.

15. FRIDAY. Good. You may wake up feeling a little worried. If it is a health matter that is bugging you, make an appointment for a check-up. You will probably find there is nothing amiss. Your mental faculties should be working overtime. You are really on the ball today, so should be well ahead if plans are to be made. Use your wits to make progress at work. Suggestions for greater production may win you a bonus, or keep you in line for future promotion. Consider family security. If you know of any way in which you can improve pension rights for yourself or employees, this could be a good time to make arrangements for implementation.

16. SATURDAY. Good. Be single-minded in the morning. Today is another day when you should know where you are going and make it clear to all. A new contract or a new job may be started today. This is quite an important day and you should see that a new broom sweeps clean. Get rid of any outstanding work in order to make a clean start. Someone in authority may think along the same lines as yourself. Make a deal and seek to establish some sort of precedent that will help in the future. You will be capable, so can be left in charge of a job to be done. New methods can be applied safely. This will save time and labor. A relative can give solid support. Move on and enjoy the fruits of partnership once you are sure of your ground. You could be going places.

17. SUNDAY. Disquieting.   Conditions at home can be troubled. Plans for the weekend can be upset. This will put everyone at odds with each other. Nothing is easy today. A chance remark can set one against another for no apparent reason. If your partner appears to be unreasonable, try hard to understand the reason why this should be. Something may explode or burst in the domestic area and this can upset all meal arrangements. You do not like to go without a meal, so will know what to expect. It may be best to resign yourself to some shortcomings. A cuddle will do much to relieve some of the tension. You will feel for someone later in the day, so can be gentle with them.

18. MONDAY. Quiet.   A day off from work would be appreciated. Weekend worries can have left you out of sorts or totally washed out. Look after others close to you. Today is not the day for thinking too much about your own ends. Consider the legality of some action you propose taking in the near future. A lawyer may be helpful. Take your partner fully into your confidence. This is another day when it may be better to have two opinions if things are to run smoothly. A colleague could be a little slow in keeping up with your progress. You can afford to take it easy and match production. Avoid getting out of step, whatever you do. Someone you love may be totally dependent on your presence.

19. TUESDAY. Good.   Today is a day for coming to grips with the big questions. There could be a marriage. For some, the day will end in agreement on the future date. Feel happy and at peace with all. Partnership may seem a splendid thing. Make a settlement on someone you love. It is advisable to look after the financial support of your loved ones when all are in a position to understand what you intend. A joint holding can be sold at a profit. Take positive steps to settle an outstanding property deal. A child may need a home after marriage. You may be pleased to have the chance at a home you have worked hard to establish. Nothing is gained by being negative.

20. WEDNESDAY. Exciting.   Enter into negotiations about a partnership. If you are not yet ready, at least consider the positive possibilities of a merger or liaison. Expansion above the small time or local level seems well-starred. You have a good sound footing so should be able to persuade anyone who doubts your potential.

Publicize your assets. A leading legal type should be able to give valuable assistance and advice if a takeover is to be considered. A parent is in a position to assist in a foreign venture. Consider the prospects for business development. Family plans for holiday travel could be furthered.

21. THURSDAY. Variable.   Someone at home can get over enthusiastic. You may have to clear up the damage. Provided you do not get disheartened by the action of others, you are in a strong position to manage. Personal plans should be pushed ahead. Give yourself as much publicity as possible in order to develop interests. A student may come to your notice as a budding partner for the future. Look well ahead, because there are no limits to the possibilities of the moment. It is essential you drive on with your plans. Some may think you are obsessed, but that is not going to worry you. Traveling should be to your advantage. A family expedition can take you far away from home.

22. FRIDAY. Good.   Today is a day for ideals. A marriage can be arranged or a partnership confirmed as a going concern. Legal advice offered by a top notch lawyer should be accepted gratefully. You will see many sides of a question. If you are prepared to forget and forgive, you could make someone very happy. A day to be philosophic, yet just. Use your judgment well. A long-standing arrangement can be made with someone influential. Local families strengthen ties through marriage. The educational progress of someone in the family will astound you. Give every encouragement to someone who is starting to learn from scratch. A friend may pass a driving test. This is the point to have a celebration.

23. SATURDAY. Disturbing.   It is best to go your own way if you have an objective in view. Get to the top and stay there, no matter who will decry you. Determination is the order of the day. An influential business partner may take a dim view of your progress. Do not be misled by objections, as this could be a clear sign of envy. A personal project can be difficult to get going. Domestic opposition to your outside activities may show up through bad temper. For the best result, you must go ahead and get any unpleasantness dealt with as quickly as possible. There is no sense or time to spare, in dragging things out. Best have a blow up and clear the air. A domestic boiler could give trouble. Be careful!

24. SUNDAY. Variable.   You will find it difficult to unwind today. This is likely to annoy the family. If business has to receive your full attention, get on with it and make your partner or loved one accept the fact. First things must come first. Look to your reputation. This is no time for weaklings. For your own security it seems essential you get down to business and force matters along. A partner could be slipshod which could mean extra work for you. Take no chances with someone who says they will ease your burden. Loose talk can cause no end of domestic strife. You should consider yourself fortunate in having an understanding and loving friend at the end of the day. There will be time enough then to take things more easy.

25. MONDAY. Fair. Today is a day for plain speaking. Do not go too far, but make things short and to the point. Someone at home could be irascible. Waste no time trying to smooth it over. You may need to act quickly to get someone out of trouble. Give them a piece of your mind when all is again under control. Avoid frustration. Better do something than hang around waiting for someone else to take the initiative. Neighbors may surprise you by their spontaneous response to an appeal. Look closely into business finances. There are immediate changes to be made. Consolidate as soon as you are sure you are on the right track. Friends can be very kind in a practical way. Show your sincere gratitude.

26. TUESDAY. Variable. You could be at full steam. A great deal is going for you. There is only one fly in the ointment: you could be carried away or may try to expand too quickly and overreach yourself. Ideals run high. Put them to practical use in your own community. While you may see the wider field of humanity as a goal for care and development, think of those near your doorstep. Generous actions will receive a generous response. An important person could be taking notice and will go along with your proposals. A smooth running partnership depends on harmony. Be sure your partner is kept fully involved in your social activities. In working together there is much more pleasure and satisfaction.

27. WEDNESDAY. Tricky. Come to terms with a business colleague. It could be wise to make a written agreement. A legal document may need to be ratified or countersigned. Take the advice of someone who works in the legal side of business. There could be some agreements that are not at the moment very happy. A new look or an open mind can come up with an answer. There is something wrong with an insurance policy. A settlement can be delayed from some trifling error. Obstacles are thrown up to stop you getting to the bottom of a financial problem at the office. If your date for the evening does not turn up, perhaps you have offended this person in some way. Try to find out.

28. THURSDAY. Disquieting. You could be feeling lonely or neglected. Avoid feeling too sorry for yourself. Perhaps you should do a bit of quiet meditation to get things straight. A relationship problem can have you worried. Do not let it get out of control. You will be inclined to blow things out of proportion. A headache can make you seek a dark corner to rest your eyes. A neighbor has some rather nasty things to say. You get unreliable information at second hand. An attempt to undermine your confidence should not be allowed to succeed. Be quite firm with anyone who tries to pull a fast one on you. Do not take a hurt too personally. Get it out of your system.

29. FRIDAY. Deceptive. You could be in a very sensitive mood today. If you are feeling under the weather you may force yourself into action out of sheer pride or stubbornness. There is something to work for today. Early morning blues should be endured and eventually conquered. You will feel much better once you have come to grips with whatever you have to do. Take a member of the family into your confidence. A private approach to a property manager can produce a good deal. Help someone who is looking for accommodation. A word in someone's ear can do the trick. You will have good news of someone in the hospital after a few heart flutterings earlier in the day. You should not believe all you hear, especially idle gossip.

30. SATURDAY. Good. Good news for a partner. A local personality makes it to the top. It is a time for celebration in the neighborhood. You may receive a wedding invitation. Communications between folk who have moved from the neighborhood are established through someone else's foresight. You can get a lot of private satisfaction from a relationship which has taken some time to develop. You have been keeping something to yourself and may now be a little relieved that you can soon make an announcement. Take a broker into your confidence. Make an arrangement about a will. This is not something you wish to discuss with anyone except, perhaps, those you love.

MAY

1. SUNDAY. Disturbing. Stand on your own two feet. Once more you seem to be going the whole hog, despite opposition. Problems are there and are meant to be overcome. A parent or some influential person will try to stop you. They may have the best intentions and a certain amount of justice on their side. But this will have little effect and may encourage you to press on all the more. A breakdown of a domestic appliance can pose you problems. Your partner may feel you should cope instantly and you may appear to be inconsiderate. Moving home could put you in some difficulty. You may be put out of accommodation after a dispute with the owner or landlord. Watch your step, but do not be deterred. If you know your rights, fight for them.

2. MONDAY. Fair. There is more opportunity to reason with an opponent. Be logical, though that can be difficult if you are feeling upset. Someone may try to talk you out of making a positive move. Listen, but do not necessarily follow advice. You have to weigh up the pros and cons of any proposal made today. A journey to see someone can be delayed or completely cancelled. Try to get in touch by other means. Your partner may decide to go out for the day and this will leave you in a bit of a mess. If some important person suggests you have a discussion about a merger, give it due consideration. Talking or dealing with the top brass is alright, but do not be put off by the secretaries or receptionists. Legally you should be O.K.

3. TUESDAY. Quiet. Slow down, you've been going too fast. The road ahead is quite clear since you sorted out the last batch of problems. See how you have prospered or lost financially during the last month. Time to take stock before going ahead with improvements to the home you have been considering. Avoid getting mixed up with anyone else's business. Let it be known you want the day to yourself. Any joint plans could be quite safely cancelled as you may not be in a cooperative mood. Make plans for buying in the near future but do not lay out any capital as yet. Let incoming mail wait until you feel like giving it attention. You must avoid distraction if you hope to accomplish your goals.

4. WEDNESDAY. Good. Reach a decision about income and expenditure. Let your partner know exactly where you both stand. A joint account may have to be watched. This is a point of no return, in a way, and you should complete a transaction satisfactorily. No sense in prolonging an experiment when you know the inevitable outcome. A domestic situation can be cleared up speedily with good and positive results. Make a deal with a property agent if you feel you are to make a gain. You will want to take initiative so should not wait for others to propose. There is money to be made at home for those who are prepared to work without supervision. Try your luck. It will keep you from boredom.

5. THURSDAY. Disquieting. Concentrate on essentials. You could be in for a surprise that will throw you off course if you are not direct and hard in your reaction. Let relatives know exactly what you think about something that has been proposed. Undertake no trip you are unhappy about. Traveling is not good today, so keep off the road as much as possible. Something may fall and do a little damage. You may try to do too much if placed in a difficult position on your own. If you can muster help, do so. If you have to cope with a problem on your own, take your time. You are meant to be delayed, so do not be impatient. Hasty action will get you nowhere. They say, marry in haste, repent at leisure.

6. FRIDAY. Lucky. You could feel relaxed or lazy early in the day. Things will perk up later. Luck can be on your side if you have to settle some legal question. A partner can be particularly helpful and show you the way out of a jam. Correspondence delayed will prove to be timely. Make contact with someone who can give sound advice about a possible financial arrangement. Having done the groundwork, you should be in a position to talk turkey with a senior partner. Arrangements can be made and a definite date set for an important event. There could be some talk of marriage or a merger. Those who wield the power are cooperative. This should make your job so much more easy.

7. SATURDAY. Good. Start your weekend on a positive note. Complete arrangements with family or relatives. You may have entertainment plans for later in the day. The early hours can be well spent in the market and in general flitting around to see that things are in order. You may want to do your entertaining on a grand scale since you are never one to do things by halves. Making contact will become easier as the day goes on. If you are not at home yourself, you could be enjoying a housewarming at a friend's. There could be good news to share about a home or a property recently acquired. Antique hunters could be in luck just as the weekend trading is near its end.

8. SUNDAY. Disturbing. Changes will have to be made. You may feel insecure. If living in rented accommodations there is a possibility of eviction. Do not look for an argument. If you are at the receiving end, expect little quarter. Set yourself to look after things in your own way. A senior partner once more seems set to disrupt your activities. You may feel you are getting nowhere. If leaving your house for the day, see that all is secure before going. Valuables should not be exposed, either in the way of showing off your possessions or due to carelessness. All too easily you may rub someone the wrong way. This will do you no good, especially if it is a person on whom you may depend in the future.

9. MONDAY. Lucky. Some blessing can come to your home. An engagement may be announced. Home buyers should find this a good day for settling in or settling a mortgage. Where joint affairs are under discussion, see that all parties are given a fair hearing. Funds can be boosted through a last minute sale of land. You may feel like going out on the town with your loved one. Let your hair down and take a chance if you are in too much of a hurry to make prior arrangements. Most things will fall into place. You have the timing and the touch today. If you are a gardener, people will say you have green fingers. Make firm friends with a neighbor. A specialist can give you advice about a work of art.

10. TUESDAY. Fair. Be careful what you say when relaxed. On the whole, you should have a good day. Careless actions or careless people could start you off on the wrong foot. If you have to do research, do not skimp. Someone can distract you and you will miss the mark. You can make yourself popular by sticking to your own particular brand of humor. Taking someone for granted will not be appreciated. As a reprisal, someone else may ape you at your worst. Partnership will pay off. Share your pleasures, and in so doing you will find they multiply. Children can give a great deal of pleasure. You have hopes for their future. You could be a little sentimental. Perhaps you are in love.

11. WEDNESDAY. Disturbing. Avoid handling other people's property. You may hear news that someone has gone out of your life. A relationship may be going through difficulty and this can depress you. Try to work your way through a difficulty. At times of stress it can help to apply yourself to a routine task until the pressure dies down. You could have a problem that seems almost too big to resolve. There are people worse off than you, so do not feel too sorry for yourself. A new job makes you put your best foot forward. Hopefully you will not have to work as hard as this all the time. Ask your partner to go a bit easy on withdrawals from the joint account. You need time to balance your savings account.

12. THURSDAY. Deceptive. Keep your chin up. Try to keep things in proportion. You have not had enough experience to know all the wrinkles, so should not think you are any worse than the next person. If you are a bit off color it may be best to have a rest. A change is frequently as good as a rest, so it is said. Look ahead to your future working conditions. A new offer should be considered. Do not leave your present employment while you are in a low. Find out all you can about other prospects and then think about it. A work colleague could be having a rough time. You may be able to help. Perhaps your partner would lend a hand.

13. FRIDAY. Good. A target can be reached. Despite all your earlier doubts you should succeed in your aims. A job well done should give you satisfaction and possibly a bonus at the end. Be sure to get on with repairs to property while you have the cash and the good will. A partnership project seems all set to be finalized. Your work colleagues are having a night out at the end of this trying week. Let your hair down with someone attractive you met a few days ago. You may benefit from a legacy or someone may be grateful and give you a gratuity. Before it is too late, get in touch with a property agent. You could have a surprise visitor near the end of the day.

14. SATURDAY. Fair. Put yourself in the other fellow's shoes for a change. See things as do others, or stand back and consider what they think of you. Today is a day for sharing. By the evening you will feel you have done the right thing and are, indeed, a lucky person. The urge to really extend yourself can lead to success if you are competing. In some way also, you should learn to give as well as take. Do not enlarge or exaggerate in order to impress others. Someone is bound to come along and cut you down to size. Weekend shopping should be done with a purpose. Save money and time by buying big, but don't go too mad. Something romantic may happen. A neighbor appears most attractive.

15. SUNDAY. Variable. Today is not the day for half measures. Disputes can arise and be resolved if you are purposeful. Parents seem to be of the same mind, though this may not always appear to be for the best. A joint project should be started now if at all this year. There will be an obstacle to surmount right at the beginning, but get on with what you have to do. You are bound to tread on some toes. Provided your own are covered, you can make a start. Something is likely to come to a head in the home. Parents can give their blessing on a departing child going out into the world. Check the foundations of any property you are considering buying. Do not be rushed.

16. MONDAY. Quiet. Take a breather and prepare your ground for the next round of activity. Research seems to be essential. This is right up your street. Get down to the nitty-gritty. A joint account can be strengthened, though it may be necessary to add something from an outside source. You may feel you are in for some criticism later on. If so, get yourself prepared with the answers to questions expected. Check up once more on your insurance. Your monthly call from an agent reminds you that something new may have to be considered. If you thought about a new policy yesterday, get on with the details now. You could be a little moody. Thoughts of the future are inevitably bound up with the past. But don't dwell on that area or you will stall.

17. TUESDAY. Variable. Clinch a deal. Someone may try to wield the big stick, but you have something to go for. You could do some good when handling the estate of a client. Any contact with the public through their finances should be to your advantage. Thoughts will not stray today. A parent is not at all happy at the way you behave. You must make it clear that your domestic policy is your affair. There is a possibility something could be overdone by your partner. Hopefully the dinner is not burnt. A property deal can be a little too much to take on at this time. The big boys may be putting some pressure on you. Seek your own terms.

18. WEDNESDAY. Mixed-up. Thoughts of someone far away can keep you going. If you cannot travel at least no one can stop you from thinking. Write a loving letter. Use your charm to persuade someone you have all that is necessary. Plug a line you are trying hard to sell. Publicity should pay off if you spot the right market and can paint the appropriate picture. Traveling could be a bit of a bore. You may have ideas of living abroad. Neighborhood conditions are hard, yet there are ties you cannot ignore. A change of plans could leave you with time on your hands. Make good use of it in company you enjoy. You will feel restricted in some way, probably. If you can rid yourself of that, you will do better.

19. THURSDAY. Special. Professional advice can be sought with confidence. Examinations for professional status taken today are well aspected. A visit to one of the family living overseas will prove most timely. If exchange visiting can be arranged, so much the better. Someone with a marriage problem could ask for your advice. Give it with good intentions. There is really no problem. With your partner or alone, enroll in a course of further education. Look to broaden your outlook on life. The study of philosophy will appeal to many. A loving relationship may have to be broken. There could be good reason for two young people separating.

20. FRIDAY. Good. Get something well under way before closing business for the weekend break. Though you may be active over the weekend, others in key positions will be at home. A business project seems to be well within your reach at the moment. The help of someone who can pull strings for you should be accepted with thanks. It is a good day to make your position clear to your banker who will then be more ready to consider giving a hand out. Look ahead to greater things. You should be looking for expansion. Enlarging prospects through partnership seems the order of the day, yet there is ground work to be done by some who are in a position to help. You are in a position of trust. Make use of it.

21. SATURDAY. Disquieting. You are aware you should be making progress. The road is not easy and you can be impatient to get on. There may be some pitfalls and in your directness you are likely to make mistakes or tread on a few toes it would be better to avoid. Reputation is important. Be seen as someone who can carry a high position without making the lives of others a misery. If you are in the position of underdog you will appreciate what is meant by deprivation. A partnership can be strained because too much may be asked of one side. This is not right. Consideration should be shown if there is to be full and effective management and production. A fair division of responsibility is essential.

22. SUNDAY. Happy. Today is a day for lovers. Possibly the one day in the year when two hearts beat as one. A honeymoon may start for some. You have a desire for freedom to do your own thing, yet share yourself with another. The dilemma of young love, perhaps. For those already established in their joint world, today is a day for pleasure and communion one with the other. There could be thoughts of children. To some, children will be the center of attraction. A journey into family archives can be very interesting. Arrangements can be made that will help someone get on in the world. Look for reward through the next generation. Be glad you were in love once yourself, or still are.

23. MONDAY. Variable. You have active opponents. Friends may be divided in their views of your ability or motives. It could be most difficult to get support from a banker until you can show progress and a workable plan for the future, which you can do. You are well prepared and have laid down good foundations. Seek to publicize yourself once more. Use gentle persuasion first but be prepared to have a fist of iron within the velvet glove. It is not politic to show all your hand at once. Build up contact with an overseas market. Company finances will need this sort of expansion to counteract unwise spending. Avoid personal speculation. You can lose friends by being careless or hasty.

24. TUESDAY. Good. Be gentle with a good friend. Appreciate those who feel as you do. A personal tie can go deep, though you may not wish to get too involved. Keep it at arm's length until you are ready to make a further move. There should be a boost to company profits. A partnership or takeover can send shares through the roof. A long-standing legal argument may be resolved and put you in the clear. You are now free to go your own way. Friends should celebrate your good fortune. A partner makes the day one to remember. Joint endeavors are now beginning to pay off in a way you did not wholly expect. This will only add to your surprise and delight.

25. WEDNESDAY. Disturbing. You may feel neglected. A loved one may leave for somewhere on the other side of the world. Local surroundings are not what they used to be when you are on your own. Take comfort in your happier thoughts of days gone by. If you have a complaint, do something about it and do not become a martyr. Someone you know is in need and you are the one who can do something to help. There could be a misunderstanding over change in a shop. Do not let this get out of hand. A mistake is a mistake. Keep your own counsel if you see someone trying to cope. Do not undermine their efforts though you disagree with their methods.

26. THURSDAY. Deceptive. Few people can be trusted. Only those in authority seem to know the true values of the day. Privacy may be difficult to achieve though you are in need of somewhere to go out of the way. Be very careful what you say and to whom you talk. Local gossips are at full strength. A relative can be in trouble. There may have been too much to cope with, so the hospital is the only answer. Give assistance and love where it is needed. A driving test can be quite worrisome. Pre-test nerves are well known. Do not underestimate your abilities. If you have a lot of mail, leave it until tomorrow. There is nothing so vital that it cannot wait to be resolved.

27. FRIDAY. Variable. Complete negotiations in private. Make arrangements for some future event that is as yet secret. Private investigation can bring new facts to your notice. Keep these under lock and key until you are ready to use them. A financial adviser or broker will be able to help in time. Listen to behind-the-scenes gossip and you could hear something to your advantage. There could be news of a windfall you never dreamed of. Keep a clear head and you can make a lot of progress. You may hear of a parting of friends. A financial takeover can reveal some disconcerting facts. It is necessary to get a balanced opinion on some matter. Are your accounts straight?

28. SATURDAY. Good. Personal plans are most important. You will have no problem with either sex in getting cooperation. Sporting activities seem well starred. You may be able to travel to participate or watch. A local restriction could be lifted giving you more scope to enjoy yourself. Someone may remark that all things should be taken in moderation. You will feel able to cope with anything that comes your way. Your judgment is good. You know when you have had enough. An artistic outing can have a touch of romance. There can be something going on which is pleasant but difficult to pin down. Why worry? Enjoy yourself this first day of the weekend and forget your problems.

29. SUNDAY. Disquieting. The course of true love never did run smooth. Don't push your luck. Though you may be tempted, it is not necessarily wise to go all-out. You may have little to fall back on if you come unstuck. Keep out of trouble that can get you involved with the law. If you are in need of legal assistance, you could spend some time today weighing up the fors and againsts. A takeover could be suggested. Think hard whether expansion is bound to follow. In some way you may have gone as far as is presently possible. On the other hand it may be difficult to hand it over to a partner. There could be divided loyalties which would probably create discord and regrets.

30. MONDAY. Difficult. First things first. See how your account stands before taking on any further commitment. You have some time on your hands at the beginning of the working week to get down to brass tacks with your bank manager. This is a quiet period. You may think it is the lull before the storm. Perhaps you are a bit pessimistic. Someone is likely to make a proposal you should not accept too readily. Immediate action may be called for later in the day. Do not put your money or your emotions at risk.

An engagement present could be very expensive. If you are feeling a little unsure of yourself, it is better to pull out than go ahead with a challenge.

31. TUESDAY. Disturbing. Watch how you tread. You will not get away with anything if Big Brother can help it. Look after your money above all. A loan is likely to be refused for a sound reason. You will not agree, but will have to put up with the situation. Bank charges can be increased to hold back the demand. Try to live within your income. A senior partner in business can impose restrictions that appear to hamper your personal progress. Try to see things in another aspect. There is news of a separation. Wait and see what eventually happens. Perhaps someone has gone too far, so there must be a return to the status quo in due course.

JUNE

1. WEDNESDAY. Disturbing. Make up your mind about a present for a loved one. It may be best to deliver it by hand before a parting. Take stock of all your finances, you could be tightening your belt almost immediately. Last minute rushes can get you in a pickle. Try to moderate your language and actions if you are to be a credit to those you love. Traveling can cause some problem. Buying a season ticket may be outside your means for a day or two. Hang on to what you have for a little while. Perhaps you should be on the defensive a little. Responsibilities may seem a bit much. You are at once looking for a break and then wishing you could stay put. Today is a perplexing day. Neighbors don't help either. It will be up to you to resolve your plight.

2. THURSDAY. Deceptive. You could be in love. Things are somehow different. An early get together with someone attractive can set you up for the day. Feel free to go ahead. Let your imagination roam and you will come up with something original. A day for the artistic who should feel they have got a special message. For those with little to do, it could be confusing. You should not have time on your hands. Idle hands always get into mischief, so try to be constructive and creative. Others may not be as dependable as you think. This should not stop you from being friendly, but you should be doing your own thing and not relying on someone to carry you. Don't dream too much.

3. FRIDAY. Quiet. Tread carefully. Disturb no one. Try to complete your working week without a fuss so that you have a clear weekend. Care of minor details is essential. Ignore any major decision. This will have to wait until next week when you have time to handle more business. Local attractions seem to be quite good. An evening out at your local theater will be more attractive than a trip uptown. Neighbors have their say if you are prepared to listen. Mail is rather routine, but must be attended to. This you can see to, since the weekend is dead insofar as getting mail delivered. More can be done on your two feet than with a car. Thank goodness for the telephone.

4. SATURDAY. Useful. Domestic duties come first. Put aside personal plans for a little while until you have other matters straightened out. You could have a crisis in the kitchen. This will give you a surprise, but will open your eyes to something you had not visualized. A member of the family may be leaving home for a little while. This may be upsetting, but is the natural course of events. A parent will listen patiently if you have something to say about home and family conditions. You can be sure of understanding and support. Have a private discussion with a reputable broker. A mortgage may have to be arranged in the near future. This could solve many problems.

5. SUNDAY. Good. This could be the perfect weekend. The boy or girl next door becomes even more fascinating. An invitation home can make everything much more friendly and natural. Family are all interested in what you have to say and do. There may be a move towards setting up a home. An inspired moment can give you a clear picture of a future financial project. The last minute intervention of a friend who specializes in finance can make you feel more secure. You look forward to consolidating what you have gained today. A regular appointment should be made if you are feeling good. The antics of children around you may make you feel protective or maternal.

6. MONDAY. Fair. Get cracking on your own projects. Your imagination could be working overtime. Be determined to have your own way, though you will know better than to be forceful about it. A love letter can make you feel on top of the world. Where you have to meet people, be gentle today. You will get what you want without making a big song and dance out of it. You could feel lucky. Keep away from gambling and above all do not dip into the joint account if you think you have a winner. Over-optimism can soon be reduced to hard practicality. The parent of someone you are in love with takes a much more logical view of things than you do.

7. TUESDAY. Variable. A love affair can be severely tested. Do all you can to understand the opposite point of view. Someone is likely to throw the book at you if you get out of line, so do not push your luck too far. Handling the money of clients or customers can be a bit tricky. Keep your eyes open for anyone trying to get away with something. Expenses may give you an unpleasant jolt. You realize you must pay for your pleasures and experience. Take your medicine like an adult and feel confident that you can handle anything. A creative project should give you plenty of scope to show your true colors. Your love life may interfere with work.

8. WEDNESDAY. Deceptive. Avoid taking short cuts. Nothing is likely to come easy today, though you may think you can get away with it. You may be called up to do extra work. Fellow workers fail to turn up. There is some talk of redundancy which disturbs your plans for the future. A health problem affects a relative and you feel you must do something about it. Detail can be boring. Your mind may be on other things. This could lead to accidents. Be particularly careful if handling drugs either for yourself or to administer to others. You may be reminded during the day that you have dropped something or forgotten to do something. Do not try any adventurous diet if you care about your appearance.

9. THURSDAY. Good. Your partner has good news for you. A joint effort seems to have been a success. You will feel highly delighted. Take someone you love dearly into your confidence. Arrangements should be made for a future event. Details can be agreed quickly when you are both in sympathy. A contract can be signed giving more permanance to your work situation or to employees. Cooperative action can lead to greater things. There is some talk of a take-over or amalgamation. A member of the family announces plans that could mean a move. Prospects are much brighter. The advice of a specialist eases a health worry.

10. FRIDAY. Variable. Health treatments can do you a world of good. Modern methods linked with more traditional healing will calm you down and give you confidence. You could be able to help a neighbor or relative to get a job. Arrange for a more reliable form of transport if you have had difficulty getting to work. Make a firm arrangement about payment of salary. It is high time you got some things established on a more permanent basis. Your patience and tolerance can be tested later in the day. You could be tempted to throw the book at someone. Perhaps you should be a little more considerate. You could frighten someone off without really having wanted that to happen. Control your emotions.

11. SATURDAY. Special. You could have had a late night. Pleasure was in your mind and a night out could have done you good. Feel lucky. You have a lot going for you. Decisions can be made about settling a partnership. Some may be walking up the aisle and feeling on top of the world. A legal matter can have a happy solution. If you are in any doubt, this is a good day to seek legal advice. People are generous, possibly because you have something to give. A debt may be repaid. This will make you or someone else feel much more free. Cooperation and teamwork will get you places. Your partner must be considered on par with yourself. Make hay while the sun shines.

12. SUNDAY. Good. Put all your eggs in one basket. There seems to be a concentration of activity, probably involving a number of people near and dear to you, perhaps a family gathering or a meeting of friends. Important folk as well as the more humble join with you. This is an excellent time to exchange views. Get to the bottom of something that is probably bugging you all. A parent can have many suggestions to make that could open your eyes. It is not the time to take immediate action, nor should you close your eyes to possibilities. Clear thinking will help more than anything else. Even in your casual conversation you should pick up handy tips. Take note of all you hear and experience.

13. MONDAY. Disturbing. You may want to please. It will give you a great kick to do something for a loved one. Let your partner have the go-ahead on a shopping expedition or purchase of something long desired. You may find you have to draw the line at luxuries or gadgets sold at exorbitant prices. A mutual agreement can easily be reached. The intervention of someone looking for an easy buck should not be allowed to disturb your plans. Look out for the slick operator. An accident can slow you down. It is not worth taking chances with money or love. Children can be expensive. A holiday will need thinking about. If nothing else, you will need reservations and probably transport.

14. TUESDAY. Variable. A research project can be initiated. You have had thoughts recently on insurance for the family. Today you can suit action to thoughts. An investment can be realized. Look ahead and reinvest in something that gives a better return. You will have come to certain conclusions. It is time to regenerate an old agreement. Look to the future and take steps. Joint functions give you more scope and better prospects. A joint production will please more than two people. Later on you will hear views contrary to your own. There can be talk of exchange rates and barter. Deal with a purpose. No one is going to give anything away.

15. WEDNESDAY. Deceptive. There can be problems of communications. It may be necessary to repeat messages to avoid misunderstanding. Publicity should be thoroughly supervised or not practiced today. A weak link in the chain will produce something garbled. Students can become disheartened by examination results or difficult questions. You need to screw your courage to the sticking place when you seem to be losing your grip. As the day develops, you will gain confidence. Someone will catch your eye and that old sparkle will return. Keep up with events. Live this moment fully. Appreciate that there are two sides to every coin. Every cloud has a silver lining. Your companion is a help.

16. THURSDAY. Good. Get up and go, you should be spreading your wings. Traveling will be all to the good. Business can be expanded and prospects improved by a positive approach. Do not be content to stay as you are. There must be a better field of grass over the fence, or a larger shoal farther down the bay. Partnerships will pay off. This is the beauty of having a number of associates who can double or treble the output. Publishing is well starred. If you feel there is a need to make your qualifications appear better than they are now, seek professional advice. You will find you have support and that, legally, you are on to a good thing. Follow it up with all due speed.

17. FRIDAY. Disquieting. You are in the hot seat today. Someone is likely to have a go at you, since you are responsible. Do not take your position too much to heart. If you have something to say, avoid being pompous. If you wish to make progress, do so in a conservative manner initially. You will wish to retain the status quo in some ways but improve your position in another. Inevitably you will upset someone. You could be misjudged or seem to be going in two directions. Do not bluster your way out of a tricky situation. Better be straight to the point and admit a mistake if one exists. It is not your manner to avoid responsibility. Your reputation is all important.

18. SATURDAY. Good. Watch your step if you mix business with pleasure. You may be inclined to go a little too far and at the end of the day comes the reckoning. On the whole you have things well sewn up. Complete arrangements if cooperation with a larger body is under discussion. You should have everything to gain. Someone may turn you on during business discussions. A light-hearted interlude can make your day. Do not let this turn your head though. You could make a miscalculation, or, you could offend your partner. So enjoy yourself but get business settled before you begin to relax. Today can give you an insight into how the other half lives. Take note.

19. SUNDAY. Good. You could feel very satisfied with developments to date. Be complacent if you want. You have earned all you have received. There could be some temptation to dwell on business matters. This may mean talking shop with associates or spending a little time in the morning at your desk. Provided you are reasonable, there should be no problems. A banker friend may give you some good advice when in your club. Developments in the financial world may justify your earlier actions. The family may see you as a strong and responsible person whom everyone respects. You may not wish to become the one who must carry the burden of responsibility.

20. MONDAY. Mixed. It may take you some time to slip into your usual routine. Mechanics can leave you cold, so you will be glad of modern electronic equipment. A load can be taken off your mind by an unexpected addition to business profits. Do not ask questions. You are totally charmed by someone you meet socially. Glamour during the working day can be a bit too much. You need time to recuperate. A hasty remark can get you in trouble, but quick wits can get you out again. Superiors or other influential people have strange ideas. It will be difficult to convince them of the error of their ways. Do not seek advice on a financial matter. Wait until life is a little more relaxed.

21. TUESDAY. Variable. You may still be suffering a lovers' tiff of yesterday. Get into action with friends and people in general as soon as possible. Financial plans can be fully exploited. Cooperation should be proved a great asset. You can relax and take a bow, or at least accept credit for your foresight. There can be a legal go-ahead for amalgamation. Introduce a partner to your friends. Broaden your field or contacts and so strengthen a partnership that is just beginning to blossom. Personal funds should not be discussed, even with your best friends. There can be some odd remarks. Stand your ground and keep well clear of intrigue. If you have to speak in public, deal with hard facts.

22. WEDNESDAY. Deceptive. You could feel unsure of your ground. A tutor may give you instructions to do some extra private study. Do not feel disheartened. This could be a blessing in disguise. Professional advice may be rather unpalatable. It is pointless trying to blow your own trumpet at this stage. Keep a low profile and observe how others fare at publicizing themselves. Live and learn. Daily routine can become muddled if you decide to go away. You may find new surroundings get you confused. Just take it easy. You can settle down in due course. Someone near you may ask for help. Be practical. A kind word can go a long way. Try to understand others.

23. THURSDAY. Special. Be happy with your own thoughts today. Taking a backseat and watching others do the rushing about appeals to you. It will suit you to make the arrangements from behind closed doors or even from behind a desk. Arrangements can be finalized for the transfer of someone to the hospital. This will be a relief, after a long wait. Financial deals can be handled much more efficiently and discreetly in a private room. You wish to keep a romance secret. No one is going to catch on today. Both are good at acting out the part. Do some meditating or thinking over past events of the month. A forward step will follow.

24. FRIDAY. Good. You should have your personal finances fully buttoned up. Keep your information to yourself. There is every incentive to being discreet when handling any business or financial arrangement. A specialist should be asked for more intricate guidance. Though you like to be independent, you must look ahead and know what is likely to crop up. Two heads are better than one, especially when technicalities are discussed. A professional person of high standing will be able to boost your morale. You could be due for a journey to meet someone who is in a position of authority at an overseas branch. If possible, make the trip doubly rewarding by combining it with vacation.

25. SATURDAY. Disquieting. Think carefully about someone you are just getting to know, you could be getting obsessed without good cause. Try to find out which way this person's mind is working. It may be necessary to come out into the open and state your case. As you are noted for your direct manner, this will come as no surprise to your friends. Others may think you are being a bit rough. You may have some back-handed compliments passed about you. Do not stand on your dignity. Either ignore them or smile. This will upset more than anything else. If you persist at something you are determined to complete, you could be shattered by nightfall. Save some energy so you can have some fun.

26. SUNDAY. Variable. A happy day to develop your love life. An early start should give you precedence if there is competition. Sporting activities are well starred. Children should be encouraged to join in the fun with adults. You may have to agree to disagree with a partner. Perhaps a third party can help. It may be better to follow your separate interests so neither will feel cheated. There could be something developing that will affect your income. While there may be little you can do about it, at least you should get to know the technicalities. Pressure seems to be building up at the moment. Be careful how far you go where others are involved.

27. MONDAY. Disquieting. Consider well before spending on life insurance. This could be a day of reckoning. If new methods have been introduced, you will have to get used to the system. Best hang fire until you are sure. You could have trouble explaining things to a partner or business associate. Better to be firm now than have to impose restrictions later in the year. Something you see may appeal to you. Perhaps just this once you can buy something beautiful without letting your partner know. The surprise of an unexpected gift can work miracles, but you are taking a chance. There could be a disappointment. The bank statement does not please anyone.

28. TUESDAY. Disturbing. Today will be one that you would rather miss. Pressure seems to have built up. You are aware more than ever of your responsibilities. A positive and determined attitude will solve all, but this could make life quite miserable in the short term. You could receive a bill that is not expected and you may think is uncalled for. Children may be getting you down. A recent ailment may recur and incur more expense than you bargained for. Your love life seems to give little compensation. You may begin to wonder if you are being hard-hearted. But it may be the other half of the equation. Life can become tedious, but only when you fail to make sure it does not. If you give up, it will.

29. WEDNESDAY. Disturbing. Something has to be settled with in-laws. Your affections are stimulated. You can be very emotional. An appeal to a parent can be the last straw. If you have dealings with an overseas official expect delays and complications. Exchange rates and immigration problems will keep you on tenterhooks for most of the day. High handed action by an official can upset the neighborhood. Someone who should know better may touch on a sore point and get you going. Do not get too deeply involved with your neighbors. They could let you down at the last moment. Your personal resources are sufficient. Think of your upbringing and how you were taught self-sufficiency.

30. THURSDAY. Variable.   Your love life should brighten up. A new face in the neighborhood brings back memories. Forget your latest conquest and start anew. More friendly contacts should be made with those who share your everyday routine. It is a good thing to widen your circle of acquaintances and develop ties with your kith and kin. Your partner could have a stroke of luck. You could be thinking of travel. So long as you have the right company, there could be nothing to lose. Advice from a travel agent, supposed to know his job, is not at all clear. Check up and you may find him totally wrong. Do not get involved with people in authority because you could find yourself hopelessly entangled.

JULY

1. FRIDAY. Fair.   Push a personal project. Security is very important at the moment. It is possible you will find someone in authority can help you with publicity. This is too good a chance to pass up. All will not run smoothly. Your well-laid plans can be carried through, but you may expect some disagreement from a member of the family. Be determined to succeed. A tutor may be the most important person in your life at the moment. Persevere with studies if you are looking for higher qualifications. Nothing will be gained by hanging fire. You could be a bit lonely if away from home. An in-law sees things as do you. This is encouraging. A pleasant day for late romance.

2. SATURDAY. Variable.   Attend to domestic arrangements in the morning. There can be traveling that will take up quite a lot of your time. Family matters should be fully discussed. Keep in direct touch with parents who will appreciate a visit from you. An agent may want you to sign a statement or contract. Read the small print and ask for clarification if necessary. You will not be cheated except by your own carelessness. There could be a divergence of interests later in the day. Evening arrangements can fall through. Someone may forget or turn up late. This can mess up a joint arrangement. Impress on your partner the need to be more careful in the home. There is a danger of leaving something unlocked such as the garage door or a porch window or door.

3. SUNDAY. Good. Get out for the day. If possible please yourself and do your own thing. Something could have a strong attraction for you. A personal interest may be far stronger than any joint or shared activity. Imaginative action is possible. Use your creative talents to the fullest. Let your talent be known. There is no need to hide your light. Important people could be watching your exploits and admire your skill. Today is a romantic day for some, a day to let yourself go without losing your sense of direction. Idealistic urges should be heeded. There is probably something you can do for a neighbor or friend. You could be a bit shy in some ways and yet get publicity in another. This is a day when you can enjoy whatever you do.

4. MONDAY. Disturbing. Tread very carefully. You could be irritated or aggravated from the word go. Children can get under your feet when you are in a hurry. Travel problems are not going to make your journey any easier. It looks like a typical Monday morning. You will have to keep cool or you will be wasting a lot of time on unnecessary activities. You may feel like blowing your top. Perhaps that would do you good. There could be some need to have second thoughts before you do something that could have to last for a long time. Fight against impulsiveness. A step taken in a fit of temper or in a hurry can be difficult to retrace. Do not speculate. Hang on to your money.

5. TUESDAY. Deceptive. Attend to those things that come automatically. There could be some urgency or you may have had a restless night. In some way you may be a bit up-tight, so routine work will be helping you get back to normal. If you take any sort of sedation to calm you down in the morning you may find it is stronger than expected. You could be inclined to doze off. This could put you in a tricky position if you have to concentrate on what you are doing. Therefore, look after yourself in the afternoon, just in case. You could be misled by someone. Information you receive about a new job can be misleading. Take nothing at face value. Check on information and background. If you are not careless, someone else could be.

6. WEDNESDAY. Variable. Someone at work can turn you on. Pleasant company should make your morning fly. Keep an eye open for the boss, who may find your conduct unseemly. If productivity falls you could be in for a hard time. A balanced diet could be the answer to a health problem. Advice given by the doctor may spoil your morning. Attention by a nurse may return the smile to your face. The diet is probably not as bad as you thought. You have more room for maneuver later in the evening. Make arrangements for a date. Do not let too much water flow under the bridge if you feel you can develop something for the future. Research into the mechanics of a job should be interesting. Find out how it works.

7. THURSDAY. Good.   See you get value for money. Whatever you apply your skills to, whether in home or workshop, see you are properly remunerated. A day to get down to the nitty-gritty. Pull no punches. You are on firm ground and seek only your right. Some may be rewarded without fuss, while others may have to fight all the way. In the end you will succeed, so do not think you are wasting your time. After the tension of application, you will be able to relax. Good company can make the evening pleasant and possibly romantic. A colleague who has worked alongside you all day turns out to be an interesting social friend. You are glad to meet nice people in the evening.

8. FRIDAY. Good.   Make a decision overnight and stick to it. It seems best to be cooperative today. Personal interests can be safely left to wait a little while you consolidate a mutual tie. Influential people have certain plans for you to fulfill. A journey overseas could be in the process of being set up for you. Accept any good publicity you can gain. A professional's advice should be heeded. Look for expansion through cooperation. You may be able to develop along certain lines tomorrow after getting guidance today. An overseas market should be ready for development. Parents get a lot of pleasure from children. There could be an addition to the family soon.

9. SATURDAY. Variable.   You or your partner could be feeling generous. There is a need to let your hair down. Children can be fortunate. They may get more than they are entitled to, but will be grateful enough to warm the heart. You could be the recipient of a present or you could be happy to spend more than usual on a gift for someone to whom you are attracted. You will not count the cost because it is for a worthy cause and you are in a positive mood. Most folk you meet seem to be looking on the bright side. It could be the weather or the economic climate. Look ahead to vacation arrangements. If you are on vacation now, you have chosen well, as summer is in full swing.

10. SUNDAY. Variable. You may still be feeling generous. There could be a salutory reminder of the length of your purse before the day is out. Look someone square in the eye if you have to talk yourself out of a difficult situation. There is no time for dodging the issue. If you are found out that will be just too bad. Diplomacy can be your strong suit. No one is going to doubt your sincerity if you turn on the charm. A settlement can be arrived at over a joint financial venture. You may collect on an insurance policy. Money is likely to flow in, but you should look after its outflow all the more. There are unexpected drains on the family purse. Even a contingency fund could be emptied in short order.

11. MONDAY. Disturbing. Life can get complicated. You may be quite sure you have it all worked out when someone throws a monkey wrench in the works and you have to rearrange your plans altogether. Do not blow your top, though this may give you some relief. A lovers' quarrel may be over in a short while but can be damaging while it lasts. Above all, keep on your toes. You should be mentally alert. This may be why you meet problems, since you could be impatient and one step ahead all the time. Do what you think is right and if the need is there, others will eventually catch up. Look out for accidents or things dropping on your toes.

12. TUESDAY. Deceptive. You could be rather absent minded. A personal matter could be on your mind. You are inclined to get obsessed and immersed in things you think important. This can lead to some evasion of immediate facts. Your friends may have to give you a reminder to keep your eye on the ball. A local art festival can occur at the wrong time in your calendar. Examinations can take priority over all other activities. You will need to concentrate if you are to get through. Do not worry about the eventual outcome, just try to relax and wait for the right moment. Someone could be keeping something from you until a more convenient moment comes along. Let them be mysterious.

13. WEDNESDAY. Good. Today is a day of decision. Look to the main chance. This is not the time to be fiddling around on minor issues which should have been attended to days ago. If you are behind with your plans there is little point in trying to catch up now. An important decision can be made or a new initiative taken. For those in publishing, this could be a red-letter day. A new publication should be introduced on the public. From now on you should be able to take a much wider view of the future. An examination could be the open sesame to a fuller life ahead. The approval and support of parents will mean a great deal to someone just going out into the wider world of adult experience.

14. THURSDAY. Encouraging. Take on responsibility with a smile. You are now in a position to see much that has been hidden before. You could feel you have got somewhere and can exercise a certain amount of authority. Take the day in your stride. Being in charge will not keep you from being active in guiding others who are learning the job. Encourage productivity by example. So much depends on your being more than just a figurehead. Be firm and fair in all your dealings and decisions. More promotion is on the way if you make a good job of your present challenge. Make the most of support and encouragement from associates who share much of your load.

15. FRIDAY. Good. Cast oil on troubled waters. The use of diplomacy will get you where you want to be. There may be an early temptation to push ahead and override any opposition. Be firm by all means but avoid overdoing the heavy stuff. A light approach will move mountains. The pen can be mightier than the sword. Look after paying clients. Your loved ones can be a great asset. They can be proud of your public image and show it in a way that will please. Take note of the words of a broker. Artistic or valuable trinkets can be worth hanging on to. The future may look bright for you, so be sure that you make the most of your position. Guard your reputation jealously.

16. SATURDAY. Variable. Get your priorities right. Make a clean break from some financial commitment before it is too late. You should be able to consolidate a position that will see you financially secure for a little while. Rewards of business activity should be apparent in end of week returns. A new approach to an old problem can help you make your position more secure. There may be mutterings among your competitors. Jealousy will get them nowhere. Do not let down your guard when you think you have made the grade. There can be a moment of carelessness that will undo all you have struggled for recently. A partner could be inefficient and uncaring.

17. SUNDAY. Mixed. Get away from home. Have a day out with your friends. Something of special interest can get you going. You will feel you want to talk about it. Romance could be on the menu. A relaxing situation can put you in the mood to travel, provided someone else is doing the driving. From past experience consider how you can achieve some personal ambition in the next few days. Your altruistic inclinations may be aroused during your travels today. Seeing how others live may give you ideas. Your imagination is working well. You may feel like unburdening your soul on a neighbor or relative. A few tears will not come amiss.

18. MONDAY. Variable. Establish a working schedule for the day. To fit all your visits in without a good organization will be difficult. You could have been through an emotional upset yesterday or early this morning. Look on the bright side and learn from your mistakes. You should be able to get to the bottom of something that has been bugging you for a while. Study or research can solve your problem. In-laws can be helpful. Advice they offer is both well meaning and objective enough to be taken or left without giving offense. You may have to straighten out a disagreement among your friends. Do not take sides if it will upset anyone whom you love dearly.

19. TUESDAY. Changeable. A day of many ups and downs. Early on you can have the full support of seniors who see business profits going up. Cooperation comes easily from those who have something to offer and recognize your abilities. Develop as far as you can. Lend a helping hand to someone who is willing to work as hard as you. A legal matter should be happily settled. There is room for maneuver. An association to which you belong has increased membership and has a better chance of doing something for the community. There may be hard words about a neighbor. Keep your wallet closed if you are doubtful about an appeal. Watch carefully how you go.

20. WEDNESDAY. Variable. Something can fall flat early in the day. You could feel let down or depressed. An arrangement made earlier comes unstuck. You may be called upon to travel well out of town when you would rather concentrate on local affairs. A letter may contain bad news. Do not expect credit if a case is reviewed. The quiet life will suit you better at the moment. Publicity is not likely to be good. Take a loved one into your confidence. Make arrangements for a quiet withdrawal from the company. Be careful not to say too much or someone will let the cat out of the bag. Keep a date. There are some you can trust: those who keep a still tongue.

21. THURSDAY. Variable. Private business deals should be worth your while. You can make a firm friend of someone you help privately. A specialist has something constructive to say in confidence. Do whatever has to be done behind closed doors.

There may be someone in need who can benefit from your
financial support. Do something positive and say nothing. Something could be recovered you had thought long gone. An old
friend, now somewhat grayer, makes a reappearance. Recount
happy days of yore. A publisher may have unkind things to say.
In-laws are rather difficult to get along with. Do not make a scene.
You can resolve any problem given time and patience.

22. FRIDAY. Fair. You may be convinced you are right. Not
unnaturally you will feel you ought to go ahead with your plans.
Mind you do not upset someone who thinks you are over-bearing.
Trust your intuition which is usually correct. The rational scene is
not bound to be the true one. Neighbors could be sensitive to your
needs. If you feel you are up against it with someone in the higher
bracket, seek an intermediary. Influential people have a way with
them. If you are lucky enough to encounter a professional with his
hand on the right strings, listen to what he has to say. You could
hear of someone receiving helpful marriage guidance advice.

23. SATURDAY. Good. You may find it difficult to settle
down. Weekend duties may come first and this could bore you.
You will want to be on the road or as far away from your usual
environment as possible. Studious types should find this an ideal
day to get down to personal production without interference.
Look up your in-laws who will be pleased to welcome you and
your partner. A letter from someone overseas can intrigue you.
Look up times of flights and be ready for an opportunity to make a
visit. You are perhaps feeling a little lonely where you are at the
moment. There are greener pastures over the hill. Why not investigate? Nothing ventured nothing gained.

24. SUNDAY. Variable. There could be some obligation to
work today. Your boss will be appreciative. There is quite an attractive bonus at the end of the day. Make a positive decision
about your health. You are better being active than hanging
around waiting for things to improve. Wastage goes on all the time
if you do not restock your larder. Think of this in financial terms
and you will understand the basics of economics. The joint account
may need some reinforcing. Either you or your partner are going it
a bit strong. You will feel happier when you know you can do
something about it in practical terms. So go ahead and give it your
best shot.

25. MONDAY. Quiet. Get back into your routine slowly.
There could be some impediment to cope with before you really

get going. A financial problem may have you thinking and not coming to any satisfactory conclusion. If you feel you are getting nowhere, let it rest. Without the necessary impetus there will be no helpful change. You could get into a situation you may later regret. Keep tabs on all that goes on around you, even if you have lost the main interest. You could feel shut out in some way. A loved one may be leading you astray. You find it difficult to keep up the pace or to keep in touch. But do not let this overwhelm or distract you.

26. TUESDAY. Disturbing. Everything may seem to happen at once. The morning can be busy. You seem likely to get responsibility thrust on you whether you like it or not. Cope with emergencies in your own way. You could have to stand on your own feet, so there is no point in calling for assistance. Put a flea in someone's ear if they bother you with minor problems. A financial crisis needs sorting out right away. Be prepared for a dispute at work. Instant reaction may either help or hinder the solution. You must act as you feel. Expect little cooperation from troublemakers. A lightning strike can disrupt returning traffic. You are not in the best of moods.

27. WEDNESDAY. Quiet. You could be glad of a break. If possible avoid routine. A trip away from your immediate environment will perhaps give you a chance to catch up on mail and the little things that mean so much in everyday life. Visit some of your local friends. Catch up on the news and generally get back into the swim. A recent separation may have left you feeling low or uptight. It is time you tried to get out of it. So take time to think things out, but do not waste a good day for getting back to normal. The possibility of some recognition in the near future can inspire you to take it easy and prepare yourself. Be open to new developments and ready to act.

28. THURSDAY. Variable. You could be in a quandary. Those in authority will not fully agree with your plans. But they seem to support your methods. You will have to puzzle out the best approach. It may be you are not seeing things as clearly as you should. Pressure can build up and confuse the issue. You have done the ground research and there is no reason why you should progress. If handling property, a sale should be possible. Someone with more influence may be bidding against you. Your finances are in good order. Do a bit of checking. Find out the reason for a deal not going through. It could be a lucky day for you or your partner, despite the odds.

29. FRIDAY. Sensitive. Look after your basic interests. As long as you do all necessary work to finish off the week you should be in the clear. Employers are full of energy. New schedules can be in hand for the coming month. A productivity scheme should encourage fellow workers. There can be a lot of talk during the day when the news leaks out. There could be negotiations in hand regarding a take over. This is a good day to seek the advice of a city broker. With spare cash in your joint account you have room to expand. Do not stay in one place or put all your eggs in one basket. It is time to use your intelligence. The tax man can be beaten if you go about it the right way.

30. SATURDAY. Variable. Put your money to good use. Look ahead before going shopping. It may be wise to lay in a stock for a rainy day. Invest in your own property. A long-term project should be undertaken rather than one where you look for a quick return. Try to build money up. The family proves to be a true support when you are in need. You could be pleasantly surprised how they understand your problems. It seems others have been through difficulties also. Swapping experiences can be enlightening. You will feel better for the chat. Relaxation can be difficult. You may be too tired to enjoy it. An engagement may be broken. Someone is likely to forget. It could be hard to find a suitable form of amusement. You are hard to please.

31. SUNDAY. Quiet. The frustration of yesterday can put you out of the running. Spend your time doing those things that give you personal pleasure, though there may be little to show for your efforts. Getting the facts will intrigue you. A mutual interest in research can keep you in touch with a business colleague. Knowledge is something you can utilize at any time. Take an interest in the outside activities of associates or the family. You will be remembered in years to come for the way you handled other people's affairs. Speak your mind in public if you are asked to give your personal version. You will be respected for your opinion. It is a good day to get your message across.

AUGUST

1. MONDAY. Variable. Resources can be pretty thin. There could be doubts about a holiday. Outlay on children's necessities may have left you short of cash. This will be a temporary holdup. The main thing is to avoid wasting more or chancing your arm trying to raise funds in a hurry. Just accept the situation and do not make it worse. A constructive approach will ensure replacement of funds if you cooperate and get down to hard work. A partner is optimistic about your future. This will boost your morale. There may be a difference of opinion with a head of business. Be straightforward, even if you appear to have no support. You are not wasting time in explaining.

2. TUESDAY. Variable. A relationship may be difficult to maintain. There is some chance of a separation. This could clear the air and give you time to think. Positive steps should be taken at work. Recognition can be rightly yours if you go direct to the fountain head. Positivity will get you all you want. Do not be put off by the negative attitude of partners or those who should know what makes a business tick. While it is certainly no time to be taking risks, there is plenty of scope for anyone with initiative. Look for promotion. Look for more business. Someone may give you poor advice. There may be a slip of the tongue that can cause a great deal of trouble. Be careful what you say.

3. WEDNESDAY. Deceptive. Colleagues can lay down their tools. There can be a problem getting around on public transport. Causes of delay are not clear. You are at loggerheads with no one, so can keep clear of trouble. You may hear of a marriage breakdown. This is unexpected news. Be sure to follow instructions implicitly if given a new job. Though you are quite clear of your own position, someone close to you can be doubtful. Reassure a loved one about money. As long as you are able to produce, there will be no problem. Insure against loss after learning of a robbery. Look after wages which may be short or can get pilfered.

4. THURSDAY. Disturbing. Your partner could be in a romantic mood. You will like to please, so may forget the duties that lie ahead. Problems have to be solved. Your peace will soon be disturbed by someone in authority. There may be some warning of trouble. Uncooperative attitudes will put you on your guard. A long standing disagreement can come once more to life. Try to keep personal problems away from business. Look after your reputation. If you have to be firm, that is better than submitting weakly to every demand imposed on you. A message can be deliberately mislaid. If you are to make the most of the situation you must be straightforward. Do not upset the man at the top more than you can help.

5. FRIDAY. Quiet.   Adopt a cooperative attitude to all around. No matter what you have to do, there will be room to listen to others and to accept any offers of help that come your way. A partner will fall in line with a request. You seem to be working up to a point of some importance connected with a relationship. This will make you feel you have time to spare and opportunity to do good. The full effect of good will may be seen later in the evening. It could be a lucky evening for some. You may realize a hope. Be generous and you will be fully repaid in kind. It seems appropriate to expand a joint interest. The family funds should be increased.

6. SATURDAY. Good.   Your partner may be fully occupied for most of the day. This will give you time to attend to other matters. You need to consider the future as it affects your dependents. It may be convenient late in the day to meet someone with knowledge of insurance for advice. Make arrangements for a medical check-up for your partner or one of the family. Someone close to you is considering military service. This rather excites you. An employer or supplier seems keen to spread his contracts. Cooperation or sub-contracting with a large corporation is being considered. You should find this will provide an opening for you.

7. SUNDAY. Variable.   Tie up loose ends. Your reputation may depend on the manner you put yourself across. A public appearance should go well if you are properly briefed and understand your subject. Leave no stone unturned if you have to prepare for a business meeting tomorrow. Your partner can have some interesting sidelights to focus on a joint interest. Take note of all information that comes your way today. Provided you do your homework properly, there should be no need to worry about the immediate future. If you are careless or waste your time, you could feel unlucky at the end of the day. Time may be running out on something. A difference of opinion may come to light.

8. MONDAY. Deceptive.   You should feel at ease and responsive. If you have things in perspective, you should be able to handle whatever comes your way. A relationship can have particular meaning. You feel at one with someone close to your heart. Some will appreciate your composure. Others will envy you. Be gentle and loving to those who are short of affection in their lives. Be short and to the point with those who will not pull their own weight. There is no reason to put up with shoddy workmanship or assistants who try to take over. You in your turn will realize you get more out of people by kindness and courtesy than by being arrogant or abrasive.

9. TUESDAY. Good.   Be efficient. Get on with your job and progress at your own pace. There is plenty of scope for major or minor operations. Attention to business overseas should be maintained. Once more you seem obliged to have your facts right. Dependence on long-term or well established connections will be necessary. You may achieve nothing spectacular, but can get yourself into a comfortable position before taking on more responsibility tomorrow. Attend to last minute publication. The publicity angle is most important. If you are preparing for examinations, this could be your last opportunity to look up references. A teacher or some other professional person can be helpful if you bother to ask.

10. WEDNESDAY. Quiet.   Make your presence felt quietly. You must not hide your light. Neither should you make any demonstration to attract attention. Aspirations will be high. You will feel you are going places so have the confidence to carry anyone who needs to be convinced. Later in the day can be more rewarding than the early part. By then you should have persuaded someone to rely on your judgment. Someone may wish to invest in a project you have recommended. You can either give or take advice. An insurance policy is to reach maturity and you must decide how to make use of this money. Look well ahead. Act positively, especially when considering the welfare of others.

11. THURSDAY. Fair.   Be firm and direct. Nothing is gained by hanging back today. A work situation needs an immediate decision. This will be to the satisfaction of both management and labor, whichever side you are on. Keep your ear to the ground in order to keep up with current thinking and attitudes. There could be changes right now and you can keep abreast of the times. An opportunity to improve working and office conditions can be taken. New equipment will speed up production and ease someone's work load. Improve your prospects and your reputation by word of mouth. Use all your mental faculties to develop and stabilize what you have already achieved.

12. FRIDAY. Good. A day for initiative and firm progress. An important venture can be started with confidence. This could be the high point of the year for some. Parents can be fully in support of your efforts today. Success seems assured. It seems a case of putting all you have into this unique desire to be recognized. Some will be married. Some will take over management of business. From now on you must develop whatever is started. You will have a solid foundation from which to start. Older heads will give sound advice. Finances can be strengthened as you take the plunge into a new world. Those seeking the bright lights should be sure they are sustained by a good bank balance. Be more original nowadays.

13. SATURDAY. Variable. A day of possibilities. Much will depend on your sensitive response to those around and to conditions. While all may not be as it appears, you have the ability to recognize what is genuine. Friends can be unreliable though some will be very perceptive. You can be careless or thoughtful. There will be opportunity to show your love and you may also try to show off to your disadvantage. Neighbors can be on your wavelength, though they will not make a fuss. An associate will try to get you out of your depth, probably with the best of intentions. You should be on your guard for wise fools. Someone can be very loving. You too will feel romantic. Show it. Why not take someone out for the evening? Find some special entertainment, and then have dinner.

14. SUNDAY. Disquieting. Think carefully about someone you are just getting to know. Friends come in two categories, you may think. There is some need to judge and be judged. You could be a little too casual with someone and find you have made a mistake. On the other hand someone may take your friendship for granted and come unstuck. Appreciate the company of those who seek only peace and quiet on this day of rest. The family funds may not stretch to a journey for parents and children. You may feel a bit disappointed. Better be safe than sorry. There could be other complications that suggest you are better off the road today. A casual word can cause trouble between friends.

15. MONDAY. Disturbing. News from abroad is not heartening. The pressures of business can hit you as soon as you get to the office. Money may be hard to come by. Play it cool. Risk nothing. Look for security in tried methods and outlets. If you come to a dead end, let it rest for a little while. There is no sense in banging your head against a wall. It is frustrating to be denied access to some place you wish to visit. There could be a romantic disappointment. Someone can go out of your life for a while. A few tears can relieve the tension. A neighbor turns out to be a mischief maker. You appear to be learning the hard way, so be philosophic and try to keep calm. If you are under the weather, take it easy.

16. TUESDAY. Deceptive. Try to practice mind over matter. So much may seem out of proportion, you should try to relax in order to cope. You could be worried about a relationship that seems to be on the rocks. A confrontation may be necessary. You will wish to keep your affairs private. This may not be possible when interested parties have other ideas. If you can detach yourself from the quarrels or distorted love life of others, you can have a peaceful day. Do nothing deceptive or secretive. Underhand methods may be practiced against you. Do not sink to that level yourself. Your inner thoughts are important. No one can steal your dreams.

17. WEDNESDAY. Good. Have quiet confidence in your ability to persuade. The art of diplomacy should be practiced in business and in the home. Cooperation with someone of importance will get you a private agreement that is more valuable than an open statement to the press. Publicity should boost profits. A personal plug will go down well and can have repercussions over a wide field. Make travel arrangements that can benefit you personally as well as the business. A loved one can be particularly cooperative. Traveling with someone you admire will make you feel you are getting somewhere. It's nice to know that you're on compatible terms.

18. THURSDAY. Good. A parent can offer support if you are in need. People in authority show they recognize your personal qualities. Do not expect any great demonstration. Sound, practical encouragement is all that is necessary. Official clearance for a personal financial deal will ease your mind. There could be some problem about getting in touch with relatives. You will be relieved to make contact, though the method may be rather dubious. Trust to the intervention of someone who wishes to remain anonymous. Deeper motivations can lead you to some action that is not completely understood by those around you. It may be difficult for you to explain. But you know deep down what you are about.

19. FRIDAY. Variable. A lovers' quarrel can upset your routine. Other people's problems seem to impinge on your privacy. You would like to get on with your own life, yet there are interruptions you cannot sidestep. There is a move at the top to introduce new methods into business. You are all in favor which can mean more money in the bank and that can't be bad. When someone of importance is prepared to stake their reputation on your reliability you should feel proud. Someone you love may be traveling far today. Have healing thoughts as this person may suffer from travel sickness. An in-law is in trouble and may need urgent medical attention. Try to help.

20. SATURDAY. Disturbing. Do not try to buy your way out of trouble. There could be some sort of ganging up on you. The odds may be stacked against you, but do not get depressed even though your reputation may seem to be at stake. An official will disagree with your personal plans. This may be expected under the circumstances. If you think about it, you may realize where you are pushing too hard. There is a temptation to go it alone, perhaps unwisely. Consider well the financial implications, if nothing else. Unsympathetic people may upset you, but there is no reason why you should spoil your chances even further by going wild.

21. SUNDAY. Fair. A health problem can vanish overnight. Feel free to do anything you want. Your sense of duty is strong today. It is an ideal time to help someone out with a financial problem. Gardeners should make the most of a free day to get the best from their crops. A pet will prove to be a winner at a show. Put some of the prize money towards your little friend's future. You may hear rumors later in the day that upset you. Friends are not all they seem. Sarcasm is the lowest form of wit and you can do without coarse comments from anyone. Look after your purse if you are socializing in the evening.

22. MONDAY. Variable. Come to grips with a personal problem. You may be concerned about your resources. Future activities and development may depend on your financial support. There is probably no need to worry, but you should make absolutely sure of your position. Keep a firm grip of your assets. You will soon have the opportunity to expand. You are looked upon with favor from the top brass. A boss may keep you in focus as you make your way up the ladder. Provided you are responsible and not a stick in the mud you have really no fear for the immediate future. It depends on you as is only right it should.

23. TUESDAY. Deceptive. You have problems of communication. In truth, you may be feeling lazy and not want to go anywhere. A health matter could keep you from concentrating on essentials. If you are not thinking clearly, do not let it upset you.

You have a need to dream or use your imagination. This will not suit everyone. Some will want you to get on with a job, which you will find difficult to master in your present frame of mind. Try to be choosy. News from abroad may confuse you. You could be wishing you were far away from this everyday routine. If at work, watch your step or the boss may think you are dispensable.

24. WEDNESDAY. Good. Make good use of your car. A lot of ground may need to be covered in a short time. Arrangements should be made about a transfer of business capital. You appear to be in the right position to act as go-between in a major transaction. Use your natural skill to get agreement between associates. An interest in a public project is stimulated when you meet people in the neighborhood. You appear to have the interests of local folk at heart and are a natural speaker on this topic. Relatives you have not seen for some time may drop in on you. There are all sorts of things to talk about. It will be a happy day. You will never have a dull moment.

25. THURSDAY. Fair. Family fortunes can improve. The value of land or property should be increasing. Develop family interests. Married couples may be planning a family increase. A partner could have a stroke of luck which will benefit the whole family. Attend to home repairs. Those who work at home should have a productive day. The health of someone close to you is greatly improved. The use of a limb is restored. You could be inclined to take on too much if you are in a generous mood. Determination to complete a task could make you rather intolerant. Mind you do not offend someone near and dear. If you're feeling tense and irritable, keep to yourself.

26. FRIDAY. Good. Buy something of value for the home. An initial down payment can set the seal on a long-term transaction. Look after your basic security. Think ahead in financial terms and prepare constructively for the future. You could secure a home mortgage. Improvements to property already started can be continued. This may be a long job but it is well worth completing. Property values continue to increase. If buying or selling get the best terms you can while the market is reliable. Elderly people will have sound advice to give on home and family. Think about methods of home security. Valuables should be kept under lock and key or in a safe deposit box.

27. SATURDAY. Disquieting. You have competition. Your love life can be blighted if a parent takes umbrage. Creative talents can be blunted because someone in authority refuses to give you a chance. Family funds do not stretch to cover the expense of a holiday at the moment. You could feel frustrated and want to get away from it all. It will not help matters to be undisciplined. Children can get into trouble. This could be an expensive exercise. Risks may have to be taken, but where possible should be avoided. Personal plans can go well if you persevere. You could be in love and that will ease the way considerably. Use your imagination if stumped.

28. SUNDAY. Disturbing. Be very careful what you say. Conversation with people outside can lead to misunderstandings. You may slip up or may hear something that disturbs your peace of mind. A recreation has to be cancelled because arrangements have been overlooked. Traveling to see someone is postponed. You will have to make your own amusement and arrange your own travel. Take no advice on investment or speculation. It is better perhaps to keep your money in the bank. Entertainment can be very expensive. You may find more than the invited guests turn up at a gathering. It may be necessary to reduce servings of food. You do not like to be cheap, but there are such people today who crash parties.

29. MONDAY. Variable. You should have high hopes for the future. A new job can be a lifesaver financially. Promotion gives you more incentive to get on with what you are doing. A one-track attitude will pay off. You have little use for colleagues who do not act quickly. If you tread on someone's toes today it will all be in the cause of progress. A positive attitude will get you what you want. You feel good to be able to cope. Do some investigating into the files. Knowledge of the past will give you an idea what the future holds. You could be misled by some of the information given. Do not take all for granted. There could be a problem traveling later on. The activity of the day can have worn you out. Have a well-earned rest.

30. TUESDAY. Fair. A loved one may be feeling out of sorts. You may have to cancel a journey because of this. A malfunction at work can leave you in a jam. You should be able to consolidate a considerable gain. Future prospects look good if you can maintain present output. There could be an emotional parting from an airport. Take things as they come and you will be in the clear. An influential person is right on your wavelength. You may find it hard to accept that an official has a soft spot. An interest in the arts is supported by a sponsor with business funds to spare. You could be instrumental in securing a large contract for your firm. The profits could be out of this world if the deal is properly handled.

31. WEDNESDAY. Fair. Cooperation is essential. You will have to make a decision before being able to channel your resources properly. Understanding support comes from different quarters. You seem to be popular with business people who have money to lend. Local sponsors also are willing to do their little bit. If you make it clear you have no axe to grind, you could have a very rewarding day. A legal question seems more likely to receive the correct attention. You may feel obliged to state your case with some force. Objective people will see your point and can arbitrate to bring about a happy solution. An important friend proves a point to your satisfaction.

SEPTEMBER

1. THURSDAY. Good. There is no need to push for what you want. Be gentle and courteous. Folks around you will be cooperative. A partnership can be particularly happy. You could be going away on your honeymoon. A journey overseas to see someone very close to your heart can make you forget all worries and problems. The future looks great. Someone will remember marriage vows and be glad. Do all you can to please people. You have nothing to lose and a great deal to gain by looking after someone. Get someone to help you prepare for an examination due in a few days time. You will find it much more relaxing to exchange questions and answers with someone you know.

2. FRIDAY. Variable. Take heed of inside information. An opportunity to make a good investment can come your way. Give your broker the go-ahead. You should be able to give assistance to someone in need. A family matter can be sorted out privately. No one need be inconvenienced. Make arrangements for care to be continued if you are not able to do as much as you would like on your own. The mechanics of a new job will intrigue you. Get to the bottom of the process. A look behind the scenes can open your eyes. Someone with business interests may take a special note of your personality. There could be something developing that you cannot quite figure out at the moment.

3. SATURDAY. Good. Sit back and take note today. Things you started a little while ago can be showing promise. There may be little to see on the surface, but underneath lies growth and expansion. A partnership seems to be blossoming. Your joint resources can have a boost through an inheritance. Be generous with those you love and who are presently a bit low on funds. You should be in an understanding mood, so you will appreciate the problems of others without having to wait to be told. Not much will miss your eye. Though some may think you are being idle, you will not be bothered. Quiet confidence will give you the ability to choose what is best for you and your partner.

4. SUNDAY. Quiet. Finish off getting the family accounts straight. Care of dependents can take up some of your time. The main part of the day may be spent with the in-laws. You could be a bit bored and wish to get away from the domestic scene. Go out with no particular plan in mind. A mystery trip could be relaxing. There can be time for study if you feel so inclined. You could be a little unsure of facts. Rather than worry, you could find it helpful to look up some information. A quiet period can help you relax. Someone close may be a little under the weather. It may be better to have a day in bed, or at least resting, rather than going out for the day.

5. MONDAY. Variable. It may be necessary to travel some distance today. You will hate having to make an early start. Once you get going, all will be well. Instructions can be a bit garbled. Private information could be misleading. Someone may have a job for you that needs instant attention. You cannot be in two places at once, so can feel like blowing your top. Get your schedule sorted out before you make a move. A business trip will be taken care of by a financial wonder. Appreciate someone in a place of authority who knows what is going on. A hasty start may mean you leave something behind. Concentrate on your angle and you will get the rest into perspective eventually.

6. TUESDAY. Good. You feel you have the world at your feet. Yes, you could be in love. Be kind and generous to all around you. Your love will be returned in full. An outing or a fashion show will really get you going. Someone lovely or handsome comes into your life. They may seem to have dropped from heaven. You are in the mood and looking for someone to share an interest with you. Get out with those you trust or who have an interest similar to your own. If you treat everyone as an equal you will offend no one. Your polish is noticeable and you could have many admirers. The evening is naturally meant for love and romance. Not a day to be on your own.

7. WEDNESDAY. Variable. You are once more in the hot seat. If called upon to arbitrate, be firm and positive in your judgment. Someone may try to push you around. Have none of it. Put any shirker in his or her proper place. It is not the day to stand on ceremony. In the main you will find people are cooperative. This will apply particularly where things need to be done. Employees can be keen to get on and secure a bonus. Employers have the right ideas about management and can get the best out of staff. A business deal could mean more work and possibly increased money for all concerned. Make private inquiries if you have to make a decision.

8. THURSDAY. Quiet. This could be the quiet before the storm. It may not be clear which way the chips will fall. You can feel something is brewing and possibly have some idea of the consequences. Retain your composure. A number of people may be dependent on you and will look to you for guidance. See that you have your house in good order. You are likely to be fully exposed at any investigation, so you should be open and above board even though there may be little going on. A day for show biz folk to make a hit without knowing why it should be. Give credit where it is due. You cannot afford to look down your nose at anyone.

9. FRIDAY. Disquieting. Be firm in your business management. A hard decision can mean a reward you have been waiting for. Personal funds should be made more than secure if you handle your affairs properly. Trust your inspiration if you have to make a quick decision. You could be pleasantly surprised by the reaction of a specialist. It could be time to lay in a supply of basic necessities. While the weather is good you should prepare for a rainy day. There could be a panic at business. Funds appear to be in short supply. There is talk of wastage or embezzlement. A friend could get out of hand. A partner is a bit of a spendthrift, spending joint funds without prior approval.

10. SATURDAY. Good. A dream may give you an idea. You feel you can achieve something. Follow up a hunch with direct action. A friend gets you involved in a project that brings back memories. Family ties are strong, even when you are away from home. You will realize this is a day to be remembered. Something important is almost bound to take place. Initiate something. It is time you made up your mind and decided how to spend your free hours socially. Parents put you in touch with an association of friends who are pleased to meet you. Official support should be sought if you are trying to get a community project agreed.

11. SUNDAY. Disquieting. Take care. Avoid doing anything hasty. You may be indecisive at one moment and full of fight the next. When frustrated you should try to do something constructive. If this is beyond you, just sit tight. Traveling and people can get you down. A shortage of money may make you feel out of it. Try not to be bitter. It certainly will do no good to be envious. Someone you know may be tempted to dip into the till at the office. A heavy hand can make life very difficult. Older people are in no mood to give guidance, even when you offer to give them a day out. It seems you may have to draw in your horns a little. First things must come first.

12. MONDAY. Deceptive. It may be better to stay away from work. Your views will not be acceptable to some of your colleagues. A family affair can give much happiness. Let everyone know how you feel. Something needs to be exhibited. A joint business arrangement should be announced. While informality and private attention to detail will get the best out of conditions, keep your wits about you. Someone could be jealous and trying to undermine your progress. Lies or doubtful information should not be acted upon. There will be at least one major decision to make. Be confident you can handle it. You have wise people around you who are perfectly willing to help.

13. TUESDAY. Good. Your mind should be much more clear. Now you have made your decision, all will seem straightforward. A day to follow up and continue to press on in one direction. Get down to some hard thinking in the privacy of your room. You will not want to be disturbed. Personal matters must come first before you can be of assistance to others. Even so, you may feel you should look after someone you know. Make a discreet journey or leave a note so that you keep in touch without making a fuss. Memories of the past may help you to cope with the details of the day. Think back to understand how your forebears coped with a particular problem.

14. WEDNESDAY. Quiet. Confidence should have fully returned. The recent period of meditation or quiet thought should have made you appreciate your assets. A financial agreement can now be completed. Take the quiet advice of someone in government service. You should try to be one step ahead early in the day. By the afternoon you are ready to make an appearance or a personal statement. Doubts you had about the future should begin to disappear quite early. Once you see how things turn out in practical terms, you will feel much more secure. It will come to you that most problems are in the mind. If you are practical you can deal with anything.

15. THURSDAY. Fair.   Try hard to implement personal plans. In your natural manner you will not give up easily. You could get obsessed by something you feel you have left undone. In the process someone may be upset. You could have a boardroom dispute on your hands in no time at all. An admirer may be difficult to please. A great deal may be asked of you which you will try hard to supply. The strain can do you more harm than good. Perhaps the conciliatory intervention of colleagues can smooth out difficulties. It seems you have happy and cooperative folk around you, but you may only see one side of the coin. That could be only what they want you to see.

16. FRIDAY. Good.   You could keep impressive company. Social connections seem to be of the highest order. Your involvement in society functions may have some side effects. You could begin to feel you are a cut above the others. This is not good for your reputation and you should try to curb the desire to show off. Keep to the main point and you will soon act in your usual manner. Important connections should be made with people in business or in the city who know the ins and outs of finance. Your personal views may be sought and accepted. This could be a feather in your cap. Stand up for your rights if you have the opportunity to make your position clear to someone in an official position.

17. SATURDAY. Variable.   Books can be difficult to balance. You have no real problem with money, but as much can go out as comes in. Concentrate, therefore, on adding to your funds. If your partner insists on spending you may have to accept the fact for today. There are great opportunities to put your best foot forward and hit the high spots. This can apply to work or to play. You should be popular. With something in your pocket to spend, you are on top of the world. A happy relationship seems to exist between management and labor. You could meet someone during business hours who really turns you on. Married couples may decide to spend heavily on something for the home.

18. SUNDAY. Disquieting.   Reactions are uncertain. Once more you may be torn between orthodoxy and heresy. If caught in a crisis there is no knowing how you may react. Try to get someone along who will hold your hand. A good influence can keep you from making a fool of yourself. Traveling can produce hazards, but you may be able to choose the best places to visit. Avoid being implicated in any act that attracts the attention of authority. In your present frame of mind, a brush with the law could bring out the worst in you. A parent may have some direct comments to make about your spending. You could be confused and not too happy about the future.

19. MONDAY. Deceptive. Working conditions may be chaotic. From the word go you will realize there is something amiss. Take on no responsibility without a firm guideline. Colleagues are uncooperative. Messages received are garbled. Traveling can be hazardous. Foggy weather may disrupt public transport and airways. Unusual things are happening in high places. Those in authority seem to be at sixes and sevens. You will find senior administrators to be unreliable or erratic in their judgment. Try to make your way through the day by keeping a grip on the immediate situation. It will be enough to cope with. You cannot plan ahead under these conditions.

20. TUESDAY. Disturbing. You make little progress again today. There are mischief makers at work behind the scenes. You would like to get information on what is developing, but are continually put off. Telephone links can be disconnected for no good reason. Labor is uncooperative. There is talk at work about taking strike action. You could feel a bit run-down with all the frustrations of the week so far. There seems little point in trying to make progress or achieve any output. You may hear of someone with an infection. Do not get worried until you are sure you have the facts. Rumors abound, so do not accept the worst. Wait until a valid diagnosis is made.

21. WEDNESDAY. Good. Establish good connections with an official. It is high time you get your contacts in order. For too long you have been talking to the monkey when it is the organ grinder you need to get in line. A firm agreement can be reached on a business matter. Finance should be readily available for getting a project off the ground. Correspondence can be important. You may have the go-ahead from a government department. This is quite a breakthrough. Feel more secure. A joint affair will begin to show profits. If you apply yourself enthusiastically there is nothing you cannot achieve. Share your good fortune with the family. Tonight is a night to entertain and let your hair down.

22. THURSDAY. Disquieting. You could disagree with a member of the family. A clash of personalities can make you get out in a hurry. Accommodations may be worse than you expected when away from home. Make no bones about it. Pack your bags and look for new lodgings. Office conditions get you down. Petty jealousies keep on coming to the surface. Everyone feels the tension and there is little hope of production. Your date for the evening has to call it off. You have no alternative arrangements so may decide to stay at home. Even here you seem to be out of place. Pressure of work may be getting you down. Consider a more balanced routine. How about a change of diet?

23. FRIDAY. Slow. Home conditions can improve overnight. You could feel like a celebration to keep you going which could be even more expensive than you first thought. Avoid taking liberties with the property of others. A casual remark does not give you the right to use someone else's car for a night out. Careless people can get you into a heap of trouble. Children may have an early day. They get under your feet if you are trying to get sorted out before the weekend. A love letter can keep you going. Gallantry and romance still exist. Get rid of all the daily chores as quickly as possible and enjoy an evening with your lover. How about dancing?

24. SATURDAY. Quiet. Take it easy. Make the most of a day free from worry or tight schedules. Do your own thing without offending anyone. A colleague may have the same idea as yourself. An outing to watch the game seems just the sort of entertainment to relax yet keep you interested. A change is certainly as good as a rest. Healthy exercise will keep you in trim and provide you with excellent company. Games of skill always intrigue you. You have an urge to be pleasantly competitive. Be generous with those you meet. A round of golf can give you an opportunity to talk business or prospects of a partnership. If all goes well, you could carry on afterward over a meal.

25. SUNDAY. Variable. You could be worried over nothing. A relative may be admitted to the hospital. If you have to take on responsibility tomorrow do not let this get you down. Both duties will be coped with. A disagreement with a parent can make you unhappy. There is right on both sides. You may both wish the matter had never arisen. Be positive. This is not a day to have second thoughts. Friends of the family will make you feel welcome. A partnership outing can give you time to think clearly and get away from local matters that are wearing you down. Neighbors have not been very helpful so far. Perhaps old friends may be that bit more understanding.

26. MONDAY. Good. Start the week in a happy mood. There can be good news on the way about your work prospects. Company you spend the day with is particularly attractive. Someone takes a liking to you in a big way. Management announces a raise. You feel you should encourage your employees for the output recently. For a nice change, everyone seems to be treating Monday happily. Listen to someone you love, they can have something worthwhile to say. You should keep your feet on the ground and learn to share the practical pleasures. You are inclined to set someone on a pedestal. A new board member brings fresh life into the office.

27. TUESDAY. Variable. Actions of others may affect your routine. You can finish off a task to your own satisfaction. Tie up all loose ends and see that you are duly paid for your services. A contract should be settled. Look into a new venture at the same time. There could be something in what a specialist has to say. Your sense of responsibility will keep you on an even keel. Employers could be in a tail spin. There could be a confrontation between employers and employees. If called to arbitrate, be precise and to the point. You may have a unique feeling about the whole situation. Trust your intuition. Be at peace with yourself. Your partner can be feeling romantic which will help you relax.

28. WEDNESDAY. Good. You have news of official permission to form a company or complete a partnership. Activity behind the scenes is slow moving but eventually produces the goods. Influential people seem to be in a generous mood. A considerable contribution to a local charity comes from a well known personality. You may know someone who will benefit. Help your family funds by taking advice from a notable to whom you are introduced. There is talk of a merger with another large corporation. News leaks out of developments that can affect the legal structure of private companies. If you have doubts of your ability, put them aside. You should be feeling proud.

29. THURSDAY. Good. A working relationship begins to show dividends. Cooperative action gives a much needed boost to family finances. This is the time for whole-hearted participation in a venture that will affect you and your dependents for a considerable time. Look with hope and inspiration to the future. Get your everyday conditions agreed and you should have no need to look over your shoulder. New terms of employment can be readily agreed. No employer will want to lose you if you are working well. Contractors can agree to make worthwhile concessions if they see you are making a go of things in your own business. A day for progress. Some could be in luck.

30. FRIDAY. Deceptive. A firm financial arrangement can be made. Someone may endow you with a responsibility that will be well worth accepting. Be glad to welcome someone into your heart. Help to comfort or ease a burden that is obvious to all. You will not wish to be superficial when discussing a relationship matter. A long and lasting liaison could start. You may have your doubts about the motivations of important people. They keep well hidden, but their instructions continue to come out. A confusing situation can arise. There is disappointing news from a local hospital. A senior doctor may have to leave. This will be a loss to the whole community.

OCTOBER

1. SATURDAY. Variable. An important decision can be made. There seems no easy option. If there are financial complications, be considerate of both sides of the question. Stand by your principles and expect no quarter. Your partner may be difficult to handle in one way. In other ways there will be kindness and light. Make the most of opportunities to foster good relations with someone at the top. You could put someone on a pedestal. You should be able to talk or negotiate yourself out of any tight spot you hit. Do not look for an escape route when the main issues are decided. Give help to someone in need. A kind word or a quick visit can bring joy if it is said or done with sincerity.

2. SUNDAY. Deceptive. People could be talking about you. No matter what you may think, you are not getting good publicity. A moral issue could have to be faced. It seems pointless trying to dodge or think you are on a winning streak. People of authority, perhaps parents, are taking stock on the sidelines. So you should be very careful how you tread. Thoughts of examinations soon to be upon you may turn your legs to jelly. Do not be afraid. It is far better you do something practical about it. If you have been overdoing the worrying, give it a rest. Otherwise your mind is likely to go blank at the crucial moment. Compose yourself and self-confidence will return.

3. MONDAY. Disquieting. Eavesdroppers never hear good news about themselves. Though you may wish to know what is going on behind the scenes, you are perhaps better off kept in the dark. Secret negotiations will do you no good, so you should discourage those who are bent on underhanded tricks and should keep your own views to yourself. A careless word can cost a great deal. Remember the old war-time propaganda about loose lips sinking ships. You may be tempted to take an easy way out of a situation where you have to consider the welfare of others. There is no slick answer. You could be suspicious of your in-laws. Consider first who is at fault before making any comment. A private word in someone's ear may have adverse repercussions.

4. TUESDAY. Good. You should feel in top form. Nothing should be too much. Prospects at work are excellent. You should be looking for promotion or some other form of recognition. Actions can lead to a place in management. You will find you have as much to do as you can cope with. This is just what you need. A full In box keeps you going, while an empty one will make you lazy. A test of strength can make you feel good. Let them see what you can do and how expert you are at your job. Show-biz folk seem set for a busy time that will bring popularity. A takeover could be considered. You may feel you ought to expand. Conditions seem favorable, at least on the surface.

5. WEDNESDAY. Quiet. You may be left in peace to plan the future of others. Keep an eye open for what goes on in your area of responsibility. There should be no complications, but you must be ready for immediate action at all times. You must try to sound out the motivations of your staff. Take an interest in the mechanics of management which may need a quiet scrutiny prior to a shake up. If you are to be undisturbed in order to produce your best results, make it quite clear to those who serve you that you have better things to do then listen to petty requests and trivialities. Look to the main chance which lies in the future. That might be a good deal nearer than you imagine.

6. THURSDAY. Good. Take the chance to settle a personal deal. Put aside enough money to back you up in a venture for the future. Finances should be in good order. Original ideas will have put you ahead for the first time in a little while. Confirm a business arrangement that will give permanence and stability. Without financial security this year you will get nowhere. Today you should be able to do something positive to further your aims. A friendly arrangement can lead to romance. You may not wish to get too deeply involved. There is no reason why you should not try to please a friend of the opposite sex. Something could grow from an initial meeting at a dance.

7. FRIDAY. Pleasant. A message can be put over. Sensitive folk will listen to what you have to say. You will feel you are among friends who share your benevolent interests. A romantic situation is likely to develop from small beginnings. You are not at all clear what is going on, but you feel good about it. You could be asked to have a trip in a balloon. This may strike you as being fantastic. All you meet seem enthusiastic. You should be able to press on with a personal project that means a lot to you. Avoid being obsessed with something or someone. You are with friends most of the time and so should circulate. Business finances get a boost.

8. SATURDAY. Quiet. You may feel a bit negative. Perhaps you have a premonition that things are not going to be as good as you hoped. As your intuition is seldom wrong, you could operate in a low key way. Lots of minor things need attention at this point of the weekend such as last minute decisions and arrangements or shopping and visiting friends just to keep in touch. A relationship may be getting a little out of hand. Your pocket money is not going to stretch as far as you would like, so you must think about pulling in your reins even if the evening's engagements are to be kept. Use your self-control and no one will suspect anything if you are in difficulties.

9. SUNDAY. Deceptive. You could get discreet word of an illicit relationship. The family would be disturbed if all the facts were known. A partnership can benefit from your private arrangements, but you should beware of the attention of so-called friends. A third party can cause no end of muddle and misunderstanding. You could be feeling a bit shattered. Excessive activity in one area can throw you out of balance and get you feeling sorry for yourself. Have a rest if that is what you need. Do not depend on neighbors to help you out in a crisis. A telephone could be out of order or the lights go out, leaving you in the dark.

10. MONDAY. Good. A day for quiet satisfaction. You will have little thought for the outside world and its problems. You can see what lies ahead and be able to make your mind up without pressure or fuss. It could be a case of putting your eggs in one basket. No one is going to make you change your mind. A highly sensitive condition exists around you. You may feel you are being protected and have not a care in the world. How romantic can you get. There is no limit to the depths of love you feel for someone or for humanity in general. The decision to do something positive can make you feel free, yet you will wish to give and give and give.

11. TUESDAY. Good. Complete the details of a financial arrangement. The long term agreement you planned should now be finally cleared and made known to those who are concerned. A change could be essential if you are to operate properly. Discreet inquiries made about procedure should have been positively answered. You can go ahead along lines suggested by an expert. A private consultation with someone responsible and a bit eccentric gives you encouragement to do your own thing. A debt can be cleared which will ease your mind. Past commitments can be reconsidered in the light of new developments. Responsibilities taken on are rewarding.

12. WEDNESDAY. Fair. Suddenly you are in love and there's no point in asking why. Someone may totally obsess you. As you are not one to do things by halves, your friends will think there is no hope for you. Romance can develop with a near neighbor or with someone you previously considered a casual friend. Emotions are difficult to control. You may upset someone or stir up jealousy in another but this will not deter you. Saying a loving farewell may have you thinking of the past. Family ties can be strong. Be gentle with someone you love. Conceal your passion, which may be a bit too much for someone more delicate than you. You must be yourself, now as never before. Consider the feelings of others.

13. THURSDAY. Quiet. Personal priorities need your attention. It may not yet be clear what the day holds for you. Do not let this deter you from looking after your own interests. There is nothing selfish in this. You will be less dependent on others if self-sufficient. Quite soon you may be considering how to improve your finances. Other things may have to be settled first. Be sure of your identity and the way you must act in order to get what you want. A friend can be cooperative. You could be paying more attention to one person in particular. This may keep you in an introspective mood. Clear your mind if you are to make plans for the future. Use your intuition.

14. FRIDAY. Variable. A partner can let things get out of proportion. If money is at stake, get a quick grip of the situation before you lose more than you bargained for. A contract with a large organization is not all it was cracked up to be. Before going any further you should consider pulling out. Avoid involvement in the financial affairs of others. You could be left holding the bag. A tax demand can set you back on the defensive. Have it checked before attempting to pay. Determination to get to the bottom of a social project can make you happy. The results are good. A relationship with a helper can make your day. You may be able to forget some worries, which would spell welcome relief, at least for a time.

15. SATURDAY. Good.   Follow up a hobby on your day off. You could make more today than you do all week conventionally. Nothing should be too much bother if you are to make the most of your chances. It is essential to be reasonably discreet. You could have as many good will offerings as direct payments. Give generously to the needy. Get involved and try to get something going that will get others thinking. A late meeting with someone who can pull the right strings can lead to further developments. No need to stand on ceremony. Speak your mind freely when you are in private. There will be a ready response. A day to practice give-and-take and be glad about it.

16. SUNDAY. Disturbing.   You will find it difficult to keep yourself on an even keel today. No need to be depressed if an early start is delayed because you will make up for lost time. Erratic behavior may come from people you meet. If you are tempted to fly off on a tangent you can expect no sympathy from the more conservative types. By all means stand up for what you think is right. Keep clear of arguments that will get you nowhere. Special care should be taken at work or with work colleagues. A tool or piece of machinery can be dangerous. If you feel feverish go to bed. A constructive approach to a senior on a job payment can be wasted if you or someone else loses faith or temper. Perhaps you resent having to work today.

17. MONDAY. Variable.   You could dream pleasant dreams. Private realities can bring you back to earth. Because of interference you may find it difficult to explain yourself. Neighbors are uncooperative in some ways. On the other hand, they accept that you have the right ideas about social improvements. Take no heed of those who talk behind your back. Be determined to follow your own course. A romantic interlude should lighten your evening. Relationships are developing with a friend. Though there may be some gossip going around, you will feel comfortable and are sure you are doing the right thing. It is not quite your style to be too casual. There may be something in this.

18. TUESDAY. Variable.   A fundamental move is frustrated. Planning permission for a new home may be refused. You will try to get hold of a top official who is not easy to corner. Bide your time if no progress is possible at the moment. There could be a delay in publication of an inquiry affecting your security. A parent is not cooperative and refuses to see you. Go ahead with construction work that is agreed. You should not waste too much time waiting for officials to come round. Home industry should have a good day. A supplier provides you with material that has been delayed. The health of someone in the family is remarkable. An operation is successful.

19. WEDNESDAY. Fair. Changes in the home may now be imperative. Someone may have to move out or you could welcome someone in from the cold. There could be a problem to solve with a newly acquired property. Look to the foundations. If possible get some local history or information from the builder if still alive. Research in a library can be helpful in many ways. Private information gives you some idea of the family tree. The claims of heredity seem strong at the moment. There are pros and cons which you can resolve with a little patience and foresight. A private person may ask you to visit them. Be discreet in your movements.

20. THURSDAY. Good. Influential people can have a lot to say. In the main, their interference will be acceptable. Money could change hands to your advantage. Official blessing can be passed on a most important project. A parent who has been opposed now agrees to a marriage. The family interests will be safeguarded. You can kill more than one bird with a stone today. Wheels within wheels should ensure a great deal coming from one action. Entertain someone famous who is pleased to keep out of the limelight and be among unaffectedly natural people. If you have felt your security was threatened recently, make your guest aware. Help may follow.

21. FRIDAY. Good. Use your imagination to get what you want. Personal talents are much more effective than mass production. Last minute details can be tidied up with a bit of polish or flair. You are in a sensitive mood and will be looking for perfection. It is never easy to find, but you feel you can make the grade. A romantic interlude with someone in the neighborhood can give you ideas. Your feelings run very deep. You would like to be able to understand what it is that drives you on. Children help you relax. You can see so much in their faces and their play. You may be thinking of writing a book or a poem. Children always make interesting subjects and are bound to figure in it.

22. SATURDAY. Disturbing. There may be a lovers' quarrel. This may soon blow over or, at least, clear the air. Someone can make you sad by deciding to leave the neighborhood. You will find it hard to come by another good friend. Recent spending may have left you broke. Make up your mind to do something radical to restore the balance. Taking a chance is not on today. There is every possibility that you end up a heavy loser. Do not quibble about minor issues. If you have an original idea that needs to be marketed, get on with the job. Frustration is caused by inactivity. It may be difficult to stop once you have the bit between your teeth, so be constructive.

23. SUNDAY. Deceptive. While you have the time, consider your diet. You may be letting things get out of hand. The bright ideas of yesterday are no longer valid. Recent evidence shows a different way is better. Get down to a good old fashioned remedy if you have a health problem. You could feel too tired to do very much. Perhaps you are lacking something or may have had a strenuous night. Do not resort to drugs as treatment if you can avoid it. You may hear news that frightens you. Face up squarely to facts. If you have to go it alone or wait for someone to come along in their own time, this will have to be so. You find it hard to argue sensibly, probably because you can see both sides.

24. MONDAY. Variable. Work should show an immediate profit. A wage rise can be announced. This should put colleagues in a good frame of mind. Employers are not too happy. Perhaps it has taken official action from the government to get this through. Try something unusual to boost production. A new method or a new machine can improve output and provide a bonus. The performance of one person intrigues you. Age does not seem to hamper someone you meet for the first time. Ask this person about diet and manner of living. There could be more to this than you think. Consider trying a vegetarian diet if you are still concerned about your health.

25. TUESDAY. Variable. Today is a difficult day to make progress. You are obliged to be cooperative if you are to succeed. Personal grudges may keep you from agreeing on a schedule. Come down off your high horse if all is to be reduced to nothing. It is stupid to argue without listening to the counter argument. A matter of honor will have to be settled. Your partner will need all the support you can muster to overcome resentment. Consider in depth the implications of an offer to partner you in business. There should be something at the bottom of such a proposal. Superficialities can be ignored. Put yourself in the other person's shoes to gain a better understanding.

26. WEDNESDAY. Good. Partners are in agreement. A great day for married couples who see their dreams coming true. There may be wedding arrangements in the works. A contract can be signed to the satisfaction of all concerned. A mid-week visit to see old friends makes a lovely change. Romantic memories are stirred when you meet someone you haven't seen recently. Sporting activities give a lot of pleasure. You are in a competitive mood. Show them all what you can do. A day to show your talents to those who share your life. Children join in the games. You wish to be accommodating. This is a genuine way to show affection. It pleases you to please someone.

27. THURSDAY. Quiet. Early morning and late evening can be very busy. The remainder of the day is for whatever you care to use it. It could be an appropriate time to do some quiet research in preparation for examinations ahead. Finances should be reviewed. If you have plans with your partner regarding home improvements, see that the funds allow such expenses. There are matters affecting children that should be attended to. You may have had a lucky break early in the morning. Your partner could have done something that made you proud. Late this evening you may attend a private function to speak. You will be made welcome. Make your message loud and clear.

28. FRIDAY. Disturbing. You could be at a crossroads. There is little in your favor to give comfort. Many decisions can be made, all with the same goal in mind. A complicated day in some ways if you do not face up to the facts. A relationship can be going through a rough time. Friendly intervention may make matters worse. Financial pressures make the going hard. You must make up your mind on expenditure and income. Quite a lot can be gained from today's experience. Points of principle are always worth learning. If you feel too much is coming at you at once, take a breather. No matter what, remember that Rome was not built in a day. Don't feel compelled to be a slave to time.

29. SATURDAY. Variable. A relationship problem may still need careful handling. You may feel you ought to take professional advice on a personal matter. It should be fairly easy to arrange a meeting with someone in a position of authority. Make a clear statement of your case and leave it at that for the time being. You can be a bit muddled or can be in contact with muddled people. A journey by air may have to be cancelled. There is confusion over schedules and bookings. Keep as far away from relatives as you can. In-laws could be helpful to some extent. Even then, they are not too keen to be of assistance. A publicity feature is a flop.

30. SUNDAY. Variable. A parent is particularly loving. There may be need to return this affection. You are a little befuddled, but something in the back of your mind keeps you from making a fool of yourself. You are aware it is better to keep a still tongue. But if you are in a position to speak and be heard, it is hard to keep quiet. Guidance from someone in authority can help you help yourself. Get the go-ahead from a local dignitary for something you have sponsored in the neighborhood. Seek no publicity at the moment. Someone will get hold of the wrong end of the stick. Your intuition is not particularly good today. You may be trying to be logical.

31. MONDAY. Good. As good a day as any to get up and away. It's vacation time. Personal interests should be publicized. If you have anything of your own creation to display, get it out. A journey to see someone you love should be undertaken without delay. You are going to be admired. See you are properly equipped to handle crowds of well-wishers if you are in show biz. This could be a popular night. Make the most of your charisma. Glamorous folk can join you during the evening. You could feel particularly fortunate at being where you are, in the right place at the appropriate moment. If you are in a position of trust, do all you can to please and satisfy.

NOVEMBER

1. TUESDAY. Fair. Someone may try to take you down a notch. Look after your reputation as if it were gold. Pressure can build up from an influential source. You could be given a rough ride. A quiet word with a well-wisher can put you in a better frame of mind. Meet someone you admire in a break period. You should be aware that someone thinks highly of you despite the adverse conditions of the moment. An associate seems to be on a lucky streak. Your partner can have great news for you. A secret agreement seems paying dividends. There is some talk of a takeover that will mean better prospects in the days and weeks to follow.

2. WEDNESDAY. Good. Today is a good day for money matters. An event which furthers your career may take place. This could alter your circumstances for the better. A new interest can take up your private time. Interesting people greet you in a place you have not visited before. You could have a heavy bill to pay, but have the resources to cope. This will give much satisfaction. Because of your reliability you are in the limelight. Do not fail to make your point. Good publicity should come easily. Complete a transaction with an intermediary. You should have the upper hand and be able to dictate suitable terms of agreement.

3. THURSDAY. Variable. Avoid getting involved witth people who are stupid or bitchy. Pretend to be out if you want to avoid irritation. You feel you get saddled far too often with unwelcome friends. They really push their luck, taking you for granted. A kindhearted acquaintance can make you feel much more secure. You are in tune with one person in particular who thinks as do you. Get on with an important letter to a romantic friend. Catch up on your phone calls. You may be in a restless mood. It is difficult to find peace and contentment without getting involved with a near neighbor. If you have been feeling rather poorly, get out with friends who understand you need a break.

4. FRIDAY. Disquieting. The cards may be stacked against you. It may be very hard to get what you want. Someone in authority seems to have a bee in their bonnet. You will find it difficult to move them from an obsessional attitude. Let it rest until a more suitable moment. A personal target seems far off, but do not let this get you down. There is light at the end of the tunnel. All you need is perseverance and patience. If you feel you are being taken over, play along for a while to lead someone on. You can get something out of an arrangement provided you let a senior think you agree with his policy. It would be foolhardy to challenge someone who has, at the moment, the upper hand.

5. SATURDAY. Variable. You could feel let down. A romantic interlude may turn out badly. There could be tears. If you feel sorry for someone do not get depressed about it. It is better to do something positive. Write a letter and get it out of your system. A money problem can hit you early in the day. Shopping may be restricted. You could see something you need and be unable to buy it. This is not the end of the world. There will be another opportunity some other time. A private party with those you share most of your hours with can make up for all the mishaps of the day. A partner is in luck and shares good fortune with you.

6. SUNDAY. Good.   You need to have a quiet day. Stop worrying about others. Just let them take care of themselves for a change. Keep a balanced diet today. You may begin to appreciate the importance of looking after the finer points. Feel happy about giving a private party. Be selective in your choice of company. You could feel quite cheerful. Someone tells you a secret which you may find hard to believe. Don't repeat it. This is for friends and loved ones only. Plans can be under consideration behind the scenes. You know there are no more details to tidy up. This is your chance to relax before the big day. You are in love and know it and you can't hide it.

7. MONDAY. Good.   Today is a good day to consolidate your gains. A personal project looks likely to be adopted by a backer with money. Before the day is out you can come clean and make an announcement. Early on it is best to remain in the background to get everything under control. A bureaucrat is particularly hard to pin down until you give him no alternative. The change of attitude is remarkable. You feel at last you have made the essential breakthrough. Look well ahead. Short-term agreements must take second place today. It is the lasting contract that has to be completed. By the evening you are well established in your role and sure of your future plans.

8. TUESDAY. Challenging.   Speak your mind. Let colleagues and those around you know where you stand. Something has to be dealt with urgently. What may appear to some superficial takes on a different meaning for you. Local affairs can be important. You must get it clear how you want to be recognized by your neighbors. One individual is like you in appearance and manner. Establish a relationship that is going to withstand outside pressures. You could be attracted to someone glamorous right on your doorstep. This could be the start of a new romance. There should be no difficulty in making yourself known. A look can speak volumes. Be gentle and understanding.

9. WEDNESDAY. Good.   Today is a day for early decisions. If it is your birthday, make firm resolutions about what you are to strive for during the coming year. It should be a day to remember. A personal project will mean more than anything else in your calendar. The past may appear a bad dream to many. From today forward you can leave all that behind. Go out into the world minus that chip you had on your shoulder. A personal victory should make you feel good. There could be a quiet moment in the day when you are completely alone. Reflect on the past. Remember that what you do in the future is largely determined by your knowledge up to the present day.

10. THURSDAY. Variable. Use your money wisely. A boost to your funds through hard work should not be taken as a hint to go wild. More can go out than comes in if you do not set yourself some limit to spending. Be active. Either sport or work will keep you in trim. Someone may comment on your appearance. Try to live up to the compliment. There is a possibility you may be promoted, but at the moment this is hearsay. Do not ruin your chances, nor build up false hopes. An associate is forgetful. You find yourself working overtime to keep abreast of progress. It's a good thing you are feeling fit and full of vigor. If necessary, you could keep going for hours longer and not be tired.

11. FRIDAY. Good. You feel a lot more cheerful. Someone you love may let you in on a secret. Money from reserves can be used without fear. There will be more where that came from. Be glad to have someone behind you who will bolster up your courage when you are in doubt. Make no secret of your affection for someone who respects your confidence. Listen to the voice of your conscience. It could be an emotional day and you can learn a lot about yourself through contact with someone who understands. Thoughts of love can make you dreamy. Be practical in your demonstration of affection. Go to someone who may need the love and support you can so readily provide.

12. SATURDAY. Disquieting. Screw your courage to the sticking place. You may feel financially restricted. On the other hand you may be determined not to spend your hard-earned money. A work situation can get out of hand. If you speak out of turn you can expect a quick reaction that may leave you gasping. Jump to it in emergency. Look out for accidents and do not expect anyone to do the right thing. A responsibility may land on your shoulders through the carelessness of others. You are well able to cope, though you will, no doubt, complain. Something could fall and frighten you. Try to get your priorities right or you could do a lot of traveling for very little return.

13. SUNDAY. Deceptive. Personal likes and dislikes come to the fore. You may consider this is your day of rest and no one should interrupt your peace. Seek quiet to give a chance of meditation. Thoughts of the past play tricks with you. You may have dreamed in the night and spend some time trying to unravel the hidden portent of a message. Give it time. Relax and you will get the message. Being rather inscrutable yourself, you know that appearances do not always matter. Be sensitive to those around you without getting involved. Someone should be on your wavelength and trying to communicate. Visit relatives who will be pleased to see you and hear the latest news.

14. MONDAY. Variable. Someone you like can be in the hospital. You feel upset. A visit can be wearing, but you feel it is necessary. Your intuition serves you well in a difficult moment. It is time you did something about getting local coverage in the press. A visit to someone of importance may be good for you. Perhaps you can get the ball rolling on a neighborhood project. Official correspondence needs a firm and immediate answer. Strike while the iron is hot as some local official seems to be cooperative. Personal plans can begin to materialize if you make the right contacts. A small personal victory makes you feel good. It may not amount to very much, but for you it is a coup.

15. TUESDAY. Mixed. Get active cooperation with a working partner. It is essential you get things straight about a schedule. The security of the whole family may depend on your ability to see the wood through the trees. So keep a clear head and insist on making progress. Future planning for the family is wise. Job prospects should be safeguarded. Look after pension rights. Your partner may have more to offer towards the joint resources than given credit for. A member of the family has a rather miraculous improvement in health. This cheers you up considerably. Some jealousy creeps into family matters later on. You could rub someone the wrong way. Do not leave the house unguarded this evening.

16. WEDNESDAY. Variable. Home hunters may hear good news from a discreet friend. Property may be scarce if you are looking for accommodation. A parent may be unhelpful and discredit your efforts. You feel your security is threatened by someone who wields authority. Look for assistance behind the scenes. The head official may be blustering to hide inefficiency. More practical consideration comes from those who help and organize without getting the limelight. A meeting with someone you cared for in the past may give you a thrill. The day can be marred by the intervention of someone with more power than you have at the moment. Do not feel resentful. That achieves nothing.

17. THURSDAY. Rewarding. Youngsters do well and deserve a pat on the back. Throw a party and let everyone have a good time. Neighbors show feelings you had not previously recognized. A romance could be developing with one of your family and a near neighbor. Promote your artistic talents. Show-biz folk should have an instant success in a small town. You may feel particularly drawn to someone. It is difficult to stop looking. You may feel a little possessive about this new interest in your love life. Try to get what you are after by using your imagination. Actions can speak louder than words. Get into the rhythm. Be attractive. It always pays to look your best, no matter what you do.

18. FRIDAY. Good.   Look after the minor details and the main issues will sort themselves out. Involvement is right up your street. Personal interests should be readily interpreted for the benefit of all. Give a demonstration of your talents. An exhibition of works of art or a dramatic portrayal will fit your bill. Arrange an evening's entertainment. Children will want to participate in whatever you have to amuse them. A teacher may have words of praise for a bright child. Use all the skill at your command to make a personal point. There will be opportunity to achieve something by talking. A travel agent can be suitably impressed and find you a late booking that you did not dare to believe you would be able to get. It pays to put your trust in someone else.

19. SATURDAY. Variable.   Make up your mind to be positive. The early hours are best for action. Make a lively start to the day. Get out before the main shopping rush gets under way. There may be little in the way of direct cooperation. Once you have got going it may attract a following. Your enthusiasm can be infectious. Prospects should improve. There is hope of a partnership bringing good results, but you will have to show enthusiasm today if you are to impress others. A bit of good luck may come your way while you are showing your strength. Problems with late night transport can get you locked out. Try to control your feelings. Someone you know feels ill when out for the evening. Be considerate even if you are upset.

20. SUNDAY. Quiet.   Take a welcome breather. You could be shattered after yesterday's activities. There may be some problem ahead that you need time to consider. It is the ideal time to prepare. Get schedules sorted out and preparations made before the start of your working week. A health matter can be handled with care. No need to make a fuss. What the patient needs is rest and quiet. Be a good nurse to someone who works hard on your behalf. There are lots of little jobs to do around the home. Recently you have not taken much interest in your pets. They appreciate you when you have some spare time to relax and take more interest in their well-being.

21. MONDAY. Good. Come to terms with your work mates. An agreement can be reached. Results could be surprising. You may have to do some slick talking or negotiating. In the end the unorthodox attitude can produce the right answer. Consolidate improvements gained. Look ahead and establish a firm financial arrangement for something you are going to do for a customer. A partnership matter may have been discussed recently. Having got the financial side sorted out to your advantage, you should settle any other outstanding problem. Get it down in writing and settle any legal points while you have a capable person there to keep you right. An appreciative letter will help a partnership along.

22. TUESDAY. Variable. Your affairs may be the subject of some activity. Tax officials or financial operators may have something to say to you after today. A money matter could be hard to determine. You may be asked later to refund an overpayment or make good some shortfall. Let it sweat until the answer is quite clear. If a compromise is necessary with a partner over a money matter, do not make too much fuss. Someone behind the scenes can do you a good turn. A sudden change of fortune can give you the money you need to meet an obligation. Visit someone in the hospital. Make a contribution to the funds while you are there. React helpfully to an urge on the spur of the moment.

23. WEDNESDAY. Variable. You could be in luck. A partnership should be proving lucrative. To keep this going you must be prepared to work. A boost does not mean all is settled and you are on easy street for life. A banker may shatter your dreams and your confidence. Take the well chosen words of someone who knows the ups and downs of the money market as a warning. You could be reminded of your responsibilities for someone else. So far you may have been carried by a willing partner. It may be time to look at the situation through the eyes of someone more objective, just stop awhile and consider. There is no need to doubt your future. Just don't get carried away.

24. THURSDAY. Good. Neighbors may need help. An older person in the family could need your help. Give advice willingly, even though you are much younger. A get-together with friends and neighbors could brighten up someone's life. You could feel more sure of yourself once you are accepted. Your personal charm will work wonders. Age does not bother you when you are looking for people to chat with. Someone will be in a serious mood and could propose marriage. Give due thought to the matter if that is necessary. You could have been waiting and be quite prepared for the request. A love letter may be read and re-read. Hang on to the words and the sentiments.

25. FRIDAY. Disturbing. A shopping expedition may have to be cancelled. There may be uncertainty about money. You could be a bit concerned now that Christmas is only a month away. Have a serious talk with your partner before doing anything extraordinary with your joint funds. A monthly pay check may be delayed. This is something to be expected occasionally. Local restrictions may prevent you from doing all you plan. Give it time. You could be asked to travel away for the weekend on a job. A neighborhood get-together will have to go by the board. Personal charm can get you out of trouble. You could have a nice traveling companion. A foreigner may attract you.

26. SATURDAY. Good. A lot of yesterday's problems are sorted out. Put aside doubts that may carry over. Traveling is well-starred. Do your own thing and get away for the day. Above all, travel with purpose. A near relative may come to visit you for a fairly long stay. This will bring back memories and childhood recollections. Today is a good day for meditation. Studies can be rewarding. You have the ability to get to the heart of the matter right away. Family ties with in-laws give you and your partner a warm feeling. An employer or main contractor comes up with more money for a job well done earlier in the month. The monthly check is as you expected, even though you had your doubts.

27. SUNDAY. Good. Another pleasant day to reflect on the past. As the future is the most important factor, you are not idly ruminating. Plans for future development should be considered. Be self-confident and you will go far. You may have wind of promotion coming your way before the end of the year. If you are on vacation, it may soon be time to return to your duties. Make the most of your last few days abroad. A lucky break in the evening can make your day. You may be recognized by someone in good company. Your ego really gets a boost. A partnership is recognized as a going concern which gives you new encouragement. You can afford to be generous. Others reciprocate.

28. MONDAY. Variable. Build up your good reputation. Press on with work you have to do. See that the labor force is happy and productive. An added stimulus of a bonus before the year's end should produce results. The financial position should be good. You are assured by your bank manager that development costs can be covered. Make all necessary arrangements for the future if considering a business deal. Much activity and rearrangement can take place if you are altering your own business. Minor details are important when relating work to payment. Suppliers and subcontractors are helpful if you deal with them directly. You have no time to waste. Influential people will step in if required and help out in a practical manner.

29. TUESDAY. Quiet.   A day to relax and regain your composure. A late night surprise could have thrown you. Forget all that. You made ground yesterday and have a lot of loose ends to tie up right now. A supervisor position will give you more time for looking without having to exert yourself. People are bound to come to you for advice or encouragement, which you can give. Get yourself prepared for a long hard day tomorrow. You could be the center of attraction though you are not aware of the fact. A feeling of aloofness or objectivity can keep you from being involved in the daily whirl. Your mind can be on higher things. It is essential to consider where you are going.

30. WEDNESDAY. Variable.   You must think carefully about someone you are just getting to know. If you are in doubt, do some investigating. Romance is well-starred. Your dreams may be coming true. There is a danger of getting into company that you will regret later. New acquaintances may have you on a bit of string at the moment. You know this cannot go on, but do not wish to be unfriendly. A business arrangement can be most rewarding financially. Cement ties with a local dignitary in a well-established business. You need the advice of older people. A specialist can give you something to think about. Keep your wits about you if you want to make a quick profit.

DECEMBER

1. THURSDAY. Good.   A friend can be rather affectionate. But if you can keep a clear head you may not get too carried away. You could be annoyed with someone who keeps on enquiring about your earnings. Let a person in authority deal with any enquiries. An important document may have to be signed. There should be improvement in business returns as the Christmas period draws near. Personal attention and application is readily forthcoming if you see some reward or gratitude in return. A dance can be particularly pleasant. You are in good company. There could be developments here. Be sure you remain in charge of the situation if someone becomes too ardent.

2. FRIDAY. Variable.   A partner can keep you out of trouble. Be glad you have someone to keep a watchful eye on you. Expenses may be heavy if you do a particularly heavy day's traveling. Local involvement can get you into all sorts of trouble. You could be held up or asked to pay high membership fees for a particular social occasion. A helping hand from a close associate can get you out of a mess. Your partner can be rather affluent at the moment. Local prices could be high, so it may pay to travel a little way out of the neighborhood to shop. You might want to spend generously to please a loved one. You should be sure you know what size or style this person would request.

3. SATURDAY. Deceptive.   Don't push too hard. Don't take anything for granted. All depends on your ability to see your way through or around the variety of jobs you have to cope with. If you keep at it, the confusion will gradually pass. If you try to do too many things at once, you are likely to blow up and achieve nothing. There may be some opposition to your plans. Try to face this philosophically. If you get worked up you will lose your natural rhythm. Perhaps you are a bit under the weather if you had a big night out last night. Once that has passed you should be in good form. It is better to rest than to try something beyond your capabilities. You could have an accident. Look after local matters.

4. SUNDAY. Deceptive.   Take time to think about a personal relationship. You could feel you are on to something that has got real meaning. It is not your style to treat such things lightly when you may have thoughts of marriage in mind. A straightforward an-

218

swer could elude you at the moment. Take a dear friend into your confidence if you feel this is something you should do. Otherwise keep your own counsel. Only you appreciate your deep down feelings. There is always a possibility that you may be expecting too much in too short a span of time. Contain your impatience and let everyone think you are fully under control. It's just a case of thinking positively and acting that way.

5. MONDAY. Good. Personal efforts will be appreciated. Be kind to someone in the locality who has your interests at heart. If they seem to be taking life a little too seriously, cheer them up. In return, a joint approach to some little neighborhood project will ensure success. Keep in touch with the media. Try something original if you want to attract attention. Original work will appeal at this time of the year when people are looking for something different. A letter written to stir up reaction could have unexpected results. You should be starting something on a sound footing, though some may say you are a little too adventurous. Nothing ventured, nothing gained.

6. TUESDAY. Disquieting. Look after your own interests. If anyone needs you, let them come to you. You should be highly charged today so will have no need to advertise yourself in any way. Your charm and charisma should work wonders. Despite your latent strength, you could be inclined to take too much on yourself. This may mean you are loth to delegate duties when you really should be watching and not working. Your manner can be a bit overpowering. Let someone in on your plans a little bit rather than keep them at arms length. It may be you are strongly attracted to a particular person. Do not make this too obvious. A little bit of mystery is essential in any romance.

7. WEDNESDAY. Disquieting. You may be at sixes and sevens today. If things appear to go awry, let it pass. Today is one of those days when you feel like a square peg in a round hole. Someone is likely to let you down. This could be a neighbor or a workmate. Get to work under your own steam. Transportation could be unreliable. An arrangement may fall through at the last minute. It will be a good idea to have duplicate keys handy and a reserve set put aside in case of emergencies. Someone is likely to challenge you on a point of order or a legal matter. Keep out of trouble as far as you can. It will be unwise to risk a brush with the law.

8. THURSDAY. Good. Exciting things can be happening in your daily routine. The chances are you are feeling on top of the world after a poor spell recently. Efforts will be recognized. Colleagues are pleased to see you in good trim. There is some talk of a pay increase or a bonus before the end of the year. The Christmas rush gives you plenty to do and you have little time to stand and stare. An operation recently performed on a colleague seems to have been very successful. So much has been achieved in a short time after years of medication. Take the initiative today if you want to get on. Think ahead and think quickly. Get your foot in the door and then you'll be in your element.

9. FRIDAY. Good.   Get on with all those letters you should be writing. You could receive important news that will affect your future plans. There may be some need to get to grips with a local matter that involves the elderly. Get acquainted with up-to-date methods of display if you intend giving a lecture or talk. The media could be interested and turn up in strength. Before midday get your financial situation in order with your bank manager. You will have little time later on to look into money matters. It is the end of the office week and you don't want to be caught short over the weekend. An extraordinary person crosses your path in the evening. Do everything you can to talk and exchange ideas.

10. SATURDAY. Deceptive.   You could be taken for a ride. Someone will think you are a sucker and try to con you. Be extra careful when shopping. With business livening up, there is ample room for the slick operator. An attempt to make yourself a bit wiser may not come off. Resist the temptation to look after something that is supposed to be in need of care. You may be the one who is suffering before the day is out. Appeals to your generosity may be disregarded. If you see one you see the lot. A day at work may be called for. This will get you down when you have so much else to do. Grin and bear it. Your reward may be in heaven. Hard cash can be short.

11. SUNDAY. Good.   Feel sure you are in good company. A proposal of marriage is in the cards. A gathering of relatives can have surprising results. You meet someone who finds you attractive. Make the most of this opportunity to cement immediate ties. The boy or girl next door looks like a treat. Enter enthusiastically into any local event that gets you better known. If you have been feeling lonely of late, this seems a good day to break the ice with your closest neighbors. Traveling around should be pleasant provided you have the right person beside you. There could be news of an addition to the family. A partnership is developing and you are glad a couple you know are having an easier time.

12. MONDAY. Successful. Take time to get into your stride. The main push comes late in the day. A target can be reached if you get a move on. That decorating you thought may be delayed until next year should get done after all. Preparations behind schedule can be speeded up. This should make you feel better. A member of the family is given a new job. A little more income will help over the Christmas period. Pressure begins to mount up in the evening. It may be necessary to take work home in order to keep up with immediate business. Be careful when taking on something entirely new. A break in routine can be more than you really need. But you have your mind made up, so it would take a lot of dissuading to change it.

13. TUESDAY. Variable. A loan may get you out of a domestic jam. Feel happier because you have something organized that has been worrying you for a little while. Schedules can now be agreed. A senior member of the family is glad to help you financially. This boost to your income should give you the security you have longed for. An official helps to get a mortgage through in time to start the new year in a home of your own. Because of other attractions you may have to cancel a date. It seems a shame. You hope you have your priorities right. Someone is rather jealous of your progress. You find it hard to settle down away from home. One of the family feels miserable over a romance that is fading.

14. WEDNESDAY. Fair. A shake-up could do a power of good. Straight talking can clear the air in seconds. Be original in your thinking. There may be intense activity in the neighborhood. A gifted person passes through and leaves everyone thinking along new lines. Stir yourself if you wish to make the best use of your talents. You may be torn between enjoying a romance and getting down to purposeful development of a natural gift. Perhaps you can make the most of both. A flair should be developed. It is pointless keeping something hidden. Children impress you with their knowledge. An artistic young person makes a great hit at a local exhibition to the delight of the community.

15. THURSDAY. Good. Favorable trends should give you an easy day. There may be little to excite you, but you should make progress with something that gives you pleasure and relaxation. Feel happier that you have things under your control to your personal satisfaction. Insist on doing your own thing quite early in the day. Your friends and family will know where they stand and can leave you in peace if that is what you want. You may hear of an addition to the family. Something from the past comes to light again. A talent of a former generation is happily resurrected. You get inspiration from a photograph. Relax and let things sink in. You may feel like a new person.

16. FRIDAY. Variable. A romantic boost to end the working week. You may hear of a birth or pregnancy that gives you a thrill. A love affair looks more than promising. You have thoughts and plans ahead of the present moment. Settle a legal matter amicably. Be sure to react positively if asked out this evening. Agree early in the day. You may not get a second offer. Later on people seem to be unhappy or unwilling to mix. You could be left on the shelf if you do not act sociably. Someone with an unusual sense of humor can disrupt your evening. A poor car service can cause complications late in the evening. It does not pay to use unqualified labor.

17. SATURDAY. Disturbing. Hasty action can get you in a heap of trouble. Take your time if you have a lot on your mind. Personal initiative is needed, but should not be overdone. Relatives get under your feet when you are trying to get something working properly. If you blow your top in the wrong company, you will have a sensitive person up in arms. Your romantic life can be blighted because someone is a little bit impetuous. Learn to be tactful through the mismanagement of others. Working Saturday will be the last straw. Try to concentrate on what you are doing. There could be careless people about who will make dangerous mistakes. Have you checked the car since your last mishap?

18. SUNDAY. Good. Things fall into place. Cooperation is seen to pay off handsomely. You and your partner are praised by a parent or grandparent for a fine job, well done. The annual share out of a money market is more than usually productive. With the support of parents, make a decision about marriage. All in all you seem to be ready to take on responsibilities not previously held. There may be exceptional news of a merger. A major decision could have to be made this weekend. It is no time for beating about the bush. The far-reaching consequences of increased dual responsibilities gives you hope for the future. Partners amaze you with their strong qualities.

19. MONDAY. Disquieting. Be direct with some and gentle with others. If you get your types mixed today, you could end up being disliked badly. A direct confrontation may need to be resolved. It may be difficult to get cooperation in some quarters. Perhaps you are using a sledgehammer to crack a nut. Associates do not seem to be very cooperative when presented with a straight choice. Use your intelligence if you see a client is ready to take business elsewhere. There are more ways than one to do a deal. Your mind may be on other things. A romantic encounter can have you day-dreaming. Transfer some of that gentleness into your immediate task. Be gentle and friendly.

20. TUESDAY. Variable. This could be your lucky day. A cooperative gamble may pay dividends. Keep your head above water by being a good mixer. Show someone close to you that you have their interests at heart. Standing aloof will get you disliked. Neighbors can be rather offputting. You may have doubts about their intentions. Keep your own thoughts clear and look for wiser counsel if you are in that sort of need. A legal matter can come to a head and be happily settled. Don't listen to gossip. Some folk may be rather speculative. You could have a good laugh to yourself about some of the things you hear. It could be a romantic day.

21. WEDNESDAY. Good. Now is the time to think carefully about your future. Your health improves. Press on with what you think is right. Make the best of present opportunities. Take immediate action if you think you can improve your job prospects. Something may come to light in research you have undertaken. All depends on your enthusiasm and application. The health of a partner is the turning point of a working agreement. You feel happier with someone to support your efforts. As the end of the year draws near, consider your prospects for the future. Make positive plans. See someone about job security and profit sharing. Such things are important later on.

22. THURSDAY. Disturbing. Influential people are hard to convince. Someone with power and publicity can be a thorn in your flesh. In-laws could give you a hard time. There seems no good reason why this should be so. You may feel you should stand on your own feet. The full meaning of such a change in your social status may not be realized until now. An autocratic teacher may make it difficult for you to study. Approaching exams may be worrying you. A long journey can present difficulties. Passports or visas may be questioned by officials. There seems to be a lot of red tape today. A separation can make you feel cut off. Someone on whom you have relied in the past must now leave you to stand on your own feet.

23. FRIDAY. Deceptive. You may have a lot of ground to cover at the end of this working week. The relief of closing up for a holiday may be a little too much. Traveling problems are likely to emerge during the day. As ever at holiday periods, public transport and airways are heavily booked. Hold-ups are likely. Stick to routine as far as you can. That which has been tried and tested should still see you through in the long run. Attending to minor details will begin to tell on some. You could be forgetful, having too much to do. Schedules may have to be altered or discarded altogether. Play it by ear. Despite pressures, delays and possible mishaps, you have something to celebrate at the end of the day.

24. SATURDAY. Variable. An extra start is indicated. For those who are positive and have something essential to do, a day to complete final preparations. For those returning home after a late night, possible mechanical problems. See you have a full tank of gas before you start. There could be a verbal dispute in the early hours. Careless actions can lose you friends. If you keep cool you are OK. If you dash out to do some extra shopping you may forget your purse or have it stolen. So try to get your priorities right and keep organized. The late evening seems the right time to share your feelings with those around you. Look forward to the coming day with happiness. A job will be well done and all eventually in its place.

25. SUNDAY. MERRY CHRISTMAS. Greet the day knowing all is as it should be. If you are host or hostess to a family gathering, play your part with due decorum and the true spirit of the occasion. Older members of the family play an important part in the festivities. You may be pleased to have someone many years older than yourself under your roof. Welcome visits from old friends nearby in the course of the day. Nothing is going to make you dash about or get in a flap for the next twenty-four hours. There may be some reminiscing over past years and how the year has gone for family and relatives you see today for the first time in months. Relax and enjoy the nostalgia engendered.

26. MONDAY. Variable. Make the best of present opportunities. You feel you have met someone who is the tops. Show you are someone to be reckoned with. It will do you good to get some fresh air in your lungs. This is traditionally a day to let yourself go after the excess of yesterday. Enjoy showing off. You may either show your muscles or apply all your charms to get what you want and attract attention. They say that pride comes before a fall. Only if you go too far. Be genuine, loving and aware of your rightful place. Only if you become overbearing will you lose out. Someone may tread on your toes or offend your pride. Why worry? You could be at work. That could be a whole lot worse than anything you might endure concerning your pride.

27. TUESDAY. Variable.   A day of mixed blessings. Some may have to return to a normal schedule. A partner may hit the high spots and threaten to ruin your reputation. Be careful with whom you are involved during the day. You could let your hair down when you should be thinking of more serious matters. A legal problem may have to be dealt with promptly. There may be some difficulty getting hold of the right person to sort things out. Careless talk may get you into trouble. Eventually you will be able to see what is going on. A new found friend can open your eyes. Make plans for an original approach to local affairs. This could be an interesting year ahead. Join in the social whirl once you are organized. You don't want to get left in the lurch.

28. WEDNESDAY. Fair.   Friends surround you. They extend from the socially well known to the glamorous. Festivities carry on well after Christmas. Most folk seem to be enjoying all that the locality has to offer. You could be in love. You could also be taking some things very seriously. Someone may comment on your faraway look. A friend could land you in debt if you are careless enough to sign a blank check. Be extra careful in your casual relationships. You have such a lot going for you at the moment. Treat everyone with the same care and attention. A favorite could do you a disservice. Do not be fooled by appearances.

29. THURSDAY. Good.   Prospects are bright. Cooperative action pays off. A business deal can be settled before the end of the year. This will button things up nicely and exceed your expectations. Maintain and increase contact with local trade outlets. Everyday relationships are vital at this time of year. Relatives join in a social get-together with you and your partner. This could be an introduction to better times ahead for fall. Look for local support to get a communal project off the ground. Your advice may be sought on a matter of company finance. Take partners into your confidence. It is essential to keep everyone who matters in the picture to get more complete information.

30. FRIDAY. Disturbing.   Most folk seem to be unsure of their way. It could be end-of-year nerves. Try to be of service to all who ask. But expect no special thanks for your good work. There may be an emergency and hospitals near you have a busy time. If you can help, do so. Problems may seem to be building up, but this is largely a state of mind. Do something practical. Keep your own counsel. You may hear lots of rumors and meet many disturbed people. There is no good reason why you should not rise above the difficulties that seem to develop. Important and respectable folk seem out of touch. Someone you know may be in need of help.

31. SATURDAY. Variable. The end of the year. See it out with someone you love who knows how you feel. A parent may be confused. There may be some question of getting in touch with an important person that might have to be shelved. It is impossible to get hold of a communications expert at a crucial moment. Little guidance comes from top people. They appear to be unsure of the future. You have no such doubts. It is time to relax and put the old year into its right perspective. Forget old arguments. Look forward to new hopes and better relations in the year to come. Forget about work. Spend the evening and your money on something and someone worthwhile. Happy New Year!

October–December 1987

OCTOBER

1. THURSDAY. Variable. This should be a good time for getting written agreements and contracts from others. Attempts to get go-aheads or planning permission from influential people or bodies can meet with success. Scorpio people can take a vigorous part in negotiations and discussions. Don't wait for others to make the moves in business activities. It will be far more advantageous to take the initiative yourself. Don't take a backseat. Put your point of view forward in no uncertain terms. But the health of Scorpio people will be more vulnerable. You cannot afford to push yourself to the limit. Take it easy. But it can be essential to tackle dull and dreary tasks.

2. FRIDAY. Satisfactory. You should get from well-placed people the help you need to tie up the loose ends of long-drawn-out projects. Then you can get new ventures on the road. Today can see the ending of one phase of activity and the beginning of a new. But do not turn your back on past experiences before you have wrung them dry of all useful lessons. You should be able to avoid future pitfalls by examining past mistakes. Capitalize on past successes. Make the most of previous ups and downs. Conditions are likely to become increasingly advantageous for property dealing as the day goes on. But Scorpios can be in a rather serious and concentrated mood that others can find hard to take. Try to unwind somewhat and communicate with others.

3. SATURDAY. Good. The early part of the day is good for making secret arrangements to meet loved ones. It will be easier to set up romantic liaisons that you want nobody else to know about. But it seems that for certain Scorpios the time has come to break off existing attachments. Again the morning is the best time to let those concerned know that it is all off. It will be worth getting into top gear for those Scorpios who have to work today. The more work you get done, the higher can be the rewards. If you can beat deadlines by taking work home and completing it over the weekend, well and good. Your efforts will not go unnoticed. The agility of your mind today will make all mental activities quicker.

4. SUNDAY. Challenging. Scorpios have a happy day to look forward to. Leisure and pleasure pursuits can give you all the relaxation and enjoyment you are seeking. Time given to hobbies and favorite pastimes will be most rewarding. Creative energies will be high and should be challenged into imaginative activities. Scorpio sports people will be in good form and can gain both satisfaction and success in their sporting endeavors. In fact, you can be favorably surprised by your own performance. Scorpios who are looking for romantic partners can be presented with opportunities for meeting such people. But once the opportunity becomes available it will be up to you to make the approach.

5. MONDAY. Sensitive. There can be unexpected bills to meet now. The affairs and needs of children can cost more than you had anticipated. Outings and entertainments can become very unexpectedly expensive. You may also have to spend more then you can afford to keep loved ones happy. Contacts helpful to financial plans can be made through social situations. Scorpios can use their charm to win over influential people. Let others know if you are impressed with their achievements. They will be more willing to help you in consequence. Friends can spoil romantic occasions by getting more interested in your sweetheart than you like. Keep personal arrangements to yourself. Then if things do not work out well, you won't have to explain.

6. TUESDAY. Deceptive. Scorpio workers may have to shoulder extra work loads due to the absence of colleagues. And this is not the best day for you to have to cope with additional responsibilities. You could find yourself in a rather dreamy state. You will probably prefer to sit staring into space rather than knuckling down to hard work. But it is important that you snap out of it and apply yourself diligently. Employers will not take kindly to your wasting time and idle chatter. They will want to see you earning your money. Don't rely too much on the help and support of people in prominent positions. It may be impossible to make contact with them when they are most needed.

7. WEDNESDAY. Productive. Recent or current efforts at work can win unexpected rewards and notice. This can give your self-confidence and self-esteem a great boost. Scorpios should make every effort to fulfill the trust employers put in them by giving them extra responsibilities. Your newfound assurance will help you to adapt to new situations. Try to live up fully to the expectations others have of you. These developments should put you on top of the world. You are likely to be in a cheerful and efficient mood. There won't be many situations that you find difficult to handle. But underneath your gaiety there may be a slight feeling of sadness that is difficult to pinpoint.

8. THURSDAY. Mixed.   Imaginative and original projects are likely to receive both encouragement and practical help from loved ones or the people you work with. Business and emotional partners will be in a most cooperative mood. They can make all the difference to the success or failure of your projects. They can have excellent suggestions and insights to offer if you are planning advertising campaigns or publicity stunts. They will have a keen sense of just what is likely to draw the greatest attention. There will be stronger bonds of affection and support between Scorpios and their sweethearts or spouses. But Scorpios may have to keep their forceful natures in check. You have a tendency to be overbearing and to expect to get your way.

9. FRIDAY. Disquieting.   You will again get far more done and to greater advantage by working along with others. Go all-out to recruit the cooperation of others. Lend a hand where you can. Solo attempts will provide disappointing results. There is no point in trying to strike out on your own. Put purely personal goals aside for the time being. But it may be difficult to ascertain where you stand with certain people. And others will more easily misinterpret what you are saying or what your intentions are. You can bypass a lot of trouble by speaking and communicating more distinctly. Making your position absolutely clear would also help to clear the air of any misinterpretations.

10. SATURDAY. Successful.   Legal disputes are best handled through unofficial channels. Settle disagreements out of court whenever possible. Everyone concerned stands to gain by amicable arrangements. It should be possible to avoid heavy lawyer's bills by direct contact with other parties. If others have asked you to take care of their finances or to handle their investments, don't draw undue attention to the fact. Proceed with such affairs as unobtrusively as possible. It is by working in the background that you can gain the greatest advantage for the interests of others. It may be best to invite influential people out for dinner if you have important business to discuss with them. Support will be more readily forthcoming under informal circumstances.

11. SUNDAY. Satisfactory.   Avoid touchy issues when speaking to loved ones. They will quickly take the bait if you bring up contentious subjects. Minor money matters can assume gigantic proportions if you attempt to thrash them out now. Such topics are best avoided as nothing whatever will be settled. But this is not to say that Scorpios should avoid going over family accounts in private. Get a good, solid picture of your resources. Then you can discuss the situation with loved ones at a more harmonious opportunity. You will be well equipped to deal with any mental activities later on. Important people will be happy to see the results of any research you undertake.

12. MONDAY. Mixed. The mail can bring news that causes some anxiety. Events in distant places may not be going to plan. Tax problems are likely to occur. You may get notification of higher tax bites than you had anticipated. It would be well to review insurance policies to ensure that they still cover all your needs and possessions. But don't make hasty changes in this department. Get professional advice if necessary. Neither should you introduce new banking arrangements in a hurry. It could be that a pay raise is in the pipeline for your spouse so that family resources would get a welcome boost. Your own job prospects can seem more optimistic. These should come first and foremost on your agenda.

13. TUESDAY. Manageable. It would be unwise to put your trust in people in faraway places. Nor should you trust those who come in from overseas. Such folk are unlikely to stick to their word or stick to arrangements. They will be more easily distracted by personal affairs. It would be safer to deliver messages and packages by hand, wherever possible. Some people may impart wrong information so that packages can go astray in the mail or be incorrectly delivered. Don't hold to a narrow point of view now. Step back and take the widest perspective possible. You should be well placed to ascertain possible future trends. Don't lose sight of long-term objectives because of immediate minor problems.

14. WEDNESDAY. Disturbing. Writers and advertisers may have problems to contend with today. The people who make decisions in the publishing field will have their own and not your interests at heart. Hopes can be dashed as a result. The plans of Scorpios can meet resistance from employers. But even though you are forced to set new objectives for yourself and new ways of achieving them, the opposition you have met may come from selfish motives. Superiors may be purposely leading you up the garden path. Despite that, exciting plans and possibilities for the future are filling your mind. However, you must not allow them to make you neglect current responsibilities.

15. THURSDAY. Productive. You would do much better to drive straight to the heart of the matter than dither about on the fringes. The time has come to make clear decisions and to act on them. You cannot afford to put things off any longer. It will be up to you to supply the initiative and drive to get employment matters or business affairs on the move. Don't wait for others to wave the magic wand. Working conditions are likely to get more and more dreary if you leave it to circumstances to bring about change. You will have to make some extra effort to alter the trend. You may meet old faces and friends from the past who can do you a good turn. Scorpios are attractive to the opposite sex.

16. FRIDAY. Mixed. It will be easier for Scorpio people to make blunders today that could lose them the respect of business associates. You will need to employ all the subtlety and tact you can muster to avoid making mistakes. You may be saying all the wrong things, and generally putting others off. It would be a mistake to attempt to impose strongly held opinions on others. People will only see such crusades as intrusions. Keep your ideas to yourself, at least until someone shows a genuine interest in hearing what you have to say. Commercial operations that have taken an age to establish themselves can at last begin to show signs of returns on invested time and capital.

17. SATURDAY. Lucky. Today should be good for meeting prominent people under informal circumstances. Influential friends can be made during social events. Such acquaintances can stand you in very good stead in your business and employment affairs. The backing of newly formed friends can help swing decisions and events your way. Financial assistance may be forthcoming through them. Self-employed Scorpio workers or business people will have excellent opportunities for increasing their earnings and profits. And those Scorpios who are employed by others can also be offered many chances for increasing their income. But people you see only now and again can be difficult to track down.

18. SUNDAY. Enjoyable. Scorpios will enjoy making the social rounds today. You will be in your element among large numbers of people or family and social gatherings. Friends can make lively companions. Activities shared with them can become adventures. And some Scorpios may be looking for romantic partners. The introductions friends may arrange could put them in touch with compatible new people. Serious love affairs can be the result. In fact, for Scorpios who do not want to commit themselves at this stage, new attractions may have too many strings attached. Partners can have greater expectations of romance than you. You may have to reveal that you are only interested in a casual affair.

19. MONDAY. Disappointing. Bad news can come by phone or letter. This will be akin to letting the fox into the chicken coop where business finances are concerned. Disappointments and reverses are likely in commercial operations. But Scorpio business people must keep their heads. The situation can only worsen if you act impulsively or give way to panic. But you may be able to contain the problem if you keep cool and act sensibly. You may come close to realizing heartfelt desires. Failure could occur through not having sufficient funds available. High hopes can be thwarted at the last moment. Friends and acquaintances may request loans.

20. TUESDAY. Deceptive. Scorpios may feel they are going around in circles today. Things are unlikely to go according to plan. People and situations can turn out to be very different from your first impression of them. You can be led up blind alleys and down dead ends. Undercover operations can backfire. Secret dealings are best avoided. Others may take unfair advantage of the hidden nature of such activities. Transactions should be conducted in the full light of day. People can arrive at very wrong conclusions where your generosity or willingness to help is concerned. Wrong motives can be attributed to you. Feelings can become very volatile later on. You will have to try to keep the lid on tempers.

21. WEDNESDAY. Good. Today will be favorable for attending to details and tying up loose ends. It is by clearing the decks of minor matters that you can pave the way to bigger things. This should be a good time for balancing the books. You should make every attempt to collect monies you are owed. It is a day for keeping your prejudices in the right perspective. You can lose valuable opportunities because of bigoted attitudes. The point is that useful offers or propositions can come from strange sources. If you can keep an open mind you may be on to a winner. Suggestions from such quarters can have very profitable consequences. A tour of shops and stores could reveal useful items at reasonable prices.

22. THURSDAY. Important. Although there won't be much happening today the time can be used to great advantage. Don't be lulled into laziness or inactivity by the unusually slow conditions. The absence of pressures and demands make this a perfect day for getting your affairs in order. Clear away any backlogs of letters, paperwork, and accounting. Make preparations to swing into action when the momentum gets going again. This will be a good opportunity for streamlining procedures and introducing new methods. All overdue projects should be rounded off now. It would be a good idea to look back over recent weeks and months to see where you could have made more progress.

23. FRIDAY. Challenging.   Scorpio people won't have much trouble in pushing ahead with their personal plans and goals today. In fact, by pulling out all the stops you can accomplish more than you thought possible. An inventive streak should prevail in your thinking. You will have both the inspiration and the enthusiasm to launch new ventures. And just as important, you will have the determination to see them through to a fruitful conclusion. Get your brainwaves into action. Don't opt for the old and familiar ways where there is room for expansion and invention. But Scorpios can easily ruin their chances by using unnecessarily harsh words. Needless to say, other people are put off by such criticism.

24. SATURDAY. Rewarding.   Today offers a favorable and unexpected turn of events in employment matters. This can bring advantages and financial gain to Scorpio workers. Keep on your toes so that you can make the most of any opportunities that come your way. The satisfaction afforded by regular work can make this an enjoyable day. Contrary to expectations, routine employment activities are unlikely to be dull and dreary. But other people will more than likely fall in with the wishes and wants of Scorpio people. So there is a good chance that you will want to sit back and take it easy. You would be better advised to remain alert and active. Health should be in tip-top form. Keep it that way.

25. SUNDAY. Exciting.   Scorpios can be particularly adroit in handling background maneuvers and manipulating events from behind the scenes. Keep in the shadows now. Don't draw undue attention to your activities. Cultivate contact with those of your acquaintances who have inside information. Such sources can provide valuable knowledge. If this is acted upon, it will give extra impetus to your money-making schemes. Scorpios can fulfill their humanitarian urges by collecting money for worthy causes. But with mental energies in a particularly sharp state, some Scorpios may feel like retiring into seclusion. They may want to pursue intellectual and other interests that require full concentration.

26. MONDAY. Manageable.   Financial conditions are likely to be in a state of flux. There can be rapid ups and downs and shifts of position. With so much change it will be difficult to make certain judgments and assessments. It would be wiser to wait for more stable times before committing large sums of money or making important financial decisions. But consider the other side of the coin of change. It also means that it will be much easier to introduce new methods and procedures into working practices. Seek ways to minimize drudgery and monotony. Workers will be quick to adapt to new approaches. And if Scorpio employers want to introduce new pay arrangements, this would be the time to do it.

27. TUESDAY. Misleading. The day should be good for making contacts by phone, letter, or short trips. Communications can be an avenue to success. But all news and information must be passed on with care. People will quite easily misinterpret the information and get it all wrong. Ensure that you do not leave room for such misunderstanding. Messages of extreme importance should be double-checked. Take pains to express yourself clearly. But others may also use garbled words or make unclear or misleading statements. It should be unwise to act on what they try to tell you. At least withhold action until you are sure that they have got it right. Scorpios should draw on their rich funds of imagination.

28. WEDNESDAY. Sensitive. Loved ones will be in a congenial and cooperative mood. It will be easier to discuss important topics with them or lay plans for the future. Journeys or visits to interesting places in their company will give great pleasure. But if you are separated from sweethearts by long distances, a love letter or phone call will bring you closer together. Scorpios will find it easier to express their thoughts and feelings in words. It may be difficult to keep your mind on regular employment activities. Don't hesitate to approach superiors if you have a favor to ask. They will be in a sympathetic mood, and will more than likely to grant your requests. But don't try to manipulate them.

29. THURSDAY. Mixed. Scorpios may have to face a difficult choice. It will be between catering to their own desires and preferences or attending to their home and family responsibilities. But you would be well advised to sacrifice personal wishes. Give family members the help and support they need. You may not even have domestic duties to handle. But the need to complete jobs or projects already in progress can prevent you from giving time to preferred activities. You have succeeded in obtaining planning permission or other official go-aheads on property matters. But even so, real estate transactions are unlikely to fulfill their early promise. Writers of fiction can win publishing success. But it won't be a snap. Competition will be fierce.

30. FRIDAY. Manageable. You may well have extra time in which to work. Even so, it can be to your financial advantage to get jobs finished at the earliest possible moment. It is by beating schedules that you are likely to win the favorable notice of employers. You should do your utmost to pay off old financial debts or any others. It could be that feelings of obligation to others are slowing you down without your fully realizing it. But with a clean slate you will probably feel much lighter and freer. If you are bothered by health symptoms this is a good time to seek the services of medical doctors or specialists. Problems can often be nipped in the bud through timely and expert advice.

31. SATURDAY. Fortunate. Scorpios can luxuriate in some easygoing conditions today. There will be plenty of time for rest and relaxation. Or you can do the things that most interest you. The day is especially good for recreational activities. These could include outings to places of interest or cinemas and theatres. Imagination will be lively, making artistic and inventive work more satisfying. There should be no shortage of original ideas. Deep-felt hopes and wishes of romantic Scorpios can come to realization today. Compatible partners can walk into your life. Love affairs can reach new peaks of fulfillment. You may receive the encouragement and financial backing of influential people for risky ventures.

NOVEMBER

1. SUNDAY. Disturbing. Once you start heavy spending for extravagances and entertainments expenses can begin to soar. You will have to keep a tight rein on nonessential spending or you will soon go into the red. Conditions do not favor speculation. Those gamblers who cannot resist trying their luck should restrict the sums they play with to very small amounts. Big bets will take you for a real ride. It will be a downward spiral if you take risks with large amounts of cash. No matter how attractive the odds are, your chances are almost nil. Scorpios may be full of lively and original ideas. These may, however, be impossible to put into operation for lack of financial backing.

2. MONDAY. Deceptive. There may be wolves in sheeps' clothing about today. Workmates, in particular, can be wearing one face but showing a different and not very pleasant one behind your back. Secret resentments may have built up against you that people express in surreptitious ways. It would be best to take nothing for granted. Keep on your toes and you may anticipate any evil intentions before they take effect. You may not be doing yourself any favors by winning the support of influential people for your personal plans. You could be sticking your neck out further than you realize. There is a chance that you are overstretching your resources. Try to step back mentally and review your finances.

3. TUESDAY. Variable.   Your mainspring can get coiled up to the snapping point before you have realized it. Nervous tension can develop through contacts with difficult people and conditions. Keep tabs on your inner state. Take every opportunity you can to relax. Let off steam in ways that do not harm your reputation. Your health will be more vulnerable to infection. Avoid people with coughs and sneezes. Attempts to make money through get-rich-quick methods are doomed to failure. Your best bet to keep money flowing into the coffers is through regular employment activities. Play it safe for the time being. Take any overtime opportunities. Employers should make more contacts with employees.

4. WEDNESDAY. Mixed.   This is not the best day for seeking new jobs or positions. The morning hours, in particular, can be bad for interviews with prospective employers or existing superiors. You are unlikely to make a favorable impression at the moment. Nor will you feel at ease with the people you work with. It would be best to keep going by yourself as much as possible without making others feel that you are shunning them. But the evening can provide a pleasant contrast to a difficult working day. Time spent in the company of sweethearts or spouses should wash your cares away. This would be a good opportunity for giving special treats to loved ones. A gourmet dinner will be much appreciated.

5. THURSDAY. Disconcerting.   Scorpios can be rather heavy-handed with people who only want to help them or draw closer to them. Be more sensitive to those who have the best of intentions toward you. You can do with all the friendship and cooperation you can muster. Beware of making enemies of people who began by liking you. The trouble is that your own inner force and drive can blind you to the positive qualities in others. You frequently try to railroad people into accepting your ideas and ways of doing things. By doing so, you may be throwing away valuable partnership possibilities. Let others have their say. Sound out the opinions of loved ones in career affairs.

6. FRIDAY. Quiet.   Be ready for a very slow and uneventful day. But at least there should be no new problems and pressures to contend with. Put business and employment activities aside as early as possible. By doing so, more time can be spent with sweethearts or spouses. This is a day for showing loved ones just how much you care. It's a good chance for making practical as well as more intimate gestures of affection. Help to lighten the load of loved ones if they have jobs or chores to attend to by giving them a hand. A little gift or treat will put a smile on their faces. The wordly wisdom of Scorpios may come to the aid of collegues or workmates who have personal problems.

7. SATURDAY. Successful. Scorpio people's delight in digging and delving can be used to good purpose now. Conditions are extremely favorable for background research and solving mysteries. Valuable information can come to light as the result of concerted investigation. Don't be taken in by surface appearances. Get down to the nitty-gritty. The most profitable work can be done away from the public eye. This is a good time for background operations. Unobtrusive people can provide aid and support. This is not a day for associating with any sort of flashy types. But if you broadcast your intentions too soon others will jump on the bandwagon or steal your thunder. The day is favorable for fund-raising.

8. SUNDAY. Manageable. Family or other mutual funds do need some protection. But it would be a mistake for Scorpios to overreact. Putting too tight a control on the spending of financial partners or other joint owners of resources would be a mistake. Keep your thinking in perspective. Avoid extreme actions. Where money is concerned you can make mountains out of molehills. Don't exaggerate problems. If you bear down too heavily on those with whom you share capital, they are likely to react themselves. One way would be by going out on a spending spree. But conditions continue to favor background study and research. The day is good for establishing family history and family trees.

9. MONDAY. Tricky. Conditions can be extremely tricky where academic affairs are concerned. You may find it difficult to make important decisions while you are treading such unsure ground. And to add to the complications, people are likely to give you wrong information. It would be best to bide your time before committing yourself one way or the other. It is probably of no avail to turn to tutors or other academic staff such as advisors. They are unlikely to provide the guidance you are seeking. Neither should you place too much trust in people in faraway places. Distant events could work out contrary to expectations. There may be some secret plotting between your spouse's relatives.

10. TUESDAY. Sensitive. The best approach when trying to win over influential people is to adopt a positive and far-reaching outlook. Demonstrate that you can look on the bright side and make the best of things. It will also stand you in good stead to show others just how wide your range of interests and abilities are. Keep an open mind on what people in prominent positions have to say. They can pass on insights and experience that you can use to great advantage in furthering your own professional interests. But employers should not rush into changes of working patterns or methods. Employees may resent new procedures being forced on them. Don't allow criticism to weaken your resolve.

11. WEDNESDAY. Difficult. There may be some infighting in family circles. Your spouse's relatives may have some bad feeling about you but be unable to express it directly. This can lead to suspicions and the buildup of tension. Scorpios can be deeply irritated by stories they receive secondhand about themselves. Some straight talking will be necessary to clear the air. The health of Scorpios may not be in tip-top condition. You could therefore experience some depression or exhaustion. Emotional problems can get you down more than usual. It is important not to exert your forceful nature over others. You will save yourself trouble by using more tact. You should concentrate on improving this.

12. THURSDAY. Changeable. Scorpios can again spoil their chances in business and employment spheres. They do it constantly by employing overly brash and forceful methods. A diplomatic, and even gentle approach should be adopted whenever possible. Treat associates with more consideration. Listen to the points of view of others. Don't ram your ideas down people's throats. It is important that you maintain a cool head when dealing with business associates or the public. Once your volatile feelings get in on the act things will go from bad to worse. This is definitely a day for keeping the more abrasive side of your nature out of sight. Contracts and cooperation can be won by showing others just how affable you can be.

13. FRIDAY. Mixed. Scorpios can begin to reap the benefits of past efforts and planning. Business projects whose foundations were laid some time ago can now start to show handsome returns on invested cash and time. Scorpios may feel like patting themselves on the back for their foresight and earlier preparations. Learn all the lessons available from such long-term operations. This is a pattern that can be adapted to similar projects again. But you may be left to rely totally on your own capabilities. While influential people will be in a cheery mood they are unlikely to be either practical or reliable. Extra efforts at work may not lead to immediate rewards. But they will stand you in good stead when the next round of promotions comes.

14. SATURDAY. Enjoyable. Friends can get themselves into all sorts of trouble and tight corners now. It may be up to Scorpios to help their pals out of dire straits. They may need a shoulder to cry on, a financial loan, or practical help. Whatever is required, Scorpios are likely to have what it takes to lift friends up out of the dumps. Give what encouragement and support you can. The day is good for cultivating contacts among designers and artists. Creative people will make stimulating company and may have professional advice to offer. Conditions are also favorable for Scorpios to put any unusual and imaginative projects into practice. Parties and social gatherings will be fun.

15. SUNDAY. Demanding. Activities shared with friends and outings with loved ones can prove more expensive than anticipated. You must strive to keep spending within reasonable bounds. Unless you put some constraints on your expenses, they will get completely out of hand. Don't overspend on sweethearts in an attempt to keep them happy. You should rely on your innate charm and loving nature for that. But it may be more difficult for everyone to keep their cool today. Tempers can flare at the slightest provocation. Old emotional wounds can open and lead to bitter arguments. But Scorpios should try to keep out of such contests and give others all the understanding possible.

16. MONDAY. Mixed. Business finances are likely to suffer reverses today. But Scorpios should be well equipped to deal with such situations, as a result of their previous experiences with these matters. You should know just what to do to minimize the bad effects of financial crises. It is by keeping cool, calm, and collected that you will be able to pick up the loose ends. And then you can get the show on the road again. But it is important that you do not devote the whole day to business and public affairs. You must find time to cater to your own needs and desires. A little solitude can have a healing effect and will help you to concentrate on problems. You may not have had an opportunity to attend to these yet.

17. TUESDAY. Important. Conditions will not be sufficiently supportive to launch new ventures successfully. But you can have great success with reshaping events and situations that have blown apart recently. It is a good time for bringing people together to effect reconciliations. It should also be good for coordinating the various strands of business operations to make a more effective whole. Pull things together wherever possible and concentrate your efforts. It would be a mistake to be lulled by the fairly easy conditions into spending a lazy and unproductive day. You can make particularly useful advances in any work requiring brain power. You should use imagination and sound judgment.

18. WEDNESDAY. Strenuous. It is possible that long-lost acquaintances will reemerge. They can bring certain benefits for Scorpio people with them. Reunions can lead to financial gain. It will be necessary for Scorpios to knuckle under in employment affairs. They cannot afford to let their minds wander in endless daydreams. Keep your mind on the job and your nose to the grindstone. This is no time to fall back on past achievements or reputation. Employers will want to see a good day's work for the money they pay. And any additional bonuses will only come on the basis of extra efforts made now. But Scorpios can also find time to give expression to humanitarian urges.

19. THURSDAY. Productive. This can be an enjoyable day for Scorpios. You may have to bide your time at first to see which way the wind blows. But it appears that the cards will fall in your favor. There should be plenty of leads to follow up before the day ends. Make the most of opportunities when they come. But at the same time, you must be careful not to tread on other people's toes while going after your goals. However, people will be more willing to forgive any inconsiderate behavior or actions on your part which crowd them out. This is a day to cultivate imaginative flair and creative talent that is lying dormant. The more you exercise that talent the better you will become.

20. FRIDAY. Disquieting. Scorpios will have the clarity of mind and grasp of events and future trends to make effective personal plans. However, conditions will not be conducive to putting such arrangements into operation yet. Build firm foundations, but delay building operations. But you can already be looking forward to Christmas. Start making shopping and gift lists and doing the first of the festive buying. Loved ones can be in an awkward mood and may behave like spoiled children. Nothing you do will seem to please them. Although there may be plenty of obstacles in your path now consistent efforts will eventually help you through to financial gain. You never quit in the face of obstacles.

21. SATURDAY. Encouraging. Some attention should be given to personal finances. You should go over your accounts to see just where you stand. But anything on the debit side will probably be offset by favorable news or developments regarding business or employment affairs. There should be sure signs of increased profits or of pay raises. Financial prospects will be looking up. You can lighten the load if you have dreary work to attend to by keeping your targets in mind. Hold the end result in front of you like a carrot before the donkey. You may have managed to turn hobbies or sidelines into additional money earners. Some extra efforts in this quarter can produce even better results.

22. SUNDAY. Variable. It looks as though financial affairs are again going to take a downward turn. It may be difficult to ward off anxieties and morbid thoughts concerning your financial outlook. New monetary demands can come up which tip the balance out of your favor. But Scorpios are likely to paint a gloomier picture than is really necessary. You must strive to keep an optimistic attitude. Past efforts, coupled with future prospects in career and business matters, should give you much hope. It is just a question of pushing through your current difficulties to more positive times ahead. Your love life can enter a volatile though enjoyable period. Concentrate on it to free your mind of gloom.

23. MONDAY. Deceptive. Scorpios may find themselves in a rather dreamy, even out-of-this-world state. You may be moved by strange and deep feelings. You will certainly be more inclined to let the heart rule the head. Your mind may be full of religious thoughts. You may also feel a particularly strong love for others. It is by following hunches and intuitions that you can give the greatest service and help to people. This is not the time to allow commonsense to prevent you from giving others a helping hand. Let feelings dictate your relationships. There may also be an urge to cast an examining eye over the way you relate to others. You can make some surprising self-discoveries now.

24. TUESDAY. Mixed. Don't get stuck in the armchair or office today. Get on the move. Short trips can be productive and enjoyable. It will be good for doing the rounds of business contacts. But you should also make sure you have not fallen behind with your letter writing. Scorpios will have a good command of language today so that correspondence can be handled well. You will also come across well on the telephone. Use of the phone can save much time and will achieve desired results. But time given to recreational pursuits or personal plans will be to the detriment of business and career interests. This is a day for single-minded efforts. There can be happy changes in your love life.

25. WEDNESDAY. Sensitive. Home and family affairs will need to be handled with a delicate touch. But this will not come easily to Scorpio people. You are more likely to jump in with two left feet and make a mess of things. Don't go at domestic affairs with a sledgehammer. Keep the feelings and needs of others in mind. Cultivate a more subtle approach. If there are important changes to be made around the home, consult the people whose lives will be affected. Don't go ahead under your own steam. And any household jobs must be done thoroughly. There may be a tendency to rush through things. But if you do, it will be a case of more haste and less speed. Also, the jobs will not be well done.

26. THURSDAY. Changeable. It will be easier than ever to whittle away the time in idle chatter. You must get yourself by the scruff of the neck and apply yourself to the work at hand. You will only get hopelessly behind schedule if you chin-wag half the day. You must find your usual, more responsible and hard-working self. Don't let others distract you with their anecdotes. But once you get involved with your work you can cover ground at a surprising rate. You may find that you easily finish ahead of time. This will be especially true if there are financial rewards for speedy work to spur you on. Any problems or tensions at home should blow over so that a more harmonious atmosphere prevails.

27. FRIDAY. Good. It is likely that processes and projects you have initiated in the past can come to fruition now. Scorpios can reap the rewards of previous efforts and preparations. Conditions at home continue to be happy and balanced. This will be all the more true if financial problems can be ironed out quickly. Loved ones will be in a cooperative and affectionate mood. Both creative energies and mental concentration are available to you right now. It would therefore be advisable to devote time to artistic and imaginative enterprises. Or you may prefer to pursue literary interests. In fact, you could get completely absorbed in such activities. This means that you have very little time left over for other things. But if you enjoy doing whatever interests you most, let the rest go.

28. SATURDAY. Disconcerting. Those Scorpios who do not have to work today will certainly be relieved to have reached the end of the working week. You will probably feel a sense of freedom and adventure. You may want to spread your wings and visit unusual and interesting places. But you must not allow your light-hearted mood to affect your attitude toward money. It is essential to remain levelheaded and responsible where funds are concerned. Any foolish usage of money will be followed by regrets. Conditions do not favor speculation. If you cannot resist playing the horses you are advised to restrict your stakes to small amounts. Larger sums will probably be lost.

29. SUNDAY. Disappointing. Plans for recreation or outings that you have been looking forward to all week may have to be called off at the eleventh hour. If they are not scrapped altogether substantial changes may have to be made in your arrangements. Children will not be easy to handle now. They can be grumpy or inclined to throw tantrums if they do not get their own way. Parents may have to exercise a firm hand. But it is essential to remain patient with difficult youngsters. Matters will only be made worse by loss of temper. Don't get carried away when spending on pleasure and entertainments. Keep your expenses moderate. Loved ones may want to drag you away from favorite pastimes.

30. MONDAY. Uneventful. You should take full advantage of this easy going day to get all the rest and relaxation you can. Those who have to work will find it is not too difficult to take things at a much slower pace. In fact, you can achieve good results at work with the minimum amount of effort. But the emphasis should be on refueling your energy and getting into better shape for busier times ahead. It will be a good opportunity for giving more attention to sensible and nutritious diets. Take a long walk in the fresh air. Loosen up your body with some exercise or fitness training. With less on your mind you should be taking the broadest possible view of the future. Determine that you will try to improve your health and minimize stress factors.

DECEMBER

1. TUESDAY. Good. Unexpected developments in employment affairs can bring benefits to Scorpios. Deadlocks in discussions on pay and conditions can suddenly be overcome. You are likely to be very happy with the outcome of any negotiations that affect your income. You must drum up a positive approach to dull and dreary tasks that have to be completed. Jobs will get done more quickly if you can handle them with a light heart. But any moaning and groaning will make them seem worse than they actually are. It may be that you are bothered with health symptoms. If so, you might get more relief from unconventional forms of treatment such as herbalism and faith-healing.

2. WEDNESDAY. Fair. This should be a good day for teaming up with another person if you have study and research activities to complete. Solo efforts in mental pursuits will tend to drag. It will be easier to get ahead by teaming up with other people, especially if you are working on the same projects. In fact, you can get into such a good rhythm with working partners that you will know what they are thinking before they express it. An excellent and intuitive rapport will also exist between marital partners and lovers. This should rule out the development of any tensions or misunderstandings. But if others do put a foot wrong Scorpios are advised not to come down on them like a ton of bricks.

3. THURSDAY. Sensitive. This will be a less eventful day than most of its predecessors. But Scorpios will have success in any legal business they have to attend to. Take advantage of the favorable conditions to confer with legal counsel on matters of concern. Give as much help and support as possible to mates and spouses. They will appreciate your assistance. But Scorpios may have to keep their wits about them in romantic affairs. People and situations may not be entirely what they first appear. It is better not to rush headlong and heedlessly into love affairs with a fast-beating heart. Some cool logic may save the day. But once your mind is at rest romance can take on a special quality.

4. FRIDAY. Mixed. It will be easier to make mistakes with facts and figures today. It would be advisable to recheck any accounting or other financial calculations you have to deal with. Large sums can be overlooked. It would be best to get professional help with tax and insurance matters. Any mistakes made in these areas can lead to dire legal consequences. Make sure that all insurance policies are fully up to date and still cover your needs. Don't risk taking a car out on the road that is not inspected, insured, and in compliance with all regulations. Requests for loans or other services from bankers can prove unfruitful.

5. SATURDAY. Difficult. You may not get official backing or the support of influential people in money matters. In fact, commercial operations may have to be called off. This can be the result of a lack of confidence shown by people who are crucial to the success of projects. Your financial prospects can take a downward turn. Plans to secure rock-solid incomes can come to nothing. Of course, any increase in the earnings of spouses can give family resources a boost. But it would be unlikely to offset the bills and debts that constantly accrue. Although the financial outlook is on the bleak side, it is essential to keep a cool mind. Anxiety will only cloud your thoughts and could easily lead to wrong decisions. You will be cutting off your nose to spite your face.

6. SUNDAY. Fortunate. The minds of Scorpio people will be particularly sharp-edged and agile today. You can derive deep satisfaction from mental pursuits and intellectual interests. Serious subjects can have great appeal for you. You may be drawn to philosophical and religious topics. It's a good time for looking into the background of exactly how things work. Scorpios should strive to get to the very bottom of matters that interest them. Having reached great depths, you will then be able to ascend to great heights. When you have gathered all the relevant facts and material you should allow your imagination to take over. Important relationships can develop from small beginnings. It may be just a casual exchange of little importance while traveling.

7. MONDAY. Changeable. The insights and broad perspective gained yesterday should enable you to adopt a very positive approach to life today. You have been able to see the deep significance of certain things. This will allow you to put details and minor irritations and frustrations in their proper place. You should have a better idea of what merits true importance and what does not. The study of profound subjects can put you in touch with deeper layers of knowledge. You may also have the urge to spread your wings and undertake long journeys. But this is not likely to meet with the approval of loved ones. High hopes of romantic plans can be disappointed.

8. TUESDAY. Quiet. This is a favorable day for contacting people in distant places. Overseas business associates may have a special need to get in touch with Scorpio business people. Foreigners will make happy companions and reliable partners. This applies both to the romantic and the commercial kind. It is good for poring over travel brochures and other information on faraway places. Scorpios may have a great urge to travel far afield. An absence of disturbances and distractions will make conditions excellent for study, research, and any work requiring long stretches of unbroken concentration. The day will be good for conferring with people who are experts in their chosen field. Take a long-term view in business operations.

9. WEDNESDAY. Mixed. New sources of finance can become available now. Scorpio business people may find new backers or raise substantial loans. Additional capital can be plowed into business projects making them more extensive and profitable. Scorpios can gain the upper hand in negotiations. Favorable new terms and working agreements can be arranged. But as the day wears on you can get more and more wound up. It continues until you come close to the breaking point. Don't push yourself too far. Take time off, if possible. You will only make blunders if you insist on continuing to work while in a tense state. Safety rules must be strictly adhered to when using tools and machinery.

10. THURSDAY. Good. The excellent past record of Scorpio employees is likely to stand them in good stead now. Positions can become vacant and superiors may well offer you promotion. Long-awaited permission is likely to arrive through official channels. It will allow you to get started on new commercial ventures. Influential people can show their confidence in your ideas by providing the necessary funding. The achievements of Scorpios are likely to increase their standing in the eyes of others. Improved reputations can be accompanied by wage increases. If you are disabled by serious illness you should go ahead with the best treatment available. The money for medical bills will be found more easily than you think.

11. FRIDAY. Disturbing. Long-held desires and hopes can come closer to fruition now. But don't expect any rapid developments. You are more likely to achieve your goals by working in a steady and measured way. Rush jobs may have to be done again. Don't look for shortcuts. Attend to everything with thoroughness. But it is still advisable to keep secret dreams to yourself until they are fully realized. It's a good day for attending parties and social gatherings in the company of friends. Your pals will make good partners in sporting activities. The feelings of Scorpios may be a little too sensitive today. The smallest remark can touch you to the quick, out of all proportion, and you may withdraw for a while.

12. SATURDAY. Fair. Scorpios should follow up any urges they have to help underprivileged or needy people. Today is good for charitable acts and fund-raising activities. You can be highly effective in getting things changed for the better through neighborhood and community projects. It's a day for giving full vent to your idealism and desire to improve the world. While friends may be in need of a helping hand, they can also be in a position to give you some welcome assistance. But the money-making schemes of your friends should be avoided like the plague. Their financial advice will have you barking up the wrong tree. There should be some pleasing developments in employment affairs.

13. SUNDAY. Worrisome. Your day or rest is likely to be rudely disturbed by worrying news concerning business finances. Unsettled conditions can affect commercial operations badly. Information about your business interests can come from unlikely sources. And just when you most need to confer with business associates they are likely to be available. They will probably be deeply involved in family or recreational activities. It may occur to you to turn to friends in an attempt to raise money to tide you over a difficult stretch. But they are unlikely to have the necessary cash. Your love life may contain disappointments due to the bad health of loved ones. You might have to work on behalf of others.

14. MONDAY. Disquieting. Scorpios may experience some rumblings in their subconscious minds. It may make them restless and ill at ease. Personal anxieties may try to rise to the surface. It would be wisest not to suppress disturbing thoughts and feelings. You must put your problems in clear perspective now. The longer you hold them down the stronger they will become. At work it may appear that there is a planned conspiracy between people and circumstances to make things difficult for you. But it is more likely that Scorpios are making problems for themselves. There won't really be obstructions that you cannot shrug off fairly easily. You are inclined to get uptight very quickly.

15. TUESDAY. Variable. A confidential approach can give the best results where personal finances are concerned. Meetings behind closed doors can bring about additional sources of income. New money-making schemes can be got off the ground. But Scorpios may have a tendency to cut off from loved ones. They, in turn, will naturally be disturbed by any lack of communication.

Keep your channels open. Officials and employers can take ages to come to decisions that affect your finances. While such delays are probably unnecessary, there is little that Scorpio people can do to speed things up. You will just have to resign yourself to a long wait. But things will work out favorably in the end.

16. WEDNESDAY. Rewarding.   There will be no shortage of creative energies and imaginative powers today. Devote as much time as possible to inventive and artistic enterprises. This is a good day for using lively and original ideas in advertising schemes. Your products or services can be brought to a much wider public as a result. It is important that you keep fully alert during regular employment hours. Opportunities can arise that need to be seized immediately. Even though you feel in the pink from a health standpoint, this is a good time to have a standard medical checkup. Health problems might be nipped in the bud. Neighbors can go out of their way to give you a helping hand.

17. THURSDAY. Confusing.   Scorpios can tend to be on the moody and irritable side. It won't be easy to predict just how you will be feeling even a short time from now. Your unstable emotional state can make routine work more difficult to handle. It will be almost impossible to stay on the beam. Gloomy feelings can color and distort your outlook. Then your problems will appear to be a hundred times worse than they really are. It may be difficult to face the world at certain times in the day, especialy early. But as the day wears on there may be an overadjustment in your mood, swinging it to the opposite extreme. You can become nervously energetic and highly strung. Try to maintain a balance between the two because either mood is far from ideal.

18. FRIDAY. Changeable.   Try to give yourself something to look forward to. Make your weekend plans with loved ones during the early part of the day. Scorpios will find it much easier to get on with siblings and other family members now. Visits to relatives can indeed be very happy occasions. Old family differences can be patched up. Others will be more than ready to forgive and forget. If you are impatient for the repayment of money you are owed a phone call can galvanize people into action. But in general, money matters will require an extremely hardheaded approach. This is no time for pie-in-the-sky schemes. It is by looking at financial problems squarely in the eyes that you will find solutions.

19. SATURDAY. Productive.   Try to put the morning to good use. If you can put in some overtime or find paying work to do, the rewards can be quite substantial. Do all you can to give personal finances a boost. A cautious approach is necessary if you are seeking financial help or advice from influential people. They can be in an up-and-down mood. But it is worth making the move, as Scorpios are likely to catch them at a good moment. You should be thinking ahead to Christmas week and making last-minute arrangements for shopping and holiday trips away from home. Check through your lists to make sure you haven't forgotten cards or presents for anyone. It is probably too late to mail cards.

20. SUNDAY. Variable.   It seems that Scorpio people are up to their necks in money matters. It is probably difficult just now to concentrate on anything else. But you should try to take your mind off the subject. Give yourself a treat or a trip out. Get involved in physically energetic activities. Time spent with loved ones may help to take your mind off the specter of many bills coming to haunt you. There may be occasion to turn to older and wiser people for help and advice. They can provide useful insights and solutions. By talking things over with them you may be able to find your way out of a tight corner. You are likely to be blessed with inspiration while attending to mental activities.

21. MONDAY. Rewarding.   Today should be good for visiting friends and acquaintances who share similar interests with you. Or perhaps they can give your personal plans a little encouragement. It is also a favorable time for sharing activities with people you like. But friends won't want you for a companion if you are in a gloomy and pessimistic mood. This is a time to show others just how energetic and positive you can be. Your drive and determination will appear as very attractive qualities to associates. If you are mixing with groups of people you would do well to turn on the friendliness and charm. Sales representatives can have a particularly productive day.

22. TUESDAY. Important.   People will be in a congenial and cooperative mood. In fact, others are likely to lean over backward to help you out of any tight spots. It should be a good time for talking over problems with associates. The atmosphere is likely to remain reasonable whatever the topic. Long journeys can provide opportunities for meeting new romantic partners. Those Scorpios who are hoping to start a new love affair are more than likely to meet people they take a fancy to. And once a prospective partner is in your sights it shoudn't be too difficult to clinch a relationship. It could be a favorable moment in time for proposing and planning marriages. Be sure that you and your intended are compatible.

23. WEDNESDAY. Disquieting. It will be more difficult than usual to maintain harmony at home. Scorpios can be rather heavyhanded and do or say things that upset other family members. Don't pour cold water on the festive spirit. It is possible that you may not feel like joining in the fun in the buildup to Christmas. But there is no reason to prevent others from enjoying themselves. In fact, you would do better to counter any gloomy feelings within yourself. Do it by encouraging others to have a good time. Shake off the blues. Don't poison the atmosphere. At work it is best to do a straightforward and efficient day's work without any frills. This is not a good day for buying and selling real estate.

24. THURSDAY. Exciting. This is a day for tying up all the loose ends before the Christmas break. Don't put energy into getting anything new started. Clear the decks. You can win the favorable notice of bosses by bringing work to successful conclusions. There is likely to be a little bit extra in your end-of-year pay envelope by way of a Christmas bonus. The sooner you can wind things up the sooner you can begin to enjoy yourself. With work behind you, you can quickly get into the Christmas spirit. Enjoy yourself at the office party or in the company of friends. Set yourself totally free of work problems for a while. Now is the time to enjoy yourself. It could be a favorable time for short trips.

25. FRIDAY. Merry Christmas! Above all, this is the day for putting all your business, financial, and personal affairs behind you. Concentrate only on having a really good time. You will be all the fresher when returning to the world of work and business. Even a short period of pleasure and enjoyment can make a vast difference. Make the most of the company of friends and family. Youngsters can be especially delightful companions now. Scorpio parents will derive great pleasure from arranging a good time for their kids. A love affair can spring up in the midst of the festivities. It would be a good idea to share Christmas activities with sweethearts. The organizational talents of Scorpios can come to the fore in arranging parties and meals.

26. SATURDAY. Disturbing. Your Christmas cheer may get a slight shake-up if you let spending get out of hand today. Bills and expenses can mount at an alarming rate. If you had to cater to all your own whims and fancies or to those of your family and friends, you will be amazed at just how fast. You must keep expenditures moderate. It will be easy to get caught up in the helter-skelter of the festive season and forget that there is a limit to what you can afford. But you should just keep reminding yourself of the mess you will be in after the holiday if you go over the top spending. Scorpios may have to cancel journeys or vacations because money has run out. Sporting activities can suffer for the same reason.

27. SUNDAY. Variable. This is a good day for completing work at home or making household alterations and improvements. Loved ones will be in an understanding and cooperative mood. You may have some catching up to do with work or studies. If so, you are unlikely to encounter opposition from mates or spouses if you want to focus on it. They won't mind your retiring for a while so that you can concentrate on it. But you may find concentration more difficult than you had expected. Your mind is likely to wander hither and yon. Strong measures of self-discipline will be necessary if you are to make constructive progress. Don't indulge in fantasies or pie-in-the-sky pipe dreams.

28. MONDAY. Buoyant. Conditions at work and in business are likely to be very much as Scorpios would wish on their first day back. The break in routine should have prepared you well to swing back into action fully refreshed. You will find renewed vigor and enthusiasm. And there will be no shortage of opportunities to be taken advantage of. Personal finances can get a boost now. There may be promises of promotion in the New Year. Business profits will be in a healthy state. There should be scope for expanding your markets and adding clients to your books. News of excellent investment returns is likely. There should be good chances for settling accounts and repaying debts.

29. TUESDAY. Productive. Loved ones and people you trust can be in an especially sympathetic and receptive mood. It would be much better for Scorpios to unburden their minds to such people than to keep troubles and anxieties bottled up. You will feel much lighter for having shared problems with someone else. Acquaintances can also provide insights and solutions that you would never have come across yourself. If you have legal or other official documents to peruse or sign it is advisable to take extra care when reading them through. Don't gloss over details that you do not really understand. Make sure you are fully in the know before entering agreements. This is basic common sense.

30. WEDNESDAY. Quiet. A less eventful and cluttered day will give Scorpios more time for being with loved ones. This is the moment to patch up any differences in marital affairs. All partnerships can be put on a more understanding and affectionate basis now. It is advisable not to put self-interest before the needs and desires of others. Fall in with the wishes of loved ones. Give what help and support you can. Self-sacrifice can bring its own benefits in the long run. Scorpios would also do well to stand back and observe the ways in which they relate to spouses and partners. You may be surprised to see just how many covert demands you make of others. Ponder this and try to find ways to be less domineering.

31. THURSDAY. Disconcerting. Today will be favorable for conferring with lawyers and sorting out any legal problems. This is not the best time to insist on making solo efforts or striking out on your own. You will achieve much better results by throwing in your lot with others. The supportive strengths of associates will make teamwork productive and enjoyable. But even joint efforts today are likely to make rather slow headway. A steady and consistent approach will achieve the desired results eventually, however. Scorpios would do well not to rise to any challenges offered by loved ones. Concentrate on the midnight festivities. Then 1988 will be at hand, another new beginning!